EUROPEAN FILM MUSIC

European Film Music

Edited by

MIGUEL MERA
Royal College of Music, UK

and

DAVID BURNAND
Royal College of Music, UK

ASHGATE

Published by
Ashgate Publishing Limited
Gower House
Croft Road
Aldershot
Hampshire GU11 3HR
England

Ashgate Publishing Company
Suite 420
101 Cherry Street
Burlington, VT 05401-4405
USA

Ashgate website: http://www.ashgate.com

British Library Cataloguing in Publication Data
European film music. – (Ashgate popular and folk music series)
  1. Motion picture music – Europe
  I. Mera, Miguel II. Burnand, David
  781.5'42'094

Library of Congress Cataloging-in-Publication Data
European film music / edited by Miguel Mera and David Burnand.
        p. cm.—(Ashgate popular and folk music series)
    Includes bibliographical references.
    ISBN 0-7546-3658-5 (hardback : alk. paper)—ISBN 0-7546-3659-3 (pbk. : alk.
  paper) 1. Motion picture music—History and criticism. I. Mera, Miguel. II. Burnand,
  David. III. Series.

    ML2075.E87 2006
    781.5'42094—dc22

                                                                    2005027803

ISBN-13: 978-0-7546-3658-8 HBK
ISBN-10: 0-7546-3658-5 HBK
ISBN-13: 978-0-7546-3659-5 PBK
ISBN-10: 0-7546-3659-3 PBK

Typeset by IML Typographers, Birkenhead.
Printed and bound in Great Britain by MPG Books Ltd, Bodmin, Cornwall.

Contents

Figures and tables

Figures

Tables

Music examples

Notes on contributors

David Burnand is Head of Music Technology and Head of the Centre for the Study of Composition for Screen at the Royal College of Music. Originally a pop musician, David has subsequently composed music and provided sound design for several films, including *Gallivant* (BFI/C4, 1996) and *This Filthy Earth* (FilmFour, 2001). His recent publications include: 'The Articulation of National Identity Through Film Music' (with Benedict Sarnaker), *National Identities* (vol. 1, no. 1, 1999); six new biographical entries on British film composers, and articles on 'Incidental Music for TV' and 'MIDI', for *The New Grove Dictionary of Music and Musicians*, 2000; 'Reasons Why Film Music is Held in Low Regard: a British Perspective', *Brio*, 39/1, 2002; the main entries on music and several biographies of composers in the *BFI Encyclopaedia of British Film* (Methuen, 2003); 'Tarkovsky's Gift', in *Soundscape*, ed. Larry Sider, Diane Freeman and Jerry Sider (Wallflower Press, 2003); with Miguel Mera, 'Fast and Cheap? The Film Music of John Carpenter', *The Cinema of John Carpenter*, ed. I. Conrich and D. Woods (Wallflower Press, 2004).

David Cooper is Professor of Music and Technology, and Head of the School of Music at the University of Leeds. He is author of *Béla Bartók: Concerto for Orchestra* (Cambridge University Press, 1996); monographs on *Bernard Herrman's Vertigo: A Film Score Handbook* (Greenwood, 2001) and *Bernard Herrman's The Ghost and Mrs Muir: A Film Score Guide* (Scarecrow Press, 2005); and a new edition of *The Petrie Collection of the Ancient Music of Ireland* (Cork University Press, 2005). He has recently co-edited *Music of the Mediterranean: Critical Perspectives, Common Concerns, Cultural Differences* with Kevin Dawe (Scarecrow Press, 2005).

Kate Daubney is the Visiting Research Fellow in Film Music Studies at the University of Leeds, and specializes mainly in the music for Hollywood films of the 1930s and 1940s. She is the editor of the Scarecrow Series of Film Score Guides, and wrote the guide on Max Steiner's score for *Now, Voyager* (Greenwood, 2000). She has written entries on various film composers for the latest edition of *The New Grove Dictionary of Music and Musicians*, and has also published an article on Billie Holiday's vocal technique in the *Journal of Gender Studies* (vol. 11, 2002). Current research includes annotating Max Steiner's unpublished autobiography, and work on the personnel of the Warner Brothers orchestras of the 1930s and 1940s.

K.J. Donnelly is a lecturer in the Department of Theatre, Film and Television at the University of Wales, Aberystwyth, where he is the convenor of the MA in Film Studies. He wrote *Pop Music in British Cinema* (BFI, 2001) and *The Spectre of Sound* (BFI, 2005) and edited *Film Music: Critical Approaches* (Edinburgh University Press, 2001) and *Music and the Moving Image* (Edinburgh University Press, forthcoming). At present he is writing a book about British film music and film musicals for Palgrave Macmillan.

Richard Dyer's research has focused on notions of entertainment and representation, and especially the relations between them. His approach emphasizes the aesthetic and historical specificity of cultural texts. He is now working principally on music and film, and especially the work of Nino Rota and the concept of pastiche. He is also currently doing work on Lena Horne, the family in the Italian *giallo* film, music in Italian neo-realist cinema, and pre-Stonewall lesbian and gay culture. His previous publications include *Stars* (BFI, 1998), *Now You See It* (Routledge, 1990), *Culture of Queens* (Routledge, 2001), *Only Entertainment* (Routledge, 1992), *White* (Routledge, 1997) and *Seven* (BFI, 1999).

Cliff Eisen is Reader in Historical Musicology at King's College London. Although the bulk of his research and publications centre on Mozart and music of the eighteenth century, he has researched, taught, and written on popular and film music as well. His recent publications include articles on Carlos Gardel and Astor Piazzolla for *The New Grove Dictionary of Music and Musicians* as well as a review of Natalio Gorin's *Astor Piazzolla: A Memoir for Gramophone*. He has also lectured on Cole Porter at the British Library.

Janet K. Halfyard is a senior lecturer at Birmingham Conservatoire, a faculty of the University of Central England, where she teaches courses on film music, and on twentieth-century and contemporary music. Her publications include papers on extended vocal technique (which she performs as well as researches) and on film and television music. She is the author of *Danny Elfman's Batman: A Film Score Guide* (Scarecrow Press, 2000) and 'The Dark Avenger: Angel, music and cinematic superheroes', in *Reading Angel*, ed. Stacey Abbott (IB Tauris, 2005). Forthcoming publications include an essay on music in the television series *Buffy the Vampire Slayer* and an edited volume on Luciano Berio's *Sequenzas*.

Heather Laing is a freelance lecturer and writer and an Associate Tutor in Film Studies at the University of East Anglia. She is the author of *Gabriel Yared's The English Patient: A Film Score Guide* (Scarecrow, 2003) and 'Emotion by Numbers: Music, Song and the Musical' in *Musicals: Hollywood and Beyond*, ed. Bill Marshall and Robynn J. Stilwell (Intellect, 2000). She is currently working on a book on music, gender and emotion in 1940s melodrama and the woman's film for Ashgate.

Miguel Mera is Senior Lecturer in Composition for Screen at the Royal College of Music. He has published widely in a range of film music subjects. Recent publications include 'Is Funny Music Funny; Contexts and Case Studies of Film Music Humor', *Journal of Popular Music Studies* (2002, vol. 14, no. 2: 91–113); 'Representing the Baroque: The Portrayal of Historical Period in Film Music', *The Consort: Journal of the Dolmetsch Foundation* (Summer 2001, vol. 57: 3–21); and 'Read my Lips: Re-evaluating subtitling and dubbing in Europe', *Links and Letters* (no. 6, 1999, 73–85). Forthcoming publications include a monograph entitled *Mychael Danna's The Ice Storm: A Film Score Study Guide* for Scarecrow Press and 'Takemitsu's Composed Space in Kurosawa's Ran' in *Film Music Reader* (Cambridge University Press). Miguel also composes music for film, television and theatre, with recent work completed for independent film production companies, the BBC, Channel 4, Channel 5, Royal Shakespeare Company, Regent's Park Theatre, and the Youth Music Theatre UK. He also serves on the BAFTA Events and Education Committee.

For his first degree **Jon Paxman** studied composition and musicology at Huddersfield University, gaining top awards in both disciplines. Thereafter he undertook a Masters degree in screen composition at the Royal College of Music, under the tutorship of Joseph Horovitz and Francis Shaw. It was during this time that he began to study the collaborations of Kieslowski and Preisner, focusing predominantly on the *Three Colours* trilogy. Jon Paxman is currently a London-based composer, working in film and television.

Phil Powrie is Professor of French Cultural Studies at the University of Newcastle upon Tyne. He has published widely in French cinema studies, including *French Cinema in the 1980s: Nostalgia and the Crisis of Masculinity* (Oxford University Press, 1997), *Contemporary French Cinema: Continuity and Difference* (editor, Oxford University Press, 1999), *Jean-Jacques Beineix* (Manchester University Press, 2001), *French Cinema: An Introduction* (co-authored with Keith Reader, Arnold, 2002), and *24 Frames: French Cinema* (editor, Wallflower Press, 2005). He is the co-editor of several anthologies: *The Trouble with Men: Masculinities in European and Hollywood Cinema* (Wallflower Press, 2004), *Changing Tunes: The Use of Pre-existing Music in Film* (Ashgate, 2005), *Composing for the Screen in the USSR and Germany* (Indiana University Press, forthcoming 2006), *The Films of Luc Besson* (Manchester University Press, forthcoming 2006). He is the general co-editor of the journal *Studies in French Cinema*, and co-author of a monograph on film adaptations of the Carmen story.

Kathleen M. Vernon is Associate Professor of Hispanic Languages and Literature at the State University of New York at Stony Brook. She has published widely on the history of Spanish cinema and culture from the 1930s to the present.

Her publications include *Post-Franco Postmodern: The Films of Pedro Almodóvar* (Greenwood, 1995) and *The Spanish Civil War and the Visual Arts* (Cornell, 1990) as well as articles treating women's cinema, cinematic relations between Spain and Hollywood, musical film, and the work of directors such as Carlos Saura, Luis Berlanga, Pilar Miró and Josefina Molina. She is currently completing a study of film and popular culture in post-war Spain, *The Rhythms of History: Cinema, Music and Popular Memory*. She is also a collaborator in an AHRC-supported research project designed to produce an oral history of cinema-going in 1940s and 1950s Spain.

Reimar Volker studied performing arts at Hochschule der Künste Berlin and obtained a degree in music education in 1995. Further pursuing the topic of his diploma thesis on music in Nazi propaganda films, he went on to study musicology at the Technical University in Berlin. In 2001 he was awarded a PhD for his work on the composer Herbert Windt. The thesis entitled '*von oben sehr erwünscht*'—*Die Filmmusik Herbert Windts im NS-Propagandafilm* was published in 2003 (wvt-trier). He is currently working for the Goethe-Institute.

General Editor's preface

The upheaval that occurred in musicology during the last two decades of the twentieth century has created a new urgency for the study of popular music alongside the development of new critical and theoretical models. A relativistic outlook has replaced the universal perspective of modernism (the international ambitions of the 12-note style); the grand narrative of the evolution and dissolution of tonality has been challenged, and emphasis has shifted to cultural context, reception and subject position. Together, these have conspired to eat away at the status of canonical composers and categories of high and low in music. A need has arisen, also, to recognize and address the emergence of crossovers, mixed and new genres, to engage in debates concerning the vexed problem of what constitutes authenticity in music and to offer a critique of musical practice as the product of free, individual expression.

Popular musicology is now a vital and exciting area of scholarship, and the *Ashgate Popular and Folk Music Series* aims to present the best research in the field. Authors will be concerned with locating musical practices, values and meanings in cultural context, and may draw upon methodologies and theories developed in cultural studies, semiotics, poststructuralism, psychology and sociology. The series will focus on popular musics of the twentieth and twenty-first centuries. It is designed to embrace the world's popular musics from Acid Jazz to Zydeco, whether high tech or low tech, commercial or non-commercial, contemporary or traditional.

Professor Derek B. Scott
Chair of Music
University of Salford

Introduction

Miguel Mera and David Burnand

Focusing this anthology on the study of European film music is an approach that is, in equal measure, both necessary and problematic. It is necessary, because writing that examines the common themes, practices, methodologies and ideologies of music within European film tradition is scarce. Individual case studies of European film scores do exist, but the vast majority of extant research has concentrated on a canon of Hollywood film music, composers and systems. This overwhelming critical bias towards mainstream American filmmaking indicates that many of the assumptions and functional models on which film music studies have been based over the last twenty-five years are at best narrow and at worst misleading. Recent scholarship, of course, acknowledges that other film-scoring traditions can contribute to a broader debate on the nature of the relationship between music and moving images, and has thus begun to redress the balance somewhat. In particular Tatiana Egorova's examination of *Soviet Film Music*,[1] Rebecca Coyle's edited volume *Screen Scores: Studies in Contemporary Australian Film Music*[2] and Anna Morcom's doctoral thesis 'Hindi Film Songs and the Cinema'[3] suggest the increasing importance of localized studies in advancing our understanding of the nature of music in film. *European Film Music* aims to contribute to this important and widening debate.

However, this discussion is complicated by the fact that the idea of a pan-European film industry has never existed in any sustained sense. In many ways European culture is defined by its diversity: diversity of language, belief systems, climate, landscape, aesthetic values and so on. When we speak about European cinema we refer, more often than not, to the cinema of individual nation states, or rather national cinemas within Europe. Individual nations within Europe may have popular cinematic forms of their own – Swedish melodramas, French musicals, Italian horror movies – but these are rarely popular across the whole European market.[4] European audiences represent diverse class, gender and ethnic identities that complicate the question of European cinema.

This conflict between national and European identities is also highlighted by the very institution of a supposedly integrated Europe, the European Union. Initially, the EU consisted of just six countries: Belgium, Germany, France, Italy, Luxembourg and the Netherlands. Denmark, Ireland and the United Kingdom joined in 1973, Greece in 1981, Spain and Portugal in 1986, Austria, Finland and Sweden in 1995. In 2004 the biggest ever enlargement took place with ten new countries joining.[5] The EU is only now beginning to approach the notion of a pan-

European organization. However, individual states are keen to retain specific aspects of their sovereignty or, as some would argue, their individual identities. This is clearly played out in the United Kingdom, where strong arguments have been made across the political spectrum about the concept of 'saving the pound' rather than signing up to a single European currency. What does a change of currency mean to individual citizens? Is it not just a case of substituting one currency for another? As Carole Burgoyne and David Routh remind us, 'The money we use in everyday transactions derives its power from that of the national currency, which is in turn partly a function of the power of the state and a symbol of national sovereignty.'[6] At the time of writing, therefore, the relationship between individual nation states and the idea of Europe as a whole is evolving, but the concept of a European cinema remains just that, a concept.[7]

With so many apparent differences, then, what exactly is it that constitutes a European film? The easiest definition is one that falls within geographical boundaries, though even here there are difficulties. The member states of the European Union would not represent the same group of nations as a political map of Europe, for example, or include the same nations that compete in European sports championships. The European Convention on Cinematographic Co-production defines a 'European cinematographic work' using a scale where 'European elements' representing at least fifteen points out of a total of nineteen are required.[8] These 'elements' are divided into three groups, as follows: creative (director, scriptwriter, composer), performing (first, second and third acting roles) and technical craft (cameraman, sound recordist, editor, art director, studio or shooting location, post-production location). An 'element' such as a European director or a lead acting role would score three points, a European composer, editor, or shooting location one point and so on. Therefore, in this context, the definition of a film's European status is largely governed by the passports of the personnel involved in the production.[9] Is a European composer as important to the identity of a European film as a European shooting location? Does a European director such as Ridley Scott, for example, celebrate the values of European filmmaking by default? Of course, no system that attempts to quantify European-ness according to birthplace of individuals can ever be foolproof, because identity depends on so much more than solely physical location. The aim of the Convention, alongside a number of other pan-European funding initiatives such as the MEDIA Plus[10] and Eurimages[11] schemes, is to achieve greater unity between European countries and to strengthen the competitiveness of the European audiovisual industry as a whole. But as John Hill has observed, what has united European film industries in the past is not so much a common identity, but rather a 'shared set of problems which certain forms of European collaboration help alleviate'.[12] These shared problems include the aforementioned lack of exportability of national cinemas within and beyond Europe, as well as problems of adequate funding and distribution. However, if we accept that cinema plays an important role in the shaping of memory and construction of identity then there must surely be shared aesthetic and cultural values beyond shared problems that unite European cinema.

It is interesting to note that this conceptual identity has been largely defined by the methodologies that have been used to analyse and theorize European films and filmmakers. In her erudite introduction to the *European Cinema Reader*, Catherine Fowler explains the seminal role that scholarship has played in the creation of the notion of European cinema. Indeed, she believes that European cinema fundamentally 'relies on discourse to create its identity'.[13] In the process of defining that identity, scholars have focused on certain areas and favoured particular approaches over others. European film research has tended to focus on individual movements or moments (such as Italian neo-realism or the French New Wave). There has been a propensity to neglect certain areas of Europe (usually the smaller countries and especially Eastern Europe, although research in these fields is beginning to emerge).[14] There has been an emphasis on high culture or 'art films' rather than films that aim to be, or which are, popular at the box office. And there has been an emphasis on the importance of a single artistic and aesthetic voice, namely that of the director, rather than an understanding of the collaborative and/or industrial processes involved in filmmaking.

One of the reasons for favouring such critical approaches is that they emphasize features that distinguish European film from Hollywood films and filmmakers. Whenever scholars attempt to define European cinema they tend to do so by positioning it against the dominant mode of practice of American mainstream narrative cinema. As we have explained above, this is partly due to the fact that latching onto an all-encompassing concept of European cinema is virtually impossible. In an attempt to explain what European cinema *is*, scholars have used Hollywood as a means of defining what European cinema is *not*. For example, Peter Wollen's important essay on Godard's film *Vent de l'est* (1970) creates a direct opposition between traditional narrative mainstream film and radical 'counter-cinema'.[15] He defines 'seven deadly sins' that Hollywood frequently commits and opposes these with 'seven cardinal virtues' that he believes are exemplified in Godard's work. Even his term 'counter-cinema' suggests that the importance and very value of Godard's filmic text is its opposition to the mainstream. Whilst it is easy to find fault with the assertion that one form of cinema can be considered sinful whilst another is considered virtuous, Wollen's categorizations demonstrate that high-art aesthetics are frequently used as the means of valorizing European film. High culture, in fact, is generally viewed as one of the few unifying factors in European cinema, so that art film acts as a repository of European identity. However, as Mike Wayne argues, we must challenge the 'arrogance, the complacency, the assumptions and self-delusion involved in an uncritical celebration of Europe as the source and guarantor of Enlightenment ideals'.[16] We must also challenge the mirror image of this position which suggests that all Hollywood filmmaking is artistically and culturally bankrupt and acts as a threat to European culture.

The prevalent argument that European cinema is threatened by the external power of Hollywood is in reality much more complicated than polarized studies would initially suggest.[17] Given the increased ease of communications, the processes of globalization, and the intricate nature of film financing, the fluency between European and Hollywood film is a vital feature of both industries and cultures. Morley and Robbins believe that the boundaries are blurred and that 'America is now part of a European cultural repertoire, part of European identity'.[18] The growth of Euro-American cinema could be viewed as a confirmation of America's cultural dominance.[19] Certainly US distributors strive to maintain their share in overseas markets and most of the major studios have established production bases in Europe. American companies such as Miramax work on acquiring low-budget foreign films or make their own big-budget versions of them, for example *Chocolat* (Hallström, 2000).[20] However, one might equally argue that Europe is an essential part of Hollywood's cultural identity. French conglomerates such as Canal + have developed close links with American partners in order to invest in films with a 'global' appeal. European cinema and Europeans have always had a profound influence on American filmmaking. The birth of what we would now call the Golden Age of Hollywood film music was masterminded and executed by European émigrés such as Max Steiner and Erich Wolfgang Korngold in the 1930s and 1940s, and European influence in Hollywood continues. For example, one of the most successful and powerful composers working in Hollywood today is the German Hans Zimmer, and directors such as the Englishman Anthony Minghella and the German Wolfgang Petersen also work within the studio system. Hollywood has always drawn heavily from European traditions in terms of style, technique and aesthetics.

> The dialogue between Hollywood and European cinema had been on-going for over a century. It has included the exchange of personnel, the exchange and interrelation of film form and content in terms of style, genre, narrative, and so on, and also trade discussions concerning the economic and cultural implications of America's domination of the European market. However, as Geoffrey Nowell-Smith points out, this conversation had often been marked by rhetoric: economic rhetoric from the US side, championing the free market and consumer choice; culturalist rhetoric from the European, which focuses on cultural and national identities and views Hollywood cinema as an hegemonic invader .... In reality, this relationship is more complex, not least due to the ambiguous position cinema itself occupies in relation to modernity .... Cinema's industrial production practices, its reliances on modern developments in technology and the position of cinema as a major form of mass entertainment make it a clear exemplar of social modernity.[21]

It is difficult enough to unravel the complexities of modernism within cinema itself, but the addition of musical modernism increases this challenge. The modernity of film technology and the technique of montage are at odds with the tendency to employ, in both Europe and the USA, older and less obviously fragmented approaches to storytelling in the cinema, for example through continuity editing. Movies most usually subordinate the artificiality of cinematography and editing to the pre-modern conventions of narrative realism. Moreover, even the most modernist of movies may use music in an anachronistically conservative way. For instance, despite the surrealism of *Un chien andalou* (1929), Luis Buñuel alternated gramophone recordings of Wagner's 'Liebestod' from *Tristan und Isolde* and Argentinian tango music to represent, respectively, romantic love and lust, in an emblematic manner that merely apes much earlier theatrical practice.[22] Thus, we have two sets of interlocking contradictions: the tension between modernism and realism within cinema, and the inconsistency between modernist cinema and modernist music. This is further complicated by the confused border-crossings of modernism and postmodernism, at least when applying those terms to individual art works.

One modernist feature found in films that are dealt with in several chapters herein is the alienation technique known as distanciation, which derived (via Brecht and Althusser) from Marxist encouragement for 'objectification' or 'estrangement' as a means of challenging mainstream ideological expectations.[23] If mainstream cinema relies on a combination of approaches, including continuity editing, linear narrative and the focus on characters that demand our support or dislike (often through the aid of music), then distanciation techniques target and subvert these methods. Musical examples detailed in *European Film Music* include: the avoidance of non-diegetic music, anempathetic music and music that deliberately underplays musical expression, as well as speculative collaborative processes between composer and director.

Modernism is inherent to the technologically enabled means of audio production in filmmaking that encourages the alliance of music and sound design as a recorded and edited form, and thus is at odds with the rehashed nineteenth-century orchestral scores typical of classic cinema, flown into the virtual orchestra pit of the movie theatre. Nevertheless, to return to an earlier issue, it would be wrong to conclude that this results from more open attitudes attributable to European or avant-garde filmmakers. The same approach to total sound design can be found contemporaneously in mainstream US cinema, for instance in *Seven* (Fincher, 1997).[24] Modernist tendencies continue to move from the margins to the mainstream, even though such 'progress' is often slow.

Having outlined some of the territories – physical, ideological, and aesthetic – that the study of European film music necessarily encompasses, we can now turn to the aims of the present anthology. Two parallel structural principles are in operation. First, the chapters contained here take us on a journey from older to newer forms of European filmmaking, covering a historical period from the 1920s until the early twenty-first century. Secondly, and as a consequence of the first principle, there is an inevitable trajectory from broad overviews to individual case studies. Historical distance often allows for greater evaluative clarity where the longevity and cultural impact of a group of texts can be explored, while it is often more challenging to draw out large issues within more recent work. Both approaches are equally valid and necessary, not least because they show the progressive development of a rich European film music heritage.

Arguably, Europe shares one dominant, momentous and painful memory, that of World War II. Unsurprisingly, therefore, many of the early chapters deal with the ways in which film music functioned and was defined before and after that war, and how cultural identity was shaped in relation to the political and social upheaval that took place. In '*Per aspera ad astra* and back again: film music in Germany from 1927 to 1945' Reimar Volker deals with the interaction of cinema, which was to become the Nazi's primary propaganda vehicle, and music, which was considered the highest art form and consequently subject to the strictest monitoring by the ultra-conservative Reich chamber. Volker's chapter provides a detailed survey of the development of German film music from the introduction of sound to the start of war, the bureaucratic frameworks for music and cinema during that period, as well as their impact on composers and on film music. Volker demonstrates that the coming of sound encouraged avant-garde approaches to filmmaking in Germany during the 1920s. This included the undisputed logic of using contemporary music for a contemporary medium; a logic that is rarely demonstrated in cinema, even modernist cinema, elsewhere and at other times.

In Italy also, the Fascist regime's exacting control over national cultural production had profound ramifications for post-war Italian cinema. Although the *verismo* movement of the 1920s can be understood as its forerunner,[25] the rise of neo-realist cinema (1942–52) was fuelled by passionate responses to Fascist repression, the Resistance, and the War. Italian filmmakers felt obliged to reveal sociocultural truths and employed amateur actors and simple depictions of lower-class life to create documentary-like objectivity. Within this contextual framework, Richard Dyer explores the distance between diegetic and non-diegetic music. As Dyer explains, the characters within Italian neo-realist films are frequently defined by diegetic music; they sing, play, dance and listen to folk songs, popular music, jazz and fragments of opera arias. However, their music – the music of the people – is rarely heard or referenced on the non-diegetic soundtrack. Dyer draws attention to a crucial dichotomy in which characters in neo-realist cinema need music to speak on their behalf, but the music that is used to do so does not belong to them. Of course, this distance is an equally common feature in numerous other cinematic traditions, but Dyer perceives it to be particularly problematic in the case of neo-realism, a movement concerned with an honest expression of ordinary people's reality. The conflict that this attitude towards music creates is a challenge to the avowed ambitions of neo-realism. A lack of genuine identification with the cinematic subjects not only distances these films from their protagonists but also from their audience.

While Dyer examines a broad range of Italian texts and filmmakers, Kathleen Vernon and Cliff Eisen compare and contrast just two of Spain's best-known directors, Carlos Saura and Pedro Almodóvar, and their respective collaborations with the composers Luis de Pablo and Alberto Iglesias. Both directors display a clear personal interest in the use of music, but they do so in very different cultural and historical contexts. The authors examine Saura and de Pablo's work between 1965 and 1972, during which the Francoist dictatorship and general modernist currents in Europe profoundly influenced their attempts to rejuvenate their national film industry. Saura and de Pablo rejected the narrative conventions and spectatorial practices associated with classic cinema and used avant-garde music, *música concreta*, or music that issued exclusively from the diegesis, usually sparsely, as a means of challenging their audience. In many ways, Almodóvar was equally reactive, but as one of the leading lights of the post-Franco counter-culture youth movement known as the *Movida*, he did not make direct reference to the ghost of the *generalísimo*, instead opting for a hedonistic liberation of the senses. According to Vernon and Eisen, however, Almodóvar's work with Iglesias some twenty years later represents a new 'normativity'[26] for Spanish film music in responding in innovative ways to the symphonic traditions of the past. Ultimately, Vernon and Eisen show how, in very different ways, these four characters have succeeded in projecting dominant images of Spanishness to Europe and beyond.

Just as Vernon and Eisen relate Spanish film music to its cultural and historical contexts, Kate Daubney demonstrates how the scoring strategies of the films that have become known as the Ealing Comedies capture the way that the British perceived their surroundings and identity in the period following World War II. Daubney argues that the Ealing Comedies satirize large ideas in small contexts and demonstrate a critical purpose as powerful as the fictional coverage of war that preceded them. Daubney, known for her influential work on Max Steiner,[27] is well positioned to comment on some of the differences between contemporaneous Hollywood and British film music approaches. She argues that the Ealing Comedies use music sparsely, with little repetition of material, and avoid the grand designs evident in so many Hollywood film scores. The function of music in the Ealing Comedies, therefore, is not so much about the representation of character or emotion, but about epitomizing a way of life or delineating an alternative fantasy vision for society.

Contrasting attitudes between Hollywood and Europe are demonstrated also in Janet Halfyard's examination of the differences between the two cinematic traditions' representation of classical music performers. Halfyard highlights two ideas that can be associated with characters who perform classical music in Hollywood cinema. First, there is a clear connection to European-identified characters who are positioned as gifted musicians but also often as the villains or anti-heroes of their narratives. Second, performing classical music often represents a threat to an American character, seducing them away from American values. This threat is often literally 'played out' through a confrontational juxtaposition of high culture and popular culture. Halfyard argues that the same opposition is not a common characteristic of European cinema, nor is there a specific association between classical music and villains or anti-heroes. Halfyard also highlights differences between male and female performers within the European and Hollywood traditions.

In 'Outing the synch: music and space in the French heritage film', Phil Powrie also considers the role of classical music, though not so much its performance as its non-diegetic ideological function (the connotation of high art), its structural function as motif, and more particularly its match or mismatch with the heritage aspect of the narrative. The combination of specially composed music and pre-existent classical music is also examined. Powrie shows how music unsettles and complicates in French heritage cinema, on occasions, functioning as more than just the reinforcement of historical location that might otherwise be expected. Rather than dress up the characters still further with slavish adherence to period pastiche, musical style and instrumentation can be at odds with historical, geographic and cultural location, thereby creating a hybrid space that is clearly postmodern.

Powrie's chapter marks the mid-point of this anthology and acts as a fulcrum for two simultaneous and seemingly contradictory obsessions that have been displayed in European cinema and European film scholarship. First, there has been a profound respect for the past. This is manifested in a museum-like aesthetic of preservation and canonization of great works and filmmakers. Second, there has been an equally forceful rejection of the cinema of the moment in order to allow for the creation of the cinema of the future. As Catherine Fowler observes, European film history has been portrayed as a series of New Waves and is 'therefore characterised by *instability*....'[28] Some of those moments of instability are elaborated in the next three chapters that examine diverse ways in which modernist, subversive principles have affected certain types of European film-scoring methods and approaches.

In 'Seán Ó Riada and Irish post-colonial film music: George Morrison's *Mise Éire*', David Cooper demonstrates that Ó Riada's score marks a turning point in his compositional style, no longer drawing exclusively on European high modernism, but now incorporating Irish traditional music. Cooper argues that this juxtaposition provides an expression of the post-colonial aspirations of a twentieth-century Ireland looking both forwards and backwards. Ó Riada's quotation of carefully selected traditional songs such as '*Róisín Dubh*', which is both a love song and a political allegory of Ireland, supports this purpose. Furthermore, Cooper argues that the resulting 'postmodern patchwork' is at least partially at odds with George Morrison's unified linear narrative, both underlining and undermining the film's function as Irish Republican propaganda. On the face of it, the proximity of traditional melodies and fragmented, strident atonality speaks of a conventional characterization technique, contrasting the indigenous and the intrusive. However, this simple opposition is made more subtle and telling by the contradictory values that can be assigned to modern music in the context of a twentieth-century Ireland looking simultaneously to the past and the future.

Modernist approaches are also explored in 'Angel of the air: Popol Vuh's music and Werner Herzog's films'. In this chapter Kevin J. Donnelly focuses on the extent to which Popol Vuh's music adds to the distinctiveness of Herzog's feature films of the 1970s and 1980s. From their background in pop and experimental music, Donnelly argues that Popol Vuh provided an appropriate and essential element of atmosphere to the long-take, spectacular style of Herzog, whilst avoiding many of the dramatic functions expected of conventional film scores, in particular underplaying emotional expression. More generally, Donnelly contends that this collaboration reveals significant parallels between New German cinema and so-called *Krautrock*.

The arguably semi-autonomous role of Popol Vuh's music in these contexts provides interesting comparisons with the more compromised experimentalism found in Angelopoulos' later films, discussed by Miguel Mera in 'Modernity and a day: the functions of music in the films of Theo Angelopoulos. Mera focuses on *Eternity and a Day* (1998), which exemplifies a shift away from the hard-line modernism of Angelopoulos' earlier work. Drawing on a wide range of commentary, including that of the director himself, Mera helps us to understand the drivers behind this transfer from modernism, to an approach that cannot readily be termed postmodernism either. The search for a fresh approach to using music in Angelopoulos' films reveals a fascinating collaborative process with composer Eleni Karaindrou. The outcome, despite the relatively small amount of music in *Eternity and a Day*, demonstrates a rejection of standard Hollywood practice leading to the development of a distinctive set of dramatic functions and purpose, especially in terms of structure, silence and contemplation. This chapter also reveals the inadequacies of conventional theoretical frameworks for the study of film music beyond the model of mainstream narrative cinema.

The last three chapters of *European Film Music* provide close readings of individual films from recent times, though from three different perspectives. Jon Paxman provides a detailed, multi-layered analysis of just one cue from Kieslowski and Preisner's last collaboration, in 'Preisner–Kieslowski: the art of synergetic understatement *Three Colours: Red*'. By concentrating exclusively on the first music cue of this 1994 film, a sequence lasting less than five minutes, Paxman reveals an impressive range of diegetic and non-diegetic musical functions within and between the narrative and sub-narrative, as well as music–image synergies that go beyond the commonplace expectations of hyperexplicity in cinema. These insights suggest a benchmark for collaborative purpose between director and composer that is rarely achieved, either in mainstream or art-house movies.

Numerous writers have problematized the excessive use of non-diegetic music in the representation of women characters, especially in Hollywood melodrama. Feminist theory has shown how women in film have been represented in terms of masculine ideologies and morals, and an all-pervading male gaze.[29] However, explorations of the soundscape in relation to the representation of masculinity remain rare. Heather Laing's close examination of Claire Denis' legionnaire film *Beau Travail* (1999) reveals how excessive *silence* is used to both represent and undermine the identity of the central male character, Galoup. Furthermore, through an intertextual exploration of the film's use of pre-existent disco music and sections of Benjamin Britten's opera *Billy Budd*, Laing shows how the opposition of music and silence further contributes to a critical representation of masculinity. Laing highlights ways in which the film's representation of repressed emotion and the battle between control and lack of control allows Galoup only one means of escape, which is to willingly surrender to music and dance, chaos and the feminine. *Beau Travail* challenges many of the conventions of 'normal' masculine emotion as it has been understood and represented by film music scholars hitherto.

In the final chapter of this book, David Burnand charts some of the decision-making processes involved in the creation of the soundscape for Andrew Kötting's art-house film *This Filthy Earth* (2001). As composer for the film he is uniquely placed to be able to comment on the nature of this process. Burnand provides a detailed examination of his compositional approaches and techniques, as well as an insight into the development of the soundscape both artistically and in its political context. This inside experience reveals that the differences between mainstream and independent filmmaking may not be as contrasted as scholars have tended to portray them.

Examples of practice-led research such as this are extremely rare in film music studies, mainly because few film composers are able to objectify their own instinctive and contingent processes. Therefore, existing testimonies tend to be anecdotal and/or often fail to provide genuine detail and critical insight. However, film musicologists have been equally reluctant to engage in the examination of process rather than product, often because of a fear that any discoveries may distort or problematize academic arguments. The inherent challenges of this type of research have been at the heart of an intention versus interpretation debate for many years.[30] But this debate is one of the most potentially fruitful and fascinating areas for development in second-generation film-music studies. It is our contention that a living art form involving living people should not rely solely on readings of the text. There can and should be a relationship between practice and research; scholars can and should be able to influence filmmakers; and practitioners can and should be able to have an input into the advancement of knowledge that goes beyond the work that they create.

It has never been our intention to provide complete coverage of European film music, nor would it be possible to do so in a single volume containing a wide range of approaches. Research in European film music is still in its relative infancy and the preferences and prejudices displayed here represent the field as it stands, and inevitably, the aspects of European film music studies that are omitted are just as significant as those that are included. For example, there is no discussion of the national cinematic traditions of Bosnia, the Czech Republic, Finland, Poland, Sweden or Turkey. There is no discussion of the work of directors such as Argento, Bergman, Buñuel, Godard, Sverák, Tanovic, Truffaut or Wajda, or of composers such as Alexandre Desplat, Simon Fisher Turner, Hans Werner Henze, Erich Nordgren, Nicola Piovanni or Rachel Portman. There is comparatively little exploration of European funding structures and how these have shaped European film music. Clearly, more work in the field is needed. We hope that *European Film Music* provides a starting point from which such research may grow in the future, and we are indebted to the authors who have contributed to this anthology. Now they must speak for themselves.

Notes

1. Egorova, T. *Soviet Film Music: An Historical Survey*, London: Harwood Academic Publishers, 1997.
2. Coyle, R. (ed.) *Screen Scores: Studies in Contemporary Australian Film Music*, Sydney: AFTRS, 1998.
3. Morcom, A.F. 'Hindi film songs and the cinema', unpublished PhD thesis, London: University of London, 2002. Due to be revised and published by Ashgate (forthcoming).
4. See Dyer, R. and Vincendeau, G. (eds) *Popular European Cinema*, London and New York: Routledge, 1992.
5. Cyprus, Czech Republic, Estonia, Hungary, Latvia, Lithuania, Malta, Poland, Slovakia, and Slovenia.
6. Burgoyne, C.B. and Routh, D.A. 'National Identity, European Identity and the Euro', in K. Cameron (ed.) *National Identity*, Exeter: Intellect, 1999, 115.
7. On 29 October 2004, the Heads of State of Government of the 25 member states and the three candidate countries of the European Union signed the treaty establishing a Constitution for Europe which would then need to be ratified by all 25 member states of the enlarged Union. In June 2005, following referenda, both France and the Netherlands rejected the Constitution. At the time of writing, it is unclear what implications this will have for the European Union as a whole.
8. See Appendix 2 of the agreement at http://conventions.coe.int/Treaty/en/Treaties/html/147.htm
9. It is interesting to see what has been excluded from this list of 'European elements', for example, a European sound-designer would currently not score any points but a sound recordist would score one point.
10. MEDIA Plus, the successor to MEDIA and MEDIA II came into being in January 2001 and aims at strengthening the competitiveness of the European audiovisual industry through a series of support mechanisms dealing with the training of professionals; the development of production projects and companies; the distribution and promotion of cinematographic works and audiovisual programmes; and the support for cinematographic festivals.
11. Eurimages is the Council of Europe fund for the co-production, distribution and exhibition of European cinematographic works. It aims to promote the European film industry by encouraging the production and distribution of films and fostering co-operation between professionals.
12. Hill, J. 'The Future of European Cinema: The Economics and Culture of Pan-European Strategies', in J. Hill, M. McLoone and P. Hainsworth (eds), *Border Crossing: Film in Ireland, Britain and Europe*, London: BFI, 1994, 67. Of course, the amount of alleviation that specific types of collaboration might provide is open to debate. For a detailed discussion of the strengths and weaknesses of the European

film business, see Jäckel, A. *European Film Industries*, London: BFI Publishing, 2003.

13. Fowler, C. (ed.) *The European Cinema Reader*, London and New York: Routledge, 2002, 1.

14. See Iordanova, D. *Cinema of the Other Europe: The Industry and Artistry of East Central European Film*, London and New York: Wallflower Press, 2003.

15. Wollen, P. 'Godard and Counter Cinema: *Vent d'Est*', in B. Nichols (ed.), *Movies and Methods Volume II*, Berkeley, Los Angeles and London: University of California Press, 1985, 500–509.

16. Wayne, M. *The Politics of Contemporary European Cinema*, Bristol: Intellect, 2002, 1.

17. See Orr, J. 'New Directions in European Cinema', in E. Ezra (ed.), *European Cinema*, Oxford: Oxford University Press, 2004, 299–317; Ellwood, D.W. and Kroes, R. (eds) *Hollywood in Europe: Experiences of a Cultural Hegemony*, Amsterdam: VU University Press, 1994; Nowell-Smith, G. 'Introduction', in G. Nowell-Smith and Ricci, S. (eds), *Hollywood and Europe: Economics, Culture, National Identity 1945–95*, London: BFI, 1998, 1–16.

18. Morley, D. and Robbins, K. 'Space of identity: communication technologies and the reconfiguration of Europe', *Screen*, **30** (4), Autumn 1989, 21.

19. Lev, P. *The Euro-American Cinema*, Austin: University of Texas Press, 1993.

20. The term 'Miramaxisation' has been coined by Ray Bingham to describe the radical reconstruction of independent film distribution following the success and influence of Miramax. Cited in Biskind, P. *Down and Dirty Pictures: Miramax, Sundance, and the Rise of the Independent Film*, New York and London: Simon & Schuster, 2004, 193.

21. Davison, A. *Hollywood Theory, Non-Hollywood Practice: Cinema Soundtracks in the 1980s and 1990s*, Aldershot: Ashgate, 2004, 5.

22. See Burnand, D. and Sarnaker, B. 'The Articulation of National Identity Through Film Music', *National Identities*, **1** (1), 1999, 7–13.

23. See Eagleton, T. *The Ideology of the Aesthetic*, London: Blackwell, 1990; Jameson, F. *Brecht and Method*, New York: Verso, 1998.

24. See Dyer, R. *Seven* (BFI Modern Classics), London: BFI, 1999; Brophy, P. *Cinesonic: The World of Sound on Film*, Sydney: Southwood Press, 1999.

25. The *verismo* literary movement included writers such as Italo Calvino, Cesare Pavese and Alberto Moravia. During the Fascist years many neo-realist writers went into hiding, were imprisoned or exiled, or joined the Resistance.

26. See Chapter 3, p. 51, this volume.

27. Daubney, K. *Max Steiner's Now, Voyager: A Film Score Guide*, Westport, CT: Greenwood Press, 2000.

28. Fowler, *The European Cinema Reader*, 7.

29. See, for example, Mulvey, L. 'Visual Pleasure and Narrative Cinema', *Screen*, **16** (3), Autumn 1975, 6–18. This remains one of the most influential texts in the field.

30. See, for example Bordwell, D. *Making Meaning: Inference and Rhetoric in the Interpretation of Cinema*, Cambridge, MA: Harvard University Press, 1991, 72; Iseminger, G. (ed.) *Intention and Interpretation*, Philadelphia: Temple University Press, 1992.

Chapter 1

Per aspera ad astra and back again: film music in Germany from 1927 to 1945

Reimar Volker

German musicality meets German technology

In 1919 the German inventors Hans Vogt, Jo Engl and Joseph Masolle developed a technique they called Tri-Ergon. It enabled the transfer of an acoustical signal to an optical one and then back again to sound by way of electrical current.[1] The first public demonstration took place in Berlin on 17 September 1922. While the general public reacted enthusiastically, the press and industry were less impressed. None of the major German film companies – including the most influential, Universal Film AG (Ufa) – showed interest in using the technique commercially. Due to the lack of support the Tri-Ergon company was forced to sell its patents to a company based in Switzerland. Not until 1925, with a much improved patent, did Tri-Ergon succeed in attracting Ufa's attention.

Yet the first ever 'talking' movie produced by Ufa and Tri-Ergon – a twenty-minute adaptation of the Hans Christian Andersen fairy tale *Das Mädchen mit den Schwefelhölzern* (*The Little Match Girl*, 1925) – was a failure, the sound cutting out only a few minutes into the film.[2] With the shadow of the world economic crisis looming, the Ufa leadership decided to refrain from costly and risky attempts at promoting and supporting sound film, especially since the company was doing rather well with silent films and had already acquired a good many theatres and investments in orchestras and theatre infrastructure. Ufa felt no need to change a system that was fully operational and financially lucrative.

Interest in sound film and the musical opportunities it offered was thus left to companies driven less by commercial than by artistic and entrepreneurial concerns. One such company was TOBIS, the Ton-Bild-Syndikat. Founded in 1928 under the musical directorship of Guido Bagier, TOBIS supported experiments in film music at the renowned contemporary music festival of Baden-Baden, where, since 1927, composers had been presenting film music composed to avant-garde films. At Baden-Baden film music was being discussed as a genre and medium in its own right for the first time. Composers explored the concept of 'contemporary music' for a 'contemporary medium', and strongly rejected the nineteenth-century illustrative music then used to accompany silent films. The concept of diegetic and non-diegetic music was discussed, as too were ideas of dramatization such as visual counterpoint. The 1928 Baden-Baden festival featured two animated films with sound by Ernst Toch and Walter Gronostay, the latter a pupil of Arnold Schoenberg's class at the Berlin Academy. Paul Hindemith also made an appearance, presenting a piece of film music entitled *Rebellion der Gegenstände* performed by mechanical piano.

One of the other composers present who was to venture permanently into the new art form was Wolfgang Zeller. Zeller had been trained as a violinist and studied composition before being drafted during World War I. Upon his return in 1919 he started composing professionally, writing orchestral music, chamber music and a violin concerto. He also worked as orchestral violinist in one of Berlin's most renowned theatres, the Volksbühne. After taking the baton for a performance he was subsequently promoted to house conductor and composer, a position Zeller held from 1921 to 1929. During that period he wrote incidental music to more than eighty productions.

For the 1928 Baden-Baden festival Zeller set the music to a work by Lotte Reiniger, a stage designer at the Volksbühne who also experimented with animated film.[3] Reiniger's *Abenteuer des Prinzen Achmed* (*The Adventures of Prince Achmed*, 1923–26), with its original silhouette style of animation, was a phenomenal success at Baden-Baden. Zeller was the only composer at the festival not to make use of any of the many synchronizing devices being tested at the time. Instead he used a stopwatch as he conducted the nine-piece ensemble that played his compositions. A contemporary critic declared that year's festival to be at the cutting edge of film music in its exploration of new musical possibilities. The following year Walter Gronostay presented music set to a film by Hans Richter *Alles dreht sich, alles bewegt sich* (*Everything Turns, Everything Revolves*), while Paul Dessau and Darius Milhaud also premiered film-related works.

For the TOBIS company its interest and support of film music paid off: Wolfgang Zeller attracted the interest of director Walter Ruttmann, who had recently been the focus of attention following the release of his *Symphonie einer Großstadt* (*Symphony of a City*, 1928). Ruttmann hired Zeller to set the music to the documentary *Melodie der Welt* (*Melody of the World*). The film was premiered on 13 March 1929 as the first ever German sound film.[4]

Meanwhile Ufa, still the largest and most powerful German film company, saw that the arrival of the talking movie was imminent. For Ufa to keep its position in the film industry it would have to embrace the new technology as well. In 1928 Ufa's CEO Ludwig Klitzsch took a team of staff members to the United States. In New York Klitzsch is said to have had an eye- (and ear-) opening experience: waiting in the lobby of his New York hotel he noticed that the thirteen-strong house-band, of which nine members turned out to be either from Austria or Germany, was playing German tunes. It occurred to Klitzsch that the combination of 'German' musicality and 'German' sound film technology could ensure Ufa's future leadership.[5]

Back in Berlin a new music department was founded at Ufa, mainly to provide soundtracks to silent films, but also to pursue new projects. Eminent composers were hired to ensure the highest musical standards. Songs were commissioned from such prominent and popular songwriters as Ralph Benatzky, Werner Richard Heymann, Friedrich Holländer and Walter Kollo. On 12 December 1929, Ufa premiered its first sound film, *Melodie des Herzens* (*Melody of the Heart*), which had initially gone into production as a silent and later was given a soundtrack by Werner Richard Heymann, another composer to have emerged from the theatre and vaudeville circuit. Born in Königsberg in 1896, Heymann studied violin and composition before being drafted. Initially he composed patriotic songs, but after his brother was killed in World War I he became an outspoken pacifist. Heymann continued composing after the war and his works were played by the Vienna Philharmonic. In the Berlin of the 1920s Heymann drifted into Dadaist circles and wrote incidental music for various Dadaist shows and plays. He also worked in cabaret where he came into contact with Max Reinhardt's legendary *Schall und Rauch*. Heymann became one of the musical fathers of this new genre that emerged in the late 1920s as left-wing entertainment featuring political songs opposing the status quo. When cabaret lost its popularity during the Depression, Heymann turned to film and took a job at the Ufa studios in Neubabelsberg near Berlin (see Figure 1.1). He started out as a set entertainer,

Figure 1.1   Werner Richard Heymann conducting the Ufa-Filmorchestra, late 1920s
Reproduced by permission of the Archiv der Akademie der Künste, Berlin

playing music to raise the spirits of silent movie actors, which led him to an assistant position under Ufa's musical director, Ernö Rapée. Work at Ufa constantly clashed with Heymann's left-wing and pacifist views, especially after the ultra-conservative media tycoon Alfred Hugenberg took over the company. In 1928 Heymann switched to TOBIS, which was still promoting film composition at Baden-Baden, but the following year he was lured back to Ufa to set the music to *Melodie des Herzens*, which received its first performance on 16 December 1929.[6]

In 1929, 224 German films were produced of which 14 were already talkies. Ufa was doing quite well and the fiscal year 1929/30 ended with Ludwig Klitzsch optimistically declaring that his company had assumed a very strong position among European sound film companies. Against the backdrop of growing political unrest, not least fomented by his nationalist and ultra right-wing boss Alfred Hugenberg, an outspoken supporter of Adolf Hitler, Ufa's archivist put on record that the company was on the path to independence from American cultural domination, resisting the cultural 'Überfremdung', or 'foreign infiltration' of American film companies.[7]

Waltzing to Weimar

With the gradual demise of silent film, individual musical responsibilities previously held by conductors and their orchestras at cinemas were quickly shifting to film producers. One of the most prolific and musically imaginative production units at Ufa was that of Erich Pommer.

After producing *Melodie des Herzens* with Heymann's music, Pommer quickly took on several more sound film productions. As a film representative Pommer had travelled extensively through Europe, where he was able to create a tight network of international film contacts. Before the advent of modern-day dubbing, Pommer simultaneously produced his films in several languages, usually French and English, using the same set with different actors and the same songs with different lyrics. He was fortunate to work with bilingual actors and singers such as the Anglo-German Lilian Harvey.

One of the next projects Erich Pommer tackled was a loose adaptation of Heinrich Mann's novel *Professor Unrat* entitled *Der Blaue Engel* (*The Blue Angel*, 1930). During auditions for the lead role, one of the accompanists caught Pommer's attention: Friedrich Holländer, a classically trained musician who had achieved prominence in the cabaret and vaudeville circuit for which Berlin was famous in the Roaring Twenties. Holländer was also a former member of one of the most popular Berlin jazz bands at the time, the Weintraub Syncopators. Pommer and the director Josef von Sternberg finally selected Marlene Dietrich as lead actress and singer, a break that sparked her international career. Holländer was hired to write four songs for the film, one of which was to become one of the first film-launched evergreens – *Ich bin von Kopf bis Fuß auf Liebe eingestellt* (*Falling in Love Again* in the English version of the film). The song was intended as a soundtrack spin-off from the outset, but the recording company was not convinced of its potential and only 200 records were initially pressed – yet the records sold out even before the film was released.[8] Because the original master copy had been thrown away, the track had to be re-recorded. Using the orchestration of Franz Wachsmann[9] – Holländer's successor as pianist with the Weintraub Syncopators – Heymann went on to write the remaining film score to *Der Blaue Engel*.[10]

Erich Pommer specialized in transferring aspects of the operetta to sound film. When the composer originally engaged for the first film of this kind failed to fulfil his contract, Pommer asked Heymann for his musical advice. Heymann quickly stepped in and provided songs and music for the film *Liebeswalzer* (*Lovewaltz*), which was simultaneously produced in French as *Valse d'amour*. The most successful film to emerge from the Pommer unit was *Die Drei von der Tankstelle* (*The Three Guys from the Filling Station*, 1930), which included a star cast and many soon-to-be evergreens such as *Ein Freund, ein guter Freund*. The film was also produced in French as *Le chemin de paradis* starring Henri Garat.[11] By 1933 Pommer had produced a total of fifteen films, all with a strong and unique emphasis on music and film songs, a style that had emerged from Viennese operetta and comtemporary popular song. He worked with directors such as Robert Siodmak, Billy Wilder, Erik Charell and Wilhelm Thiele; composers involved included Friedrich Holländer, Franz Wachsmann and Werner Richard Heymann.

Apart from the commercial interest in mass popular films, Ufa Film also paid tribute to the political inclinations of its leadership. In July of 1932 Ufa decided to introduce a new series of films that, instead of providing entertainment and diversion from the bleak outside world, would do justice to what it termed the '*Aufbaugedanke*' (the founding spirit) of its authoritarian leadership. Yet, as Siegfried Kracauer was already aware, this policy would have little effect on a company that had hitherto succeeded so well in combining various strands of supposedly opposing artistic (and political) styles.[12]

Günther Stapenhorst was chosen to lead the production of the series, which was conceived as bringing forth a new type of heroic film. That the official press releases did not yet identify a composer suggests that Ufa still had not found the right kind of music for their project. When Stapenhorst and one of his scriptwriters later attended an opera premiere, they came across a composer they immediately deemed appropriate for their nationalistic films: Herbert Windt. His artistic background was different from most of the composers employed by Ufa at the time. Windt had studied composition with Franz Schreker and had made his mark as an opera composer in the Berlin of the late 1920s. At that time Berlin was at the very forefront of modern opera, or known for infamous first performances and regular scandals at the Kroll-Oper under such renowned conductors as Erich

Kleiber and Otto Klemperer. It was Erich Kleiber who also conducted Windt's opera *Andromache* at the slightly more conservative Preussische Staatsoper. After seeing Windt's neo-expressionist opera, Stapenhorst immediately offered him the opportunity to score *Morgenrot* (*Dawn*, 1932–33), a U-boat drama set in World War I, that reaches its dramatic climax when one of the main characters exclaims that Germans may not know how to live, but certainly know how to die, before committing suicide in order to save his fellow sailors. Not surprisingly, the film was re-released at the height of World War II. The Allied forces later classified the film as 'a good production with excellent acting, nationalist and militarist propaganda'.[13]

Windt accepted Stapenhorst's offer and embarked on a career in film music. He would be instrumental in establishing a new style of heroic music, born out of the spirit of later Richard Strauss with moderately atonal influences and very heavy orchestration. It was a style that would become synonymous with that of Nazi film propaganda. This style further exaggerated what Reinhold Brinkmann has recently termed the 'distorted sublime' in National Socialist (music) aesthetics. The initial idea was to tap into the nineteenth-century symphonic tradition which established the idea of the sublime, doing so, however, in a sense that this had emerged out of the seventeenth-century distinction between the sublime and the beautiful. This, according to Immanuel Kant, was a distinction of each individual's choice. The concept and definition of the sublime lay in the subject and not in the object. By subordinating all forms of artistic expression to politics and ideology, art was in a sense depersonalized by National Socialism. Furthermore, the sublime was perceived not as a category of subjective definition but as an integral and increasingly necessary part of a work of art itself. Music and composition in particular were expected to reconnect to the nineteenth-century symphonic tradition by embracing the sublime. Film music, enhanced by its visual stimulus, obviously also lent itself to this prerequisite.[14]

Morgenrot had its first official premiere on 2 February 1933, three days after the Nazis had officially seized power. The performance, held at Berlin's Zoo-Palast, was to become an official goodwill gesture to the film industry, with Adolf Hitler and his closest cabinet members in attendance. The curtain to the film screening rose after a specially composed overture was played introducing aspects of the film music and film to come. Herbert Windt's 'serious' or 'high-art' music managed to reconcile many of the ultra-reactionary members of the Nazi party with a medium they had long written off as either communist or hedonistic and which they assumed to be controlled by Jews. The cultural branch of the Nazi party under the leadership of chief ideologist Alfred Rosenberg had long rallied against all forms of modernization and 'mechanization'; this, of course, against the backdrop of mass unemployment amongst musicians and the advent of the sound film. The *Kampfbund für Deutsche Kultur*, of whom Rosenberg was the '*spiritus rector*', published a magazine entitled *Deutsche Kultur-Wacht* which continuously warned of 'alienation' as well as 'foreign' (that is, Jewish) control and domination of the entertainment industry and with it the denigration of German cultural heritage. The film industry was one of its main targets.[15] With the help of Windt's music, to a large extent in line with what was expected of 'German' music and art, film experienced a partial rehabilitation for the reactionary right, presenting as it did a medium with high propaganda potential. Windt's music infused the images with a cultural and historical connotation which at that time was not associated with film. Not surprisingly, 'the picture was received with tremendous applause', according to *Variety*'s Berlin correspondent who reported on the premiere.[16]

When the National Socialists came to power, sound film had already been fully established as a cultural and artistic entity. Several strands and schools of film music had emerged, the most popular and successful of which borrowed from the tradition of the operetta, its film songs and dance scenes having been developed and introduced by the Pommer group with success on the national and international level. Yet just two months after the Nazi seizure of power on 30 January 1933 the film industry, now a special interest of the newly appointed Minister of Propaganda, Joseph Goebbels, was to experience the shape of things to come. On 28 March, film-industry members were called together at the Hotel Kaiserhof in Berlin where Goebbels outlined the new ideas and responsibilities of the film industry, which included enforcing 'national norms'. Such norms were to come into effect only a few days later when a national boycott of Jewish shops and businesses was announced.

A day after the boycott Klitzsch and the Ufa board decided to follow suit and immediately relieved Jewish employees of their duties. The Pommer production group was one of the hardest hit – this despite the huge financial success and international critical acclaim it had earned Ufa in its transfer to sound film. Eric Charell, director of the highly successful film-operetta *Der Kongreß tanzt* (*Congress Dances*, 1930), was among those sacked. Heymann, who was at the time conductor-in-chief of the Ufa Orchestra and composer of many songs, was promised that, as a convert to Christianity and a veteran of World War I, his case would receive special attention. However, he declined the offer and immediately emigrated, initially to Paris and from there to Hollywood, where he went on to work with such directors as Ernst Lubitsch, and to win several Oscars for his film music. Holländer, another of the early film composers, was forced into exile via Paris to Hollywood where he would later join his one-time orchestrator Franz Waxman, or Wachsmann as he was originally called. Within a few weeks the German film industry had deprived itself of some of its most talented musical pioneers.

The reliable film industry

On 20 July 1933, a law was passed establishing a provisional film chamber. Its stated goal was to ensure the 'reliability' of the entire film industry; in other words, to ensure its conformity with National Socialist principles, especially concerning race and religious issues. A few months later, the idea of the film chamber was expanded into a system that would encompass the entirety of cultural life. Underlining the bizarre theatricality of Nazi politics and propaganda, the founding ceremony of the Reich Chamber of Culture on 15 November 1933 took place at the Kroll Oper, which the Nazis had always detested for its avant-garde performances. Until its closure in 1931 the opera house had been renowned for its many premieres, including Arnold Schoenberg's *Begleitmusik zu einer Lichtspielszene* (1929) and Paul Hindemith's *Neues vom Tage* (1930).

As Eric E. Steinweis has pointed out, the Reich Chamber of Culture and its six sub-chambers governing all aspects of the arts did not emerge *ex nihilo*: since the mid-1920s there had been calls for artists' guilds of various kinds to guarantee standards and good working conditions for artists in an attempt to counter the hardship brought about by the downfall of the traditionally arts-friendly and philanthropist upper middle-class, the *Bürgertum*, and the world economic crisis. The initial idea conveyed by the authorities was that of professional self-administration under the guiding hand of the state. The first administrative directors appointed to the Reich Chamber of Culture underscored this initial idea: Richard Strauss became head of the Reich Chamber of Music and Fritz Lang was supposed to have become director of the Film Chamber before he fled the country. In the end Fritz Scheuermann, a lesser-known film bureaucrat, took the post. Chamber membership was obligatory for anyone professionally involved in the arts. The main prerequisite, however, had nothing to do with artistic performance or merit, but with adherence to Nazi racial laws. Jews were barred from membership and confined to an organization of their own, which entailed their effective exclusion from all cultural life. By 1936 the artists at the top of the various chambers had been replaced by party bureaucrats. Once the chamber had fulfilled its main aim – 'aryanization' of cultural life – it became clear that no genuine art could evolve from such a tight and rigorous system. The most talented artists had left the country and those remaining often failed to attract attention and enthusiasm. As Hermann Göring had famously stated, it was easier to gradually turn a great artist into a decent National Socialist than to turn a small National Socialist into a great artist.[17] Eventually cultural politics resorted to appropriating art, especially music, from the nineteenth century.

So where did 'aryanization' place film music institutionally and artistically, after the difficult yet promising start of this genre only a few years before? Composers of film music were forced to register with the Reich Chamber of Music unless they were employed directly by film companies, an exception at the time.[18] A special advisory board to the film chamber may have been intended to bridge this strict institutional divide between traditional film and non-film music.[19] Herbert Windt and Alois Melichar were the composers nominated as advisors, but the board never came into being. The film chamber was considered more progressive and less dogmatic, mainly due to the direct influence of Joseph

Goebbels in many controversial matters. Goebbels was a film buff who would frequently show up on set. He was also known for having affairs with prominent actresses. The music chamber, on the other hand, was far more conservative and considered itself the defender of the 'most German of the arts'. This led to continuous friction with the film chamber, particularly when 'classical' music was used in film. Music chamber officials frequently complained that sacred German music was being devalued by reckless film composers using it 'by the metre' to accompany their films. Such complaints were most likely directed against newsreels, but many prominent film composers were offended and took strong objection to the suggestion. The music chamber called for a type of 'Blue List' intended to prevent the pruning of pre-existing music. Speaking for most film composers, Alois Melichar called for the music chamber to establish specific guidelines to resolve the problem.[20] These, however, were never made – a typical manoeuvre of Nazi bureaucracy.

Film music in the Third Reich

When the Nazis took power in 1933, sound film and various styles of film music had developed enough to be appropriated for the purposes of propaganda and politics. Despite the fact that some of the most creative and inventive artists had been driven away, the film industry and its structures remained intact. Plenty of less talented musicians and directors were happy to step into the shoes of those who had been forced to go or were not prepared to sacrifice their artistic ideals for political purposes. Film production continued at the same level as before; between 1933 and 1945, a total of 1,200 films were produced. There were roughly 200 composers working for the film industry with a core of about 20 receiving most of the contracts.[21]

One of the first films to play directly into the hands of Nazi propaganda was Hans Steinhoff's *Hitlerjunge Quex* (*Hitler Youth Quex*, 1933). Much like his more successful colleagues who had left the country, Steinhoff had worked in theatre and operetta and utilized the same kind of technique and plot structures that had worked so well for the Pommer production unit. Instead of waltzes and cabaret songs, Hans-Otto Borgmann, Steinhoff's composer, focused on a marching song entitled *Unsere Fahne flattert uns voran* (*Our Flag Leads the Way*), whose lyrics were personally penned by the leader of the Hitler Youth, Baldur von Schirach. The tune was alluded to in the overture, sung in the film itself and then played again as a sing-along at the end of the film as the main protagonist mouths the lyrics while dying from an assault by a communist. A choir and marching band dramatically picks up, when Heini's voice fails him. The final lines of '*Unsere Fahne ...*' seem to pre-empt his fate and that of many more youths to come: '*Unsere Fahne ist die neue Zeit. Und die Fahne führt uns in die Ewigkeit. Ja, die Fahne ist mehr als der Tod!*' (Our flag is the new era, and the flag will lead us to eternity. Yes, the flag is more than death!). Further proof that film could act as a springboard for disseminating propaganda and ideology, *Hitlerjunge Quex* certainly helped imprint the song into the hearts and minds of thousands of Hitler youths.[22] Yet contrary to common perception, the film industry did not turn out only propaganda. Of the 1,200 films produced under the Nazi reign only a very small proportion (14 per cent) has been classified as overtly propagandistic.[23] Those films often used music drawing upon nineteenth-century orchestral and operatic traditions, and sought to emphasize cultural continuity and infuse the images of Nazi politicians and iconography with a cultural legitimacy. Windt's *Morgenrot* was a prime example, as were the other films he made with Leni Riefenstahl. In *Triumph des Willens* (*Triumph of the Will*, 1935), the epitome of Nazi propaganda set against film music often characterized as Wagnerian, Windt alludes to various renowned composers and other Nazi art-forms to provide a cultural backdrop and a means of highlighting Nazi iconography. For Riefenstahl's following project, *Olympia* (1938), Windt worked together with Walter Gronostay, the Schoenberg student who had participated at Baden-Baden.

Wolfgang Zeller was another of the Baden-Baden group of film composers who would have a successful career in the Third Reich. In addition to *Der Herrscher* (*The Ruler*, 1937), he set the music to one of the most vicious pieces of Nazi film propaganda ever made: Veit Harlan's film *Jud Süß* (*Jew Süß*, 1940). For this film he used a German folk song as a leitmotif, at times contrasting it with supposedly Jewish/Oriental melodic-minor melodies.

Zeller and Windt point to the fact that for prestigious propaganda projects composers with a background in 'high' art or 'E-Musik' (serious music) were chosen. One of the most effective means of musically driving home the point of such films was to contrast what was considered to be German music with non-German, so-called degenerate or 'Jewish' music. This technique was applied by Windt in war films, anti-Russian films and others, one of the main propaganda aims being to safeguard German culture from a supposed Bolshevist threat. In film, this point could best of all be brought across musically which in artistic and musical terms often implied pandering to the lowest common denominator for maximum effect. In this context Siegfried Kracauer's study of Nazi propaganda film is extremely interesting.[24] Kracauer does not specifically deal with the issue of music and its application as a means of propaganda, he even dismisses the capability of music as a propagandistic device in film, but his characterization and description of the soundtrack is proof of its intention and reception: In *Sieg im Westen* (*Victory in the West*, 1941) the British expeditionary force is depicted arriving in Belgium to the tune of 'We're Going to Hang out the Washing on the Siegfried Line', which Kracauer believes to be a German parody, its opening pick-up phrase characterized as, 'music imitating the chatter in a chicken yard'.[25] It is, in fact, the original version written by Jimmy Kennedy and Michael Carr.[26] Later in the film French-African prisoners of war are shown against the acoustical backdrop of ritual drumming. This, Kracauer explains, is 'Negro music reminiscent of jazz tunes'.[27] These two musical examples could probably only be perceived and interpreted in this manner when juxtaposed with 'German' music, both composed or quoted. Windt's score draws heavily on nineteenth-century orchestral music and even the marching songs composed for the soldiers to sing are taken to Schumannesque extremes in their harmonization. Probably the most telling scene is when the Cathedral in Laon in northern France is allegedly saved from destruction by the advancing German troops. As soon as the cathedral is safe the commander heads straight for the organ, takes off his helmet, puts aside his machine gun and pulls out all propagandistic stops by triumphantly playing the ultimate 'German' piece of organ music: J.S. Bach's Toccata and Fugue in D minor.

Yet, artistic interference by authorities such as the film chamber appears to have been minimal, which was probably largely due to ignorance. Some did complain, however. In one of Windt's scores for a campaign rally film, an official complaint was registered concerning a melodic minor scale in one of the themes. This 'oriental sing-song' (*orientalische Tonweise*) was deemed inappropriate for a military film portraying soldiers in action. The military high command who had commissioned the film called for the theme to be replaced by marching songs, but the film went into circulation without any changes to the soundtrack.[28]

One of the few truly experimental films produced during the Nazi reign was *Das Stahltier* (1935), commissioned by German railways to commemorate their hundredth anniversary in 1938. The film's camera work was carried out in a free and experimental Bauhaus style, while the musical score, by Peter Kreuder, went as far as to play inside the piano to imitate engine and machine sounds. The film was banned, not because of its visual effects and unusual score – which could not have been further from German song and nineteenth-century orchestral music – but because its plot reveals all too obviously that the steam-engine and transport by rail had been invented in England, not Germany.

Production of musical comedy and operetta continued and intensified. In fact, as Karsten Witte points out, the military aspects of chorus lines and variety stage show choreography reconnected with their military origins in many Nazi films, possibly even as early as the carefully choreographed scenes of *Triumph des Willens*.[29] In the field of popular music there were, however, strict guidelines that had to be applied. Jazz was officially banned in 1935 and anything remotely reminiscent of it, even instruments such as saxophones and muted trumpets, had to be very carefully employed to bypass restrictions by the authorities. With musicals and musical comedies confined to waltzes and foxtrots, or the occasional (banned) *rhumba*, the musical energy of German productions seemed subdued in comparison with their Hollywood counterparts showing in Berlin at the outbreak of World War II.[30]

Some artists from the early days of the sound film continued to work. Lilian Harvey, the singer and dancer who had come to fame in the Pommer production group, starred in a few films before she left Germany over a dispute concerning her pay in hard currency. She was succeeded by the ultimate diva of Nazi films, Zarah Leander, whose film songs achieved as much popularity as those of the 1930s. The first two films that brought Leander fame were the last to be directed by Detlev Sierck before he emigrated to the USA, where he continued to work, in Hollywood, as Douglas Sirk. Zarah Leander worked with a fixed group which included composers Ralph Benatzky, Lothar Brühne and lyricist Bruno Balz.

After the defeat in Stalingrad signalled the beginning of the end for Germany, the propaganda ministry officially held a competition for an *Optimismusschlager*, a song of optimism. Michael Jary, a composer who had previously worked with Zarah Leander, was determined to enter a song, but his lyricist was in police custody due to allegations of homosexual activity. Jary managed to arrange his release and together they wrote the song that was to become the most famous so-called *Durchhalteschlager*, a kind of never-give-up war anthem entitled *Ich weiß, es wird ein Mal ein Wunder geschehen* (I know that a miracle will happen one day).[31] The film in which the song appeared, *Die große Liebe* (*The Great Love*, 1942), was premiered two weeks after the city of Cologne had been reduced to rubble in what would be the beginning of a massive Allied bombing campaign. *Die große Liebe* was one of the most successful films of the early 1940s. Eight million people saw the film and heard its optimistic ballads such as *Davon geht die Welt nicht unter* (This won't mean the end of the world) and *Ich weiß, es wird*, both of which became classics. Depending on one's point of view, these songs could be understood either as an allusion to the so-called *Wunderwaffen* (the V1 and V2 rockets expected to change the course of the war) or as cynical and somewhat subversive commentary on Nazi propaganda. Many similar songs followed and towards the end of Nazi power the movie industry had regressed to a blend of escapist entertainment and subtle propaganda serving a society wary of the hardships of 'total war'.

One of the last films to be made under the Third Reich was a historical parable based on an episode in the Napoleonic wars. The story of the besieged city of Kolberg, which was intended as a source of inspiration and encouragement, once again falsified history by implying a historical parallel between the Napoleonic wars and the ongoing conflict. Film production on location in eastern parts of Germany became a race against time as the Red Army rapidly advanced. While German cities lay in ruins, mock cities were being built on set only to be destroyed by cannon fire, and 185,000 soldiers were taken out of battle to act as extras. *Kolberg* called for a melodramatic score alluding to German history to underline the propagandistic point of the film. Norbert Schultze, an accomplished composer who had made his mark as both a songwriter and composer, was given the task. As a songwriter Schultze had come to fame with a tune called *Lilli Marleen*, often referred to as the biggest hit of World War II. Later, intent on exculpating himself, Schultze claimed that *Lili Marleen* was an anti-war song. As had been the case for many other propaganda films, Schultze's score for *Kolberg* (1945) tapped into classical eighteenth-century music to provide its musical backdrop.

From the light back into the dark: closing remarks

Two major strands of film music emerged from the unsympathetic climate that accompanied the discovery of sound film. First there were the 'serious' composers who had a background in orchestral and concert music and were interested in the new ideas and challenges raised at the Baden-Baden festivals from 1927 to 1929. For them, the combination of film and music offered new artistic perspective, and film became a possible catalyst for new developments in composition. Secondly, there were those composers involved with incidental music who saw film as a continuation of popular art forms such as cabaret, theatre and operetta. With the help and support of producers like Erich Pommer, the latter initially enjoyed greater success. Once sound film began to be used for 'serious' subjects, opportunities for composers from a background in high-art pursuits emerged as well.

After 1933, both strands were absorbed into Nazi film production. The more serious music aspirations added credibility to cultural propaganda and the Nazis in general; the lighter variety provided an ideal means of disseminating propaganda on a wider cultural basis to a greater audience. Film music in the Third Reich had closely followed the various phases of cultural politics. After the enormous creative bloodletting that followed the Nazi's seizure of power, many of the pioneering achievements of the early 1930s, especially the film operetta and musical, became a mere springboard for propagandistic marching songs and ballads. Despite their promising start, the development of film music and film song came – with few exceptions – to a stop and drifted quickly into mediocrity. The fact that there were neither clear artistic guidelines, nor a clear institutional body responsible on behalf of the Nazi authorities, means that the question of whether film music was specifically acknowledged and applied as a tool of propaganda must remain an open one. Artistic choice seemed to lie much in the hands of individual composers, their choice of style and music often further underlining or even fortifying the propagandistic drive of the film.

While most of the outright propaganda films and their marching songs remain banned in Germany, many of the entertainment films, with their seemingly less overt and carefree songs and variety shows, are frequently broadcast on German television. The film songs of the 1930s and 1940s have best stood the test of time. Songs by Holländer, Heymann and Jary are still continuously played; Nazi film divas such as Zarah Leander still attract a lot of attention, her songs often being performed by cabaret singers and dance orchestras only marginally aware of the political climate the music and films emerged from – or fell prey to. The passage of German film music from the early 1930s into the Third Reich and its musical legacy points to the susceptibility of this art form to propagandistic appropriation.

Notes

1. Kreimeier, K. *Die Ufa Story*, Frankfurt am Main: Fischer Taschenbuch Verlag, 2002, 210 f.; Rügner, U. *Filmmusik in Deutschland zwischen 1924 und 1934*, Hildesheim: Georg Olms, 1988, 35 f.
2. Jossé, H. *Die Entstehung des Tonfilms. Beiträge zu einer Faktenorientierten Mediengeschichtsschreibung*, Munich: Alber, 1984, 208.
3. Bock, M. (ed.) *CineGraph Lexikon zum deutschen Film*, Munich: edition text und kritik, 'Zeller', 1984.
4. Rügner, U. *Filmmusik in Deutschland*, 38.
5. Kreimeier, K. *Die Ufa Story*, 214. Klitzsch's thinking underlines the prevalent notion of German superiority in music later to be taken on and appropriated by the Nazis. In this context Arnold Schoenberg's famous (or infamous) remark immediately comes to mind: according to his pupil Josef Rufer, Schoenberg characterized his application of 12-tone technique in 1921 with the following remark, 'I have made a discovery that will ensure the supremacy of German music for the next hundred years.' (*Ich habe eine Entdeckung gemacht, durch welche die Vorherrschaft der deutschen Musik für die nächsten hundert Jahre gesichert ist*.) The statement, however, has recently been refuted as an unlikely appropriation of nationalist German rhetoric. See Randol, E. 'Schoenberg: the Most Famous Thing He Never Said', *International Forum for Suppressed Music (IFSM) Newsletter*, November 2002, 13–17.
6. Bock, M. *CineGraph Lexikon zum deutschen Film*, 'Heymann'.
7. Kreimeier, K. *Die Ufa Story*, 217.
8. Rotthaler, V. 'Die Musikalisierung des Kinos. Die Komponisten der Pommer-Produktion', in K. Uhlenbrok (ed.), *MusikSpektakelFilm. Musiktheater und Tanzkultur im deutschen Film 1922–1937*, Munich: edition text und kritik, 1998, 124.
9. Franz Wachsmann was another of the composers who ventured into film by way of the cabaret and vaudeville scene in 1920s Berlin. Born of a non-musical family, he soon showed talent as a composer and took up musical studies in Berlin. In order to make a living he started work as a pianist, eventually becoming a regular member of the Weintraub Syncopaters, one of the most successful jazz and dancebands of the time. In the band he came into contact with Friedrich Holländer, who brought him into contact with the film industry where Wachsmann then worked both as composer and orchestrator. When the Nazis assumed power it became increasingly difficult for Wachsmann to work due to the race laws imposed on the film industry. After being beaten up on the street in Berlin, he emigrated to Paris and together with, among others, Peter Lorre, Billy Wilder and Friedrich Holländer, took up residence at the Hotel Ansonia. He continued to work in film in France until invited to Hollywood by Erich Pommer, where he changed his name to Waxman. Bock, *CineGraph Lexikon zum deutschen Film*, 'Franz Wachsmann/Waxman'.
10. As in so many of his other films (for example, *A Foreign Affair*; *One, Two, Three*), Holländer makes an appearance as a pianist.
11. The French version of the signature tune *Ein Freund, ein guter Freund*, entitled *Avoir un bon copain*, had its most recent screen appearance in Alain Resnais' 1999 film, *On connait la chanson*.
12. Kracauer, S. 'Ablenkung oder Aufbau? Zum neuen Ufa-Programm', *Frankfurter Zeitung*, 27 and 28 July, 1932.
13. Kelson, J.F. *Catalogue of Forbidden German Feature and Short Film Productions*, Trowbridge: Flick Books, 1996, 53. For further information and an interpretation of the film see also Kracauer, S. *From Caligari to Hitler. A Psychological History of the German film*, Princeton: Princeton University Press, 1947, 269–70.

14. Brinkmann, R. 'The Distorted Sublime. Music and National Socialist Ideology – A Sketch', in M.H. Kater and A. Riethmüller, *Music and Nazism. Art under Tyranny, 1933–1945*, Laaber: Laaber Verlag, 2003, 43–63.

15. See Hinkel, H. (ed.) *Deutsche Kultur-Wacht.* Blätter des Kampfbundes für Deutsche Kultur e.V., Berlin, 1932.

16. 'Morgenrot', *Variety*, 28 February 1933.

17. Brenner, H. *Die Kunstpolitik des Nationalsozialismus*, Reinbek: Rowohlt, 1963, 42. ('*Görings Wort lief um: "Es ist immer noch leichter, aus einem großen Künstler mit der Zeit einen anständigen Nationalsozialisten zu machen als aus einem keinen Pg. einen großen Künstler."*')

18. Tackmann, H. 'Beschluß betreffs Mitgliedschaft der Filmautoren und Filmkomponisten vom 7.11.1933', *Filmhandbuch der Reichsfilmkammer*, Berlin, Allgemeines VI A, 3 a–f, 1938.

19. Bundesarchiv Berlin, box R56 I, file 126.

20. Volker, R. *'Von oben sehr erwünscht'. Die Filmmusik Herbert Windts im NS-Propagandafilm*, Trier: Wissenschaftlicher Verlag Trier, 2003, 25–6.

21. Vogelsang, K. *Filmmusik im Dritten Reich. Die Dokumentation*, Hamburg: Facta, 1990, 261–93. Film composers were nevertheless looked down upon by 'serious' high-art composers in the music chamber and often had to put up with denigrating remarks about purported hedonistic lifestyles that their handsome salaries and steady royalties afforded.

22. Claus, H. 'Von Gilbert zu Goebbels. Hans Steinhoff zwischen Operette und Tonfilm mit Musik', in M. Hagener and J. Hans (eds), *Als die Filme singen lernten. Innovation und Tradition im Musikfilm 1928–1938*, Munich: edition text und kritik, 1999, 105. See also Vogelsang, *Filmmusik im Dritten Reich*, 297–303.

23. Albrecht, G. *Nationalsozialistische Filmpolitik*, Stuttgart: Enke, 1969, 107.

24. See Kracauer, S. *From Caligari to Hitler*. As a supplement (p. 274) the book includes Kracauer's study entitled 'Propaganda and the Nazi War Film', which was initially issued in 1942 by the Museum of Modern Art. It was intended to serve the purpose of psychological warfare. See also Sakmyster, T. 'Nazi Documentaries of Intimidation: "Feldzug in Polen" (1940), "Feuertaufe" (1940) and "Sieg im Westen" (1941)'; *Historical Journal of Film, Radio and Television*, **16** (4), 1996, 485–514.

25. Kracauer, S. *From Caligari to Hitler*, 317.

26. Rather ironically, this officially banned tune became a sort of anthem for the subversive and later persecuted 'Swing Jugend' (Swing Youth) in Hamburg, a youth group that clandestinely listened to jazz, danced jive, dressed in an English style and grew long hair. See Polster, B. (ed.), *Swing Heil. Jazz im Nationalsozialismus*, Berlin: Transit Buchverlag, 1989; and Kater, M. *Different Drummers: Jazz in the Culture of Nazi Germany*, New York: Oxford University Press, 1992.

27. Kracauer, S. *From Caligari to Hitler*, 322.

28. Volker, R. *'Von oben sehr erwünscht'*, 103. Bundesarchiv Freiburg, box RW/4, file v. 294.

29. Witte, K. 'Gehemmte Schaulust. Momente des Deutschen Revuefilms', in H. Belach (ed.), *Wir tanzen um die Welt. Deutsche Revuefilme 1933–1945*, Munich: Hanser, 1979, 31.

30. Prox, L. 'Melodien aus Deutschem Gemüt und Geblüt', in H. Belach (ed.), *Wir tanzen um die Welt*, 73.

31. Pacher, M. 'Filmschlager. Ein Stück Kulturgeschichte', Foreword in *Von Kopf bis Fuß auf Kino eingestellt*, Hamburg, 1990, 9.

Chapter 2

Music, people and reality: the case of Italian neo-realism

Richard Dyer

People in Italian neo-realist films sing, play and dance and listen to folk songs, popular hits, jazz and snatches of opera. Yet these forms of music rarely appear in the background music, which runs the stylistic gamut of concert music from mid-romanticism to early modernism. This discrepancy could just be conventional (in Hollywood and Cinecittà[1] too, people often have different music in their world from that on the non-diegetic soundtrack), but it is a gap with bitter implications for a movement presumed to be about creating a cinema genuinely expressive of ordinary people's reality.

Vittorio Spinazzola has suggested that 'production in the immediate post-war period [in Italy] was characterized by two antithetical strands: … films about the people or films for the people', neo-realism and commercial cinema.[2] While (as Spinazzola was among the first to point out) in box-office terms this antithesis can be overstated,[3] it remains the case that there is a contradiction within the neo-realist project between making films about ordinary people and a tendency to view with suspicion what ordinary people liked, a contradiction sharply registered in music.

The problem is revealed in an early (1950) defence of music in neo-realism by Fernando Ludovico Lunghi.[4] He begins by arguing that neo-realist films need music because naturalism – the mere recording of the external appearances of things – is not enough to represent all of reality. Music conveys the inner meaning. Yet as he proceeds, he also inadvertently suggests the problem that music posed for neo-realism. He describes a typical neo-realist sequence: 'countryside, mountains, sea, suffocating cities, squalid suburbs, a bit of grass, two tired, bleeding feet, a ray of goodness, a shadow of bestiality'.[5] This evokes a characteristic neo-realist opening, moving from a panoramic shot to a close-up, usually indicating that the person lighted on at the end is just one of the crowd, typical, representative, but also betraying a sense of coming from outside the world of the film. As it proceeds to make the case for the need for music, Lunghi's account compounds this sense of seeing from without: 'the camera is silent, nature is silent, man even in his language with its tired and blasphemous words, is silent. … What is lacking … is that third dimension that … only music can provide'.[6] The typical subject of neo-realism cannot speak for themself: music is needed to speak for them. But that music will not be their music.

My definition of neo-realism is inclusive. As Christopher Wagstaff has pointed out, a tight or pure definition of neo-realism is liable to lead one to omit even *Roma città aperta* (*Rome Open City*, 1945) from the account.[7] Alberto Farassino suggests that one think rather in terms of the neo-realist period:[8] while few films were purely neo-realist, 'all or very many films of the immediate post-war period felt themselves obliged to be a bit neorealistic and no-one dared oppose it', such that most were 'infiltrated, crossed, ennobled or even sullied by neorealism'.[9]

O sole mio (1946) is exemplary. It is a film built around a song title (a consistent product of popular Italian cinema since the coming of sound[10]) and the singing of its star, Tito Gobbi. As is typical of such films, it has a plot of misunderstanding and mild absurdity: Giovanni (Gobbi) sends messages to the Resistance by tapping or 'la-la-ing' them out during his radio concerts. Yet, made within months of *Roma città aperta*,[11] it is shot on war-torn location, with available or crude lighting, is simply edited, and deploys classic neo-realist iconography: street fighting, torture and the black market; dark, basic proletarian quarters, contrasting with bright German/Fascist ones; and Resistance fighters, collaborators and opportunists. Unusually, it is very sparing in its use of non-diegetic music, mostly just a few phrases over establishing shots and never behind dialogue. All of Gobbi's numbers are diegetically motivated and never involve augmented musical tracks, and he was a big star singing popular material (favourite opera arias, a Latin-American song and the eponymous Neapolitan classic). In short, *O sole mio* is an impure mix of realist and generic elements, a mix characteristic of neo-realism, although, less characteristically, it remains musically close to the tastes of its protagonists and, one may presume it presumes, its audience.

The use of non-diegetic music in neo-realism is by and large indistinguishable from the music in popular cinema before and during the neo-realist period. This is most vividly illustrated by the fact that, as David Forgacs notes,[12] the music by Renzo Rossellini for perhaps the most famous moment in the whole of neo-realism, the death of Pina in *Roma città aperta*, is recycled from his score for a battle sequence in *L'uomo dalla croce* (*The Man of the Cross*, 1943), one of the most 'overtly ideological'[13] of Roberto Rossellini's Fascist era films. Pointing chronologically in the opposite direction, Renzo's music for the Sicily episode of *Paisà* (1946) is re-used to generate excitement in a scene in which a man escapes from the police in the thriller *Una lettera all'alba* (*A Letter at Dawn,* 1949). Quite apart from these explicit borrowings, the overall approach of Renzo Rossellini is identical across official Fascist cinema, canonical neo-realism and commercial genre films; and the same could be said of Alessandro Cicognini and Nino Rota (except that, though they worked during the regime, they never did so for the official Fascist cinema).

It is not just that the music sounds the same but that its relation to the image is that established in commercial cinema in the 1930s. Often played quietly and without readily grasped melodies, music is used to provide an overall emotional feeling to a sequence: tension, drama, sentiment, tragedy. Sometimes louder music and stronger melodies heighten the emotions of a scene; rather more rarely, music underscores in the Hollywood manner, closely following the movement and minute emotional shifts within a scene. *Roma città aperta* contains all three approaches. The busy dramatic music of the opening sequence (as the Gestapo search the partisan Manfredi's flat), and the tense music behind the boy Marcello and Don Pietro leaving the church on Resistance business, are both, despite their emotional content, unemphatic, subordinated to ambient sounds and speech. However, a searingly tragic-majestic theme heightens the tragic heroism of the young boys making their way home after sabotaging a railway goods yard and then again, at the very end, after Don Pietro's execution. There is also 'Hollywoodian' underscoring. For instance, as Don Pietro and Pina leave the church carrying money for the Resistance, they both notice someone off-camera but continue to walk apprehensively ahead, the music gradually slowing as they themselves do, until the person off-camera addresses them, at which point a stinger underlines the fear that this is a Gestapo officer; moments later, mounting staccato chords build up as the man takes out his pistol, but then the music ebbs away after he takes out a note indicating he is in fact a deserter seeking shelter: each moment in the sequence is precisely underscored on the soundtrack. In all these ways, the use of music of *Roma città aperta* is, like most music in neo-realism, conventional in relation to prevalent practice.

All this provided a continuity with the cinema that was part of the putative audience's culture. I want to suggest, however, that, both in its attitude towards the diegetic music and in the latter's relation to the non-diegetic score, there is more often a distance between the films and their protagonists, and thus implicitly the audience, a distance at odds with the ambitions of neo-realism.

The people's music

There are five kinds of diegetic music in neo-realism: sacred, military, concert/opera, folk and popular hits. The first three occur pretty well where and in the form one might expect: organ and/or choir in church services, singing on religious processions, church bells; fanfares, *reveilles* and drill music; arias and popular classics sung, whistled, played or listened to by characters, at leisure or as they go about their business. Their function is primarily ambient, providing the patina of detail characteristic of realisms;[14] occasionally they serve a narrative purpose (as when the priest rings the church bells to signal to the villagers that the Nazis have left in *Vivere in pace* (*To Live in Peace*, 1947)). Folk and popular hits can have these functions too, but they also carry moral/political weight: most commonly, the more traditional – and especially folk or folkish – the music, the more highly it is valued; with hit songs conversely carrying negative associations.

Folk may be divided into two categories. The first comprises song and music presented as a product of rural and/or working communities, usually seen as unauthored and handed down. This is particularly important in the films of Giuseppe de Santis: *Caccia tragica* (*Tragic Hunt*, 1948), *Riso amaro* (*Bitter Rice*, 1949) and *Non c'è pace tra gli ulivi* (*No Peace under the Olive Trees*, 1950). Other examples include farm labourers' songs in *Il mulino del Po* (*The Mill on the Po*, 1949), the songs of builders, housewives and fishermen in *La terra trema* (*The Earth Shakes*, 1948) and the partisans' song in *Achtung! Banditi!* (*Beware! Bandits!*, 1951). (As discussed below, African-American music was also often considered a folk music.) Second, there is what one might call folkish music, songs and music that have been around so long that they seem part of a common musical inheritance. The sacred, religious and opera music listed above is often seen like this. Equally music whose origins are commercial becomes naturalized. Since the mid-nineteenth century, regional song, particularly Neapolitan,[15] had established itself as a commercial concern that was nonetheless readily folklorized, by the construction of a lineage back to the late Middle Ages and the deployment of timeworn Romantic rustic or maritime imagery in the lyrics. A folkish strain is also manifest in accordion music and amateur bands. *Ladri di biciclette* (*Bicycle Thieves*, 1948) features accordion-playing, street musicians, a barrel organ, a gypsy-like trio in a restaurant and an amateur revue. Typical of this strain is '*Mattinata fiorentina*', which features in both *Roma città aperta* and *È primavera* (*Spring is Here*, 1949). Written by the Milanese Giovanni D'Anzi and the Neapolitan Michele Galdieri for the latter's 1941 Rome revue *È bello qualche volta andare a piedi* (*Sometimes It's Nice to Go on Foot*), it celebrates mornings in Florence; as Gianni Borgna suggests, it also aspired, in the December of 1941, 'to be a hymn to peace, serenity, to the joy of living, a sort of anxious refuge while all around raged the drama of war':[16] in other words, occupying the folk space of simple, ordinary hopes and fears.

Folk is understood to be, as the folklorist Giorgio Nataletti put it, 'what the people sing naturally (without external pressures like the radio, TV, juke-box etc.)'.[17] This positive valuation of folk music is in line with the resurgence of interest in folk music in Italy in the 1940s, signalled by the establishment of the *Centro Nazionale Studi di Musica Popolare* in 1948[18] and given a Marxist inflection by the post-war publication of Antonio Gramsci's *Quaderni del carcere* (*Prison Notebooks*) and their treatment of folk culture as expression of the world view of subaltern classes.[19] In one appropriation of these ideas, collective singing embodies in its form as well as sentiments the subaltern value of collectivity, and this is clearly its role in De Santis' films: the agricultural worker's co-operative in *Caccia tragica*, the rice pickers in *Riso amaro*, the shepherd community in *Non c'è pace tra gli ulivi*. Similarly the Sicilian peasants trekking through Italy to find work in *Il cammino della speranza* (*The Hopeful Road*, 1950) keep their spirits up by singing together, while the partisans' song in *Achtung! Banditi!* is used as a (diegetic) background to a discussion of strategy, providing the emotional solidarity fuelling rational discourse. In contrast, the fishermen's work songs in both *Stromboli* (1950) and *La terra trema* express a sense of community, that is respectively untouched by or unable to resist capitalism and bourgeois values (but is in both cases implicitly superior to them). Church music too is, at the least, seen neutrally, simply part of the Italianness of ordinary Italian life, for example, *È primavera, Molti sogni per le strade* (*Many Dreams along the Way,* 1948), but also often offered as a symbol of hope, especially in Rossellini – *Roma città aperta, Germania anno zero* (*Germany Year Zero,* 1948), *Stromboli* – but also elsewhere *Un americano in vacanza* (*An American on Holiday,* 1946), *Campane a martello* (*Alarm Bells,* 1949), *Vivere in pace* and, most explicitly, in *Il cielo sulle palude* (*The Sky over the Marshes,* 1949), about the life of Saint Maria Goretti; only occasionally, and then not emphatically, is church music seen as having little to offer working people (for example, *Ladri di biciclette, Non c' è pace tra gli ulivi*). The value of opera, on the other hand, is unpredictable.[20] The good proletarian Michele in *Caccia tragica* whistles Rossini, Mondio sings 'Casta diva' from *Norma* to a guitar to accompany the young lovers Luca and Rosa as they wander in the woods in *Il cammino della speranza* and the anti-Fascist Ugo in *Cronache di poveri amanti* (*Stories of Poor Lovers,* 1954) is always 'tra-la-la-ing' opera arias; but the callousness of Umberto's landlady in *Umberto D* (1952) is of a piece with her trilling opera arias with her gentlemen callers.

Popular music in neo-realism includes songs clearly presented by the film as part of current cultural production: '*Fiorin Fiorello*', the 1938 hit sung by Giovanna in the 1942 *Ossessione* (*Obsession*); '*Ma quando tornera*' ('But when you return'), sung from a piece of sheet music in *Fuga in Francia* (*Escape to France,* 1948); the title song of *Sotto il sole di Roma* (*Beneath the Roman Sky,* 1947); and the night-club ballad '*Bambola vorrei stare con te*' ('Baby I Want to Be with You') in *Tombolo paradiso nero* (*Tombolo Black Paradise,* 1947). Equally common are Latin American and, above all, swing styles.

Pop music is nearly always associated with corruption. In *Ossessione*, '*Fiorin fiorello*' acts as a siren's song, drawing Gino to adultery and murder; later, his flirtation with another woman in Ferrara is accompanied by a dance band playing '*Piccolino come te*' ('Cute like You'). The sexual danger that the city poses to an innocent peasant girl is signalled in *Il cammino della speranza* by Lorenza, at a stop-off in Rome, being cruised by a large car blaring swing music. The world of rackets and prostitution is conveyed by both swing and Latin American music in *Senza pietà* (*Pitiless,* 1948) and *Tombolo paradiso nero*. Latin American music seems especially corrupt, perhaps because the Fascist regime had vaunted the historic unity of the Latin peoples of Europe and South America. 'Brazil' is associated with gangsterdom in both *Senza pietà* and *Sotto il sole di Roma*. In *Roma città aperta* the hit song '*A Copocabana*' (from a 1944 Rome revue) is heard in the background the first time we see Marina, the drug-dependent girlfriend of the Resistance leader Manfredi, whose inadvertent betrayal of him leads to his and Don Pietro's death.

Folk and pop music are often explicitly contrasted. *Proibito rubare* (*Thieving Forbidden*, 1948) sets '*Simmo 'e Napule, paisà*', representative of 'the heritage of an autochthonous culture apparently in the past but still alive in the social fabric of the nation', as opposed to boogie-woogie, projecting 'sectors uprooted from society and looking toward the future'.[21] In *Roma città aperta*, there is a cut directly from Don Pietro celebrating Mass with organ accompaniment to Marina tuning the radio to 'an American station playing jazz' (her words). In the Rome episode of *Paisà*, there is a cut from the bagpipes of a Scottish military band at the liberation to 'In the Mood' being played in a night club; here we encounter Francesca, a degraded prostitute, who, a flashback reveals, was at the time of the liberation a sweet innocent. A similar musically signalled slide into decadence recurs in *Un Americano in vacanza*, where the American dance music in the Melody Club is associated with the corruption of the village boy Roberto, while in *Sotto il sole di Roma*, one sign of the hero Ciro's corruption in the post-war world is his hanging out with petty criminals in the Liberty Club bar to the accompaniment of 'Brazil'.[22]

In *Riso amaro*, in a scene where rain has prevented work in the rice fields, the camera moves from a group of women singing as they play a game with stones to Silvana cutting out glamour pictures from a magazine; in the process, the women's singing is displaced by dance band music. This moment is only the most direct juxtaposition of 'good' folk music with 'bad' pop music in the film. Throughout, this opposition constitutes a dialectic of true and false consciousness. The singing of the harvesters (all women) is presented as an untutored expression of class belonging. It is first heard as they travel to the fields and settle into their temporary accommodation, an emanation of their coming together as a work force. In the fields, it is used as a means of communication, first resisting the undermining of their work and pay by the employment of non-unionized women, then later by their rallying to the support of one of their number, Gabriella, who collapses in the fields miscarrying her baby. This nasal, choral singing is thus not only expressive of collective feeling but practical in furthering the interests and supporting members of the collective; in short, it is truly proletarian and – therefore – socialist. Pop music, on the other hand, is associated above all with the character of Silvana, first seen dancing boogie-woogie which attracts the attention of the petty thief Walter. She is drawn to his gangster glamour, which she connects to the photo-romances she reads and film star pin-ups she puts over her bed. Her fascination with popular mass culture makes her ripe for corruption by Walter.

The starkness of the opposition in *Riso amaro* between politically progressive folk and corrupting pop tunes is made more complex by two things. First, Silvana is clearly a peasant woman, in contrast to the urban and, in appearance, more bourgeois character of Francesca. The twin trajectories of the film are Francesca's coming to identify with the other women, being won for the working class; and Silvana's corruption by *petit bourgeois* fantasies of glamour and crime. Secondly, few would dispute that the most memorable thing about the film is Silvana, not least her boogie-woogie dancing. This is not just star power. Mangano was one of several women who became stars through beauty contests,[23] some organized by film magazines (Mangano won the contest organized in 1948 by *Cine illustrato*), which were informed by a discourse of Italianness:[24] these were to be authentically Italian women, drawn from the people, typically sturdy and big breasted, the sign of an earthy, unaffected beauty. In other words, Silvana Mangano, playing moreover someone called Silvana, brings with her very positive and even neo-realist associations, even while she dances boogie-woogie.

The place of the score

Whatever moral-political valuation is put on diegetic music in neo-realist film, it is often not referenced in the non-diegetic score (hereinafter, just 'the score'). Here I want to consider the practices of Renzo Rossellini, whose work maintains a strict separation of diegetic music and score; Nino Rota, in whose films the score is constantly inflected by diegetic music; and, before discussing Rota, two composers with practices between his and Rossellini's: Goffredo Petrassi and Alessandro Cicognini.[25]

Rossellini, through bombastic orchestration and sheer loudness, often brings drama to images that might otherwise be lacking it. In the Florence episode of *Paisà*, for instance, there are several shots of deserted streets accompanied by hysterically urgent strings that carry on the tension of Harriet and Massimo crossing the city to find their loved ones. In one longish overhead shot, there is nothing but a boy cycling rather leisurely along, stopping to speak to someone in a jeep and pointing-off screen (not towards anything otherwise established by the film); only the high, pounding strings disguise the shot's inconsequentiality. This is an extreme, but symptomatic, point of disjuncture between music and world in Rossellini; elsewhere, the music does heighten more clearly dramatic images (the boys in *Roma città aperta*, the troops in the Sicilian and the partisans in the Po episodes of *Paisà*). Yet the music never has anything to do with the characters' own music, which is presented either as meretricious pop music or belonging to the separate world of the sacred (provided for but not by the people).[26] The score encourages us to see how heroic and tragic these people are, but does not trust their own music to convey this.

Petrassi's music for De Santis' *Riso amaro* and *Non c'è pace tra gli ulivi* is also predominantly in marked contrast to that of the characters, albeit to different ends. In *Riso amaro*, the opposition of folk and pop music discussed above is established before the introduction of any non-diegetic music. The latter occurs after Mario has suggested that the regular and 'scab' rice harvesters work together rather than compete against each other; he then discusses work and crime with Silvana and Francesca. Just as the stories of Silvana and Francesca embody the possibilities of being lost or won to the class struggle, so Mario represents the voice that can see further, the voice of the Party. His words are accompanied by spare, unmelodic woodwind – unemotive, rationalistic, a vanguardist perspective from outside the immediacy of the situation. *Non c'è pace* aims, in its editing patterns and framing and posing of actors, at Brechtian distanciation[27] and the music, in its relentless, mechanical rhythm and use of counterpoint,[28] is entirely appropriate: cerebrally exciting, but not emotionally engaging, underlining the political significance of the story rather than inviting identification with the characters.

In *Riso amaro*, Petrassi does twice allow the characters' music to colour the score. Both Mario and Walter are attracted to Silvana. When the former talks with Silvana in a barn, there are echoes of the harvesters' themes mixed in with the modernist score, as well as drum beats that recall Mario's class experience as a soldier. Mario offers Silvana the possibility of remaining true to her class, and the music reminds us of this in amongst its ruminative dialectic. Later, in a couple of Silvana's scenes with Walter, the score incorporates a pastiche of ragtime. This connects the couple to the world of American popular music and to the class corruption represented by Walter. The oddness of the example – in 1949 ragtime was a dated, almost forgotten music – also indicates the function of both it and the earlier folk elements behind Silvana and Mario. They do not invite us to feel each relationship in the affective terms that the characters might deploy, but rather to judge its political significance in relation to the social values carried by folk and pop music.

Much of Cicognini's work, especially with De Sica, is, like Rossellini's, emotionally urgent while diegetically apart. Where Rossellini evokes heroism, however, Cicognini elicits pity. The impact of his music is achieved from the repetition of a readily grasped theme. *Ladri di biciclette* establishes its main theme behind the credits and repeats it throughout the film. In the long sequence of pawning the sheets, getting the bicycle out of hock and visiting the film poster offices, the tune is repeated at the same pace by different solo instruments (clarinet, oboe, violin, cello, alto saxophone) over light string accompaniment. This is simple and *cantabile*, not keeping the audience at the awesome distance maintained by Rossellini's symphonic tendencies. At the end of the film, after Bruno has seen his father, Antonio, trying to steal a bike but then being caught, the melody reappears yet again, but fitfully, as if unable simply to repeat itself as previously. Bruno and Antonio walk off together, the tune still, as it were, trying for a complete statement. At the end, the pair are lost in the crowd and the music does come to a finish by means of a *rallentando*, but it remains harmonically unresolved, as if the inherent optimism of the earlier scenes (Antonio has got a job, he will find his bike, he is a hero to his son) cannot really ever be recovered.

Cicognini's score for *Umberto D* works in a similar fashion, albeit using three repeated themes in connection with Umberto and a fourth with the maid, Maria. However, one of Umberto's themes is an old fashioned waltz, suggestive of the old world to which he belongs, while the whole of the score for *Due soldi di speranza* (*Two Pennyworth of Hope*, 1951) is based on original themes – principally a *tarantella* – in the style of the indigenous musical culture of the inhabitants of a village near Naples. In these cases the separation between diegesis and non-diegesis is diminished, the kind of music the characters would listen to in the world of the film are echoed in the 'background' score.

In *Roma città aperta*, Don Pietro whistles '*Mattinata fiorentina*' to make contact with the Resistance; it is, however, never alluded to melodically in the score – which is, in any case, a world away from the musical culture from which the song comes. The same song provides the basis for Rota's score for *È primavera*: the title is the first few words of the song; it is heard first behind the credits, then in the first minutes sung raucously by the protagonist Beppe on his delivery round; thereafter he sings, whistles and 'tra-la-las' it on and off throughout the film. The theme is also picked up in the score, arrangements taking off from his careless elation, sometimes seeing the funny side of his exploits (for example, a twanging mandolin plus cello teases his cocky attitude towards girls), sometimes passingly melodramatic (as when, all alone at Christmas, a plangent solo violin becomes almost dissonant as his loneliness intensifies). Diegetic and non-diegetic statements of the song are intertwined: Beppe bounces up the stairs to deliver bread to a maid he knows will be pleased to see him and his singing and whistling of the tune are counterpointed by trumpet riffs based on it; his Sicilian fiancée Maria Antonia herself sings the song and non-diegetic strings take it up as she continues singing, suggesting how much she has been captivated by his sunny energy. The tune is also an inversion of the fanfare that opens the credits and occurs throughout the film and which relates to the fact that the film is mainly about Beppe during his military service. Likewise, calling the film *È primavera* (*Spring is Here*) emphasizes his youth, even while the proper title of the song ('Morning in Florence') was well known enough to underscore the regionality at work in a story of a Florentine boy, set loose by military service, winding up with wives in Sicily and Milan. In short, through the very familiarity of the song, the use of it both diegetically and non-diegetically (with often subtle riffs and inversions between them) and its clear association with the central character, *È primavera* makes no cultural distinction between those making the film and those about whom it is made – the exact opposite procedure of *Roma città aperta*. It is a procedure typical of Rota's work,[29] notably in *Sotto il sole di Roma* and *Senza pietà*.

The title song of the first of these was intended to sell the film and vice versa.[30] It is melodically and instrumentally interchangeable with hundreds of such city songs in the repertoire of the time, with lyrics that, equally typically, evoke youth, love and Rome. It is sung over the credits by rising star Claudio Villa, Roman born (in the then working-class district of Trastevere, comparable to the film's own setting in the Lateran district) and with a very light tenor voice, typical, says Gianni Borgna, of the Roman '*posteggiatore*' (singers who went the rounds of restaurants).[31] In short, the song is over-determinedly 'Roman' in its sound as well at its words.

There is a great deal of other musical material in *Sotto il sole di Roma*, and, after the credits, the song is not referenced in the score for some time. In the early part of the film, during the war, Ciro develops a relationship with the girl next door, Iris, but after the war he drifts into an affair with an older woman. When Iris hears about this, she is angry; he tries to make it up to her in an awkward scene where we are to believe they really love each other and yet in which they also reject each other. It is here that we hear again '*Sotto il sole di Roma*'. It is as if the film recognizes the extraordinary affective complexity of this kind of popular song: trite, suspect sentiments from which people can nonetheless construct real feelings. The music conveys the way emotions are caught up in – only expressible through but also always compromised by – the cultural forms available for their articulation. Later Ciro, repentant, goes looking for Iris but cannot find her, and here the song comes in on the soundtrack in snatches, never quite able to be stated while he cannot find her; when he does at last find her and says he loves her, it is a different musical theme that comes in, one not signalled as belonging to the coinage of popular romance. Only at the end do we hear the song again, rounding off the film with what may now feel a rather complacent affirmation of youth, love and Romanity.

Senza pietà makes a much more sustained use of its characters' preferred music, in this case Negro spirituals. African-American music, whether spirituals, blues or jazz, tends to be treated in neo-realism as an authentic, 'folk' expression of the black experience, an idea adumbrated by Giuseppe de Santis in 1943 in an article on '*Il jazz e le sue danze*'.[32] Often there is a sense of common cause between black GIs and ordinary Italian people, both victims of an unjust society. Joe sings 'Nobody Knows De Trouble I Seen' in the rubble of Naples, side by side with the dispossessed Pasquale (*Paisà*). In *Vivere in pace*, Joe and the grandfather, an ex-infantryman, bond when Joe plays the theme of the old man's regiment on jazz trumpet. A central sequence of *Tombolo paradiso nero* shows the 'paradise' that Tombolo represents, an idyllic encampment in the woods of (mainly black) AWOL[33] GIs and Italian women. Only at this point in the film, a moment of repose and hope, do we hear a cheerful blues sung to a guitar (as opposed to the raucous white swing heard elsewhere). The common experience of poverty and oppression can be transmuted into a sense of the universality of suffering. In *Natale al camp 119* (*Christmas in Camp 119*, 1947), a group of Italian prisoners of war in the United States remember their homeland through listening to records. At one point an Italian-American senior officer sings 'Sometimes I Feel Like a Motherless Child', while an African-American looks on benignly; gradually the Italian POWs gather round. The moment encapsulates the process of universalization of the spirituals, their presumed folk-like capacity to speak for all simple, common human emotions, uncontaminated by commerce. This was the claim made by the most internationally famous singer of spirituals, Paul Robeson.[34]

In *Senza pietà*, the spirituals express the poles of hope and tragedy that the black GIs represent for the Italian women in the film. When Angela and Gerry first meet, he sings a snatch of 'All God's Chillun Gotta Row (to Get to Heaven)' in exultation at being with her; however, when they go to speak with Angela's vicious pimp Pierluigi, 'All God's Chillun' plays on the score in counterpoint to 'Nobody Knows De Trouble I Seen', exactly catching the couple between hope and sorrow. Later, Angela has tried to commit suicide and is now being looked after by Marcella. At first, 'Nobody Knows' plays behind, underlining Angela's despair, but when Marcella starts talking about her own escape to America with her GI, 'All God's Chillun' is introduced, amplifying her hope of a better life.

Senza pietà ends tragically. When Angela is shot by one of Pierluigi's men, Jerry takes her in his arms and drives off with her in a lorry to a full orchestral statement of 'Nobody Knows'. However, as he drives recklessly along, this gives way to the hopeful 'Swing Low Sweet Chariot (coming for to carry me home)', the first time it is heard in the film. It is sung by a deep bass (very Robeson) and then a full, liturgical choir (as in classic choral performances of Negro Spirituals). This optimism, supplemented by phrases from 'All God's Chillun', ends when the lorry crashes, killing them both. 'Nobody Knows' returns, but with fanfares and heavenly choir, over a close-up of her white hand in his black. The song expresses their suffering but also, now, their transcendence.

Conclusion

It is telling that '*Mattinata fiorentina*' in *Roma città aperta* and 'Sometimes I Feel Like a Motherless Child' in *Paisà* are never allowed to appear in the non-diegetic score (not even so much as an echo), whereas they form the basis of it in *È primavera* and *Senza pietà* respectively. Renzo Rossellini's scores also celebrate the common people; in particular, *Roma città aperta* affirms the heroic, tragic, transcendent status of the protagonists no less fulsomely than does *Senza pietà*. But Rossellini never does so in the protagonists' own cultural terms. Unlike Petrassi, on the other hand, Rota's approach is not critical. His music refuses a comfortable position of moral-political certainty outside the lives and situations of the films itself, while showing the workings of popular culture in everyday life. It suggests one of the ways neo-realism might have bridged the gap between 'films about the people or films for the people'.

Notes

1. From 1937, Cinecittà in Rome was the centre of commercial film production in Italy.
2. Spinazzola, V. *Cinema e pubblico. Lo spettacolo filmico in Italia 1945–1965*, Rome: Bulzoni, 1985, 7.

3. On neo-realism and the box office see Grignaffini, G. 'Lo Stato dell'Unione. Appunti sull'industria cinematografica italiana 1945–1949', in Farassino, A. (ed.) *Neorealismo. Cinema italiano 1945–1949*, Turin: EDT, 1989, 37–44; Lughi, P. 'Il neorealismo in sala. Anteprime di gala e teniture di massa', in ibid., 53–60; Spinazzola, V. *Cinema e pubblico*; and Wagstaff, C. 'Neorealism in Italian Cinema, 1945–54', in Hewitt, N. (ed.) *The Culture of Reconstruction: European Literature, Thought and Film, 1945–50*, London: Macmillan, 1989, 67–87.

4. Lunghi, F.L. 'La musica e il neo-realismo', in E. Masetti (ed.) *La musica nel film*, Rome: Bianco e Nero, 1950, 56–60.

5. Ibid., 57.

6. Ibid.

7. Wagstaff, C. 'Neorealism in Italian Cinema, 1945–54', 72.

8. Farassino, A. 'Neorealismo, storia e geografia', in A. Farassino (ed.) *Neorealismo. Cinema italiano 1945–1949*, 21–36.

9. Ibid. 32.

10. Cf. Caldiron, O. 'Il cinema canta', in G. Governi, F. Lefevre and C. Terenzi (eds) *Tu musica divina. Canzoni e storia in cento anni d'Italia*, Turin: Umberto Allemandi, 1996, 94–8; and Venturelli, R. (ed.) *Nessuno ci può giudicare. Il lungo viaggio del cinema musicale italiano 1930–1980*, Rome: Fahrenheit 451, 1998.

11. *Roma città aperta* was first screened publicly in September 1945, *O sole mio* in February 1946.

12. Forgacs, D. *Rome Open City*, London: British Film Institute, 2000, 55.

13. Brunette, P. *Roberto Rossellini*, New York: Oxford University Press, 1987, 25.

14. Cf. Barthes, R. 'The Realist Effect', trans G. Mead, *Film Reader* 3, Evanston, IL: Northwestern University Press, 1978, 131–5.

15. See Gargano, P. and Cesarini, G. *La canzone napoletana*, Milan: Rizzoli, 1984; and Borgna, G. *Storia della canzone italiana*, Milan: Arnoldo Mondadori, 1992.

16. Ibid. 187.

17. Nataletti, G. 'La musica folklorica italiana nel cinema', in S.G. Biamonte (ed.) *Musica e film*, Rome: Edizioni dell'Ateneo, 1959, 109.

18. Jointly overseen by the Accademia Nazionale di Santa Cecilia (the Italian conservatory of music) and the RAI (the state radio and television service). One product of this in the 1950s was the film music documentary film.

19. See Straniero, M.L. *Manuale di musica popolare*, Milan: Rizzoli, 1991, 34–5.

20. Visconti's recourse to opera is nearly always ironic: in *Ossessione*, the gap between the appearance of amateur singers and the heroic, pulchritudinous idealizations of the arias they sing is a source of grotesque humour (cf. Bacon, H. *Visconti: Explorations of Beauty and Decay*, Cambridge: Cambridge University Press, 1998, 25); an optimistic aria from Bellini's *La sonnambula* in *La terra trema* counterpoints the pessimism of the film's narrative trajectory (see Chiarelli, C.G. *Musica e memoria nell'arte di Luchino Visconti*, Milan: Archinto, 1997); Donizetti's *L'elisir d'amore*, about a charlatan, sets the stage for the depiction of the commercial film industry in *Bellissima* (1951).

21. Mangini, G. 'Nino Rota, il cinema, le canzoni ovvero: "Quanta gente c'era da contentare!"', in V. Rizzardi (ed.) *L'undicesima musa: Nino Rota e i suoi media*, Rome: RAI, 2001, 137–60 (155).

22. Both the Melody Club and the Liberty Club are so named in the film, clearly linking American values to louche locales.

23. For example, Lucia Bosè, Gianna Maria Canale, Eleonora Rossi Drago, Gina Lollobrigida, Silvana Pampanini.

24. See Farassino, A. 'Il cinema come premio', in A. Farassino (ed.) *Neorealismo. Cinema italiano 1945–1949*, 140–41.

25. Other composers who worked in neo-realism but are not discussed here include Giovanni Fusco, Mario Nascimbene, Carlo Rustichelli and Mario Zafred.

26. *Accattone* (1962) also uses religious music (Bach) to suggest the paradoxical sacredness of its sordid subproletarian world, but the case is too complex to go into here (see Calabretto, R. *Pasolini e la musica*, Pordenone: Cinemazero, 1999).

27. See Premuda, E. *Il coro sulla scala. Il rapporto suono-immagine nella stagione neorealistica di Giuseppe De Santis*, Palermo: Edizioni della Battaglia, 2000, 34–5. Note also Sergio Miceli's brief discussion in Morricone, E. and Miceli, S. *Comporre per il cinema: Teoria e prassi della musica nel film*, Venice: Marsilio, 2001, 88–9.

28. It is in fact very reminiscent of Petrassi's own first Concerto for Orchestra of 1934.

29. Film composers of course work in conjunction with directors and producers, but I have here for the sake of brevity mainly written as if the composers made the decisions about the form and use of music in the films. In many cases a repeated collaboration is evident: Renzo Rossellini with his brother Robert, Cicognini with De Sica, Petrassi with De Santis. Rota's neo-realist films, on the other hand, were made with Castellani, Comencini, Fellini, Lattuada, Soldati and Zampa, and show an approach to music that remains consistent throughout all his film music output (for 157 films).

30. See note 10.

31. Borgna, G. *Storia della canzone italiana*, 201.

32. De Santis, G. *Verso il neorealismo. Un critico cinematografico degli anni quaranta*, Rome: Bulzoni, 1982, 65–8; see also Vitti, A. *Giuseppe De Santis and Post-war Italian Cinema*, Toronto: University of Toronto Press, 1996, 13.

33. Absent without leave.

34. On Robeson and the Negro spiritual, see Dyer, R. *Heavenly Bodies: Film Stars and Society*, London: Routledge, 2003 (2nd edition) and Anderson, P.A. *Deep River: Music and Memory in Harlem Renaissance Thought*, Durham, NC: Duke University Press, 2001.

Chapter 3

Contemporary Spanish film music: Carlos Saura and Pedro Almodóvar

Kathleen M. Vernon and Cliff Eisen

The decision to centre this study of Spanish film music on the works of Spain's most internationally celebrated directors of the last forty years is an approach that brings both benefits and risks. The advantage of a focus on Spain's best-known *auteurs*, with the significant exception of Luis Buñuel, is the prospect of greater meaningfulness for English-language readers of this chapter, who are more likely to be familiar with the films discussed than they would be in the case of lesser-known directors. The disadvantages of an uncritical embrace of *auteurism* – compounded by our parallel emphasis on the two composers who have carried on sustained collaborations with each director, Luis de Pablo in the case of Saura, and Alberto Iglesias with Almodóvar – is the promotion of a kind of cultural exceptionalism that reinforces the notion of the great artist who rises above national and historical circumstances to speak 'directly' to world audiences. There is also a danger, as Michel Chion reminds us, that the focus on the director-composer 'tandem' may turn attention away from the visual/aural text and textures that are the result of these collaborations, and those of countless other members of the production team, thereby reducing the films in question to a struggle between artistic personalities: 'stories of tête-à-tête, understanding or lack thereof, submission or conflict'.[1]

Where the concept and function of the *auteur* does prove useful in framing our study of Spanish film music in the context of European cinema is with respect to the specific role of Saura and Almodóvar in signifying Spain and Spanish cinema to European and international spectators. What combination and expression of 'universal' themes and values and national specificity enabled Saura and Almodóvar, at very different historical moments, to project the dominant images of Spanishness to their European neighbours? And what part did their film music play, or not play, in that achievement? Although Saura continues to make films today, this chapter will concentrate on his work between 1965 and 1972, during the last decade of the Franco dictatorship, when his cinema arguably both suffered and benefited from the regime's lurching oscillation between tentative modernization and repressive reaction. As the visible exponent of a Spanish cultural opposition much esteemed abroad, Saura's films traced a path between the demons of a tragic national history and the anguished discontents of a modern urban bourgeoisie. In contrast, Almodóvar and his cinema first came to international prominence nearly twenty years later as the standard-bearer of a hyper-modern, post-Franco Spain determined to turn its back on the past.

Beyond history and chronology, many further differences separate the two filmmakers. From the beginning of his career, Saura was received and promoted as the quintessential art cinema director. A graduate of the national film school, he took up the challenge to reinvigorate the national industry under the inspiration of neo-realism and European 'new cinemas' from a declining studio system caught between Hollywood and the pressures of Francoist ideology. Saura and his cohort enlisted the work of 'new music' composer Luis de Pablo and others of his generation whose efforts to modernize Spanish art music harmonized with other similar contemporary European currents.

Almodóvar, on the other hand, was an outsider from a socio-economic milieu unrepresented in influential cultural circles, a self-taught filmmaker who began his career with super-8 films in the context of the counterculture youth movement *Movida* centred in Madrid following Franco's death. The immediate sources for his cinema were popular Hollywood genre films and the Spanish comic populist tradition of the 1950s and 1960s. The music for his first films stemmed primarily from *Movida* sources and included punk and glam rock numbers performed by Almodóvar and Fany McNamara and co-written with Bernardo Bonezzi.[2] Almodóvar's work with Alberto Iglesias began in the mid-1990s following the director's first mainstream international hit, *Mujeres al borde de un ataque de nervios* (*Women on the Verge of a Nervous Breakdown*, 1988), and on the heels of his collaborations with well-known international composers Ennio Morricone (*Atame/Tie me Up, Tie Me Down*, 1989) and Ryuchi Sakamoto (*Tacones lejanos/High Heels*, 1991).

Despite their differences in background and approach, both Saura and Almodóvar evince a strong personal interest in music and the use of music in their films.[3] Although perhaps most visible and audible in Saura's later films, his flamenco ballet trilogy made in collaboration with dancer and choreographer Antonio Gades, the music/dance documentaries *Sevillanas* (1993) and *Flamenco* (1995) and the fiction feature *Tango* (1998), his concern with music and the use of the soundtrack to 'engender the camera track' is already in evidence in the films of the 1960s and 1970s.[4] In Almodóvar's case, his broad musical culture is on display in the range of musical sources in his films – his incorporation of Latin American and, less frequently, Spanish popular song, French *chanson*, works by Miles Davis, Kurt Weill, Stravinsky, Rimsky-Korsakov, and his quotations and pastiches of classic American scores (especially those by Bernard Herrmann) – an eclecticism also apparent in Iglesias' scores for their five films together.

It is our conviction, then, that the analysis of film music in the films of Saura and Almodóvar cannot be separated from a broader cultural history and context.

To that end we include a brief overview of the history of film music in Spain. Only recently have film critics and historians begun to devote serious critical attention to the role of music in Spanish cinema, past and present.[5] New research and recordings by prolific film composer José Nieto, currently director of the sound department at the Madrid Film School (ECAM),[6] has given greater insight into Spain's neglected 'golden age' of symphonic film composing and composers in the 1940s.[7] Contrary to the common view, held even within Spain, of the early post-Civil War film industry as a chronically underfunded operation devoted to the production of pro-Franco propaganda and escapist fluff, recent studies have come to reveal a more complex picture of a relatively successful, if minor, national industry modelled on the Hollywood studio system, one which not only included a role for symphonic film scores but also provided an infrastructure designed to support their production. Roberto Cueto's research on the period testifies to the prominent standing of the film composer, as the fourth highest paid professional involved in each film, following the director, scriptwriter and producer. Likewise, from the 1930s onwards, the SGAE guaranteed film composers separate authorship rights to their music for film.[8] Cueto and Carlos Colón Perales describe composers' efforts to create a 'national' style or school of film music based on a hybrid of traditional Spanish forms such as the *zarzuela* and *copla* (a popular, commercial song genre with strong regional folkloric accents), European symphonic music, and Hollywood and European cinema practices.[9]

In the decades that followed, despite the country's political marginalization, developments in Spanish film music also largely paralleled tendencies in the rest of Europe. The 1950s brought about a change in subject matter and modes of production moved away from genre cinema and studio shooting toward location filming and 'critical realism'.[10] With the dismantling of many of the studios, film production could no longer sustain the needs of symphonic scores. Spanish critical realism, Alvares tells us, 'required a different type of music'.[11] Cueto compares the scores for Luis Berlanga's films to the 'intellectualized populist'[12] compositions of Nino Rota for Fellini's first films. The subsequent Spanish 'new wave' directors, grouped under the banner of the *Nuevo Cine Español* in the 1960s, shared common ground with their counterparts in the world of Spanish concert music. Luis de Pablo was one of a handful of members of the Generation of '51, among them Carmelo Bernaola, Antón García Abril, Cristóbal Halffter and Antonio Pérez Olea, who combined their work as 'serious' composers with collaborations with directors such as Basilio Martín Patino, Miguel Picazo, Antxon Eceiza and later Víctor Erice and Manuel Gutiérrez Aragón, as well as Saura. By the late 1970s, however, 'new music' composers had retired from film work and the art cinema paradigm had lost its dominance. During the 1980s the majority of films had recourse to pre-recorded music and popular songs. Tight budgets resulted in ever poorer working conditions for recording and synchronization, a situation that would have been shocking to the filmmakers and composers of the 1940s. Such was the immediate context for the emergence of a new group of film composers in the 1990s, with Alberto Iglesias among the most celebrated, not only for his work with Almodóvar but also with Julio Medem (*Lovers of the Arctic Circle*, *Sex and Lucia*). The last fifteen years have seen a rebirth of the large-scale and symphonic film score, favoured by higher film production budgets, technological advances in digital recording and Dolby sound, and a new recognition for film music as recorded music evidenced in regular releases of Spanish film scores by Iglesias and others.[13]

Carlos Saura and Luis de Pablo

The young composers who banded together under the banner of *Nueva Música*, members of the so-called Generation of '51, sought nothing less than to bring Spanish classical music into the (mid-) twentieth century and out of the isolation imposed by the Civil War and Francoist cultural values and policies. Their first task was, in Tomás Marco's words, 'the conquest of lost time. In very few years they had to assimilate the ultimate consequences of Stravinsky and Bartok, atonal expressionism, dodecaphony, serialism, open and aleatory forms, graphism and electronic musics.'[14] By the mid-1960s Luis de Pablo had established himself in Spain and abroad as perhaps the most respected exponent of modern Spanish concert music, both in his growing list of compositions, which integrated a broad range of Western avant-garde practices in the development and expression of his personal style, and as a 'thinker ... [and] spokesperson for serious contemporary music'.[15]

Although de Pablo's first examples of 'incidental' music for film date from 1956, his sustained collaboration with Spanish new wave directors begins with his work in Antxon Eceiza and Elías Querejeta's 1960 documentary *A través de San Sebastián* (*Through San Sebastian*).[16] Eceiza recounts their meeting with de Pablo, 'a young musician who was working [as a lawyer] for Iberia ... he saw the rough copy of the film and told us that *música concreta* would work very well with the film'.[17] De Pablo would work with Saura on five films: *La caza* (*The Hunt*, 1965), *Peppermint frappé* (1967), *La madriguera* (*The Warren*, 1969), *El jardín de las delicias* (*The Garden of Delights*, 1970) and *Ana y los lobos* (*Ana and the Wolves*, 1972). *La caza* was Saura's first collaboration with producer Elías Querejeta, a key figure in the development and promotion of Spanish art cinema of the period, both through his ability to negotiate the bureaucratic shoals of the governmental film-subsidy system and censorship apparatus, and his creation of a standing production team that counted de Pablo among its members.

Perhaps the most conspicuous characteristic of the Saura–de Pablo film scores is the relative scarcity of music in the films. While assuming a foregrounded role, as we shall see, in *La caza*, music in the form of a composed score is strikingly limited for much of the duration of the other four films. In the absence of sustained scholarship on the role of music in New Spanish Cinema, it is useful in understanding this apparent scarcity to turn to Chion's discussion of attitudes toward film music within the European film 'modernisms' of the 1960s and 1970s. Among filmmakers such as Antonioni, Buñuel and Rohmer, Chion finds a 'fear on the part of the director of showing bad taste or kitsch sentimentality, … a distrust of ready-made solutions, pre-packaged emotions that music seems designed to produce'. Such suspicion of music's presumed manipulative function led these cinematic modernists to 'radical solutions … obviously distanced and distancing music' or the elimination of music 'in order to avoid the effect of an emotional catalyst, of precipitator of meanings and significance (saying: here you can vibrate emotionally, cry)'.[18] It seems clear that to cinematic modernists – among whom one should count Saura and his cohort – rejection of the narrative conventions and spectatorial habits associated with classic cinema, whether from Hollywood or their own national traditions, extends to a parallel suspicion toward the classic, 'golden age' film score. Thus, film music in modernist cinema will tend to be absent precisely at those moments when the classic model, as analysed by Claudia Gorbman and others, requires its presence: in providing continuity against the discontinuous nature of the visual track, underscoring narrative events, matching character moods, and cueing spectator emotions.[19]

Beyond the simple absence of music, or the reduction of its traditional role, however, there seems to be a more radical reconceptualization of the soundtrack and the place of music in the overall sonic design of the film. What de Pablo brings to Saura's films are not only the modern sonorities and fragmented structures of the European musical avant-garde but also the experimental openness of *musique concrète* and its incorporation of everyday sounds or 'noise' into the musical texture. The de Pablo scores do make use of the recognizable strategies of 'new music', most notably in *La caza*, but they do so within the context of decidedly heterogeneous film scores. Taken as a whole, the five Saura–de Pablo films draw on a range of Western musical styles and idioms, from medieval to modern, and from high-art concert traditions to contemporary pop. The mix of musical discourses within individual films responds to a generalized preference for diegetic, that is, music explicitly or implicitly sourced within the scene, over non-diegetic scoring. Thus the films frequently cede 'control' of musical choices to the characters themselves, who, as we shall see, use music in a number of different ways. All of the films deploy hybrid scores, incorporating both pre-recorded 'compiled' selections and de Pablo's 'original' composed material – although that distinction is sometimes less than clear.[20]

As suggested above, the score for *La caza* represents an exception among the Saura–de Pablo collaborations for its use of a through-composed, albeit intermittent, non-diegetic score based in new music practices. While it is not the exclusive musical referent for the film – the composed score coexists with a compiled musical track of derivative Spanish versions of 1960s US and French pop songs that emerge from one character's transistor radio – de Pablo's score plays a central role in shaping the sense of narrative inevitability that leads to the film's explosive denouement. *La caza,* Saura's third film, was and perhaps remains, the director's most internationally celebrated work, a powerful parable of the human capacity for violence and self-destruction, played out in the form of a rabbit hunt turned human slaughter on a former battlefield of the Spanish Civil War.

The composed score is deployed primarily in the first and last thirds of the film. The first section introduces two main musical cues while the latter and concluding section of the film offers five variations on a third type of music. The first musical cue accompanies the opening shot of the film, as an open-topped jeep occupied by four men traverses a stretch of arid, hilly terrain. The music begins abruptly in the middle of a phrase, as sharply rhythmic chords and percussion introduce a slightly dissonant piano melody. The effect is disquieting, jaunty but grim with clear military overtones. This first theme has elements of what Chion calls anempathetic music, music that displays a distance or detachment from the scene it accompanies. Rather than straightforward contrast or counterpoint, this anempathetic music, 'marked by a certain regularity of rhythm, a certain absence of contrasts, of intensity, fluctuations of level, of phrasing',[21] shows indifference, a lack of correspondence between events or emotions depicted on screen and life as it goes on elsewhere. In the examples discussed by Chion, the scenes in question depict horrific events. In *La caza* this initial musical cue, before the action has really begun, offers an anticipation of later scenes of death and destruction and a suggestion of impersonal forces, the legacy of war in human history, that rise from the terrain itself, initially unacknowledged by the characters.

A second musical motif is introduced shortly after the men arrive at the hunting site, as José, the owner of the land and organizer of the expedition, enters a hut looking for the caretaker, Juan. As José passes from the glaring sunlight to the shadowy interior of the hut, the music evokes a primitive netherworld, shown to be inhabited by grotesque beings, Juan's senile, bedridden mother and the caged ferrets she treats as her pets. While sharing a certain motivic harmonic identity with the jeep motif, the hut music deploys a quasi-fugal texture that with its lack of rhythmic thrust and grounded harmonies – there is no military tattoo here or marching rhythms, no clear-cut yet chromatically inflected melody – seems to float uneasily around the scene, circling back on itself. This music will recur to characterize different forms of interior dis-ease whether manifested through actual physical spaces or the troubled psyches of the characters, as revealed through a series of interior monologues.

The first hunting scene, about a third of the way into the narrative, brings the two motifs together in the longest continuous musical sequence in the film, at seven and a half minutes. After dividing up into what one character describes as military formations, the men set out in pursuit of their quarry. A flurry of drum rolls gives way to the hut motif as the men's ruminations on their financial worries and the breakdown of their friendship are heard in voiceover. When the shooting finally begins, the jeep motif recurs. In uniting the two themes, the sequence establishes the grounds for the film's denouement in the convergence of external and internal causality. But that conclusion is postponed by an extended musical and narrative pause in the action as the hunters stop to eat and rest.

When the gunfire and music recommence, some 30 minutes later, there is a notable shift in the music's relation to the action. Where the earlier musical cues seemed to emerge from the space or setting, as an element of *mise-en-scène*, this third-stage music – four false starts before the final slaughter – is triggered by a series of sonic events: untimely gunshots, the tinkling bells on the collar of the ferrets as they are sent into the rabbit holes to flush out the prey. These new musical cues, while broadly derived from the previous themes, are active and propulsive in contrast to the static character of both the jeep and hut music. Each of them is characterized by a number of traditional 'action music' devices, including forward-driving rhythms and increasingly shorter note values, rising harmonic and melodic sequences, and a build-up of volume. This final segment gives extensive evidence of what Marsha Kinder has termed the film's overall 'orchestration of violence'.[22]

The genesis of *Peppermint frappé*, Saura and de Pablo's second collaboration, derives from a pre-existing sonic event, the Good Friday 'Drums of Calanda', a day-long ritual of collective drumming practised by the inhabitants of the small Aragonese town Calanda, the birthplace of Luis Buñuel (to whom the film is dedicated). The film's protagonist, Julián, is a middle-aged, unmarried doctor in the provincial capital of Cuenca. When his boyhood friend Paco returns to the town with his much younger foreign bride, Elena, Julián is convinced that he has seen her in Calanda beating a drum during the Good Friday observance. Julián becomes obsessed with Elena, to him the very image of attractive modern woman, whose magazine representations he is shown cutting out and pasting in a scrap book to the '*Ternario*' theme from the medieval Spanish mystery play, *El misterio de Elche* (*The Mystery of Elche*), during the opening credit sequence.[23]

Both Julián and Pedro, the male protagonist of Saura and de Pablo's next collaboration, *La madriguera*, are presented as members of a contemporary Spanish professional class struggling to reconcile the traditional values with which they were educated and the promises and pressures of modern consumer society. And in both films music plays a role in expressing the characters' conflicted identities. Julián's traditionally furnished home contains the latest model stereo system on which he plays *The Mystery of Elche* and a classical period string quartet. Pedro returns from his job as an automobile company executive to a fashionable young wife, Teresa (Geraldine Chaplin plays the female lead in both films), and an architecturally ultramodern home where he listens to late Renaissance variations for cello and lute on his stereo. Both men arguably make use of Western classical music in similar ways, as a marker of cultivated good taste, but also as an exercise of rational control and a barrier against the disorder of modern life. The disruption and ultimate destruction of the rational surface of both men's lives is announced in the films by the invasive presence of non-diegetic, atonal music.

In the case of *La madriguera* it is the arrival of a truckload of traditional furniture belonging to Teresa's parents that triggers the first fissures in their placid routine. Teresa's subsequent nightmare recollection of her convent school days sees her woken by two nuns who drag her down a long hallway to an encounter with a zombie-like male authority figure. Her dream's auditory track is in striking contrast to the daytime melodies that issue from the on-screen music sources. The sounds begin with the rhythmic footsteps of the two nuns heard against a low hum of light fixtures that merges into a single sustained organ note, increasing in volume, that ends in her scream. This opening to Teresa's past sets in motion a first playful and then destructive cycle of role-playing between the couple that ends in murder and suicide. The film's two diegetic musical cues, Pedro's late-Renaissance variations and a modern romantic theme scored for guitar and vibraphone (we hear it over the second half of the opening credits and it is later identified as 'their song' when played on a record player in the climactic role-play scene in which the couple relive their courtship), serve as unsuccessful attempts to anchor their lives in the everyday against the onslaught of the irrational.

Like *La caza*, the film ends in gunshots, punctuated here by an even more explosive musical coda, a sudden outburst of organ music – not the single note of Teresa's nightmare but an all-embracing cacophony of dissonant harmonies and irrational rhythms, so overpoweringly loud as not just to signal a rejection of the film's earlier tonal music but its utter negation. The notable paucity of music in *La madriguera* – it is clearly the film with the fewest musical cues – has its own effect on the spectator/listener. If the continuous flow of the classical film score is intended to function, in Gorbman's words, as an 'unheard melody' (its effectiveness in shaping audience response to the product of its subliminal character), then the impact of de Pablo's score, when it does appear, is much more overt. Music in the Saura films calls attention to itself, whether as a visible narrative element, or an 'unnatural' and unnaturalized off-screen presence.

The first of two particularly sonically significant scenes in *Peppermint frappé* signals a decisive moment in Julián's progression from a repressed bachelor with an active fantasy life (in which respect he is more like *La madriguera*'s Teresa than Pedro) to an imaginative and calculating murderer. Julián is seen developing photographs of Elena dancing, which he took during the three friends' excursion to his country house. Both visual and sound tracks converge to suggest Julián's unbalanced mental state as we share his vision of a static image of Elena bathed in the red glare of a darkroom lamp. The red tint gives way to the reverse black and white of a negative image accompanied by a solo atonal organ – in a sense the reverse or an 'inversion' of the previously heard tonal music. Julián continues manipulating the photographic image, cropping the background to focus on Elena and then using a paper trimmer to chop his friend and rival Paco out of the picture entirely.

The film's final act stages Julián's murderous revenge on both Paco and Elena whom he once again has lured to his country house. As he prepares supper, Julián puts music on the reel-to-reel stereo system, a modernized version of the *Elche* material that initially suggests a possible reconciliation between the competing impulses in his conflicted psyche. Both diegetic and subsequent non-diegetic music in the scene serve less as autonomous musical elements than as a base or glue for the accumulation of sonorous layers, natural and man- (and woman-) made sounds, in the formation of a complex sonic texture. As the song continues Julián goes out to greet Paco and Elena, the sound of their car engine and horn juxtaposed with the music. Back inside, the sonorous structure builds as Elena and Paco tease Julián for his earlier attempts to win Elena for himself. The *Elche* material is first accompanied by Elena's tapping fingers on the drum she has mockingly given him in 'memory' of Calanda. Elena then begins beating the drum in earnest as Paco recites an Antonio Machado sonnet that Julián had read to Elena on an earlier visit, topped-off by her hummed accompaniment to the poem. Lastly, Julián pours two glasses of his signature cocktail, peppermint frappé (which the audience knows from a previous scene to be drugged), from a glass decanter containing the figure of a dancer, whose tinkling music box melody lays down a final stratum of sound. The film's conclusion sees a further sonic layering formed by the merging of 'natural', mechanical sounds and the return of the off-screen organ. When the ever-playful Elena jumps on an antique bicycle and is chased by her husband, the sounds of the squeaking wheel are matched to the organ's tones, the drug's effects made perceptible in the decelerating rhythm of the slowing bicycle–organ mix. The organ will further accompany Julián as he piles the couple's inanimate bodies into Paco's sports car and drives to a cliff where he sends the car and its two passengers crashing down below.

While marked by increasing attention to the narrative and thematic functions of music and sound, both *El jardín de las delicias* (Saura's first film to employ direct sound) and *Ana y los lobos* also give evidence of a diminishing role for de Pablo as composer of an original score. In *El jardín* the family of amnesiac accident victim Antonio Cano deploys a series of musical cues, ranging from a popular song, '*Recordar*', sung by 1930s film star Imperio Argentina, to the Spanish Republican anthem, the '*Himno de Riego*', and Rodrigo's *Concierto de Aranjuez*, as memory triggers designed to restart the shattered recall mechanism of the once-powerful industrialist's damaged brain. The non-diegetic music, which includes both composed and compiled material, serves as a representation of Cano's subjective state, expressing flights of fancy, or fear, as experienced by a mind trapped in a paralysed body.[24] One theme, highly reminiscent of the romantic 'Our Song' of *La madriguera* in its scoring and purely diatonic chord progressions (similar, in fact, to late 1950s pop music but here decked-out with a 'classical' sounding surface), evokes the pastoral setting of Cano's family estate and the garden of the film's title. It is portrayed as a form of both mental and physical refuge that nevertheless cannot withstand the assaults from without or within: neither the protagonist's family's demands nor his own nightmarish hallucinations.

One of the most interesting forms of sonic representation in the film occurs in two instances of *musique concrète* that are both implicitly tied to Cano's mental processes. The first is located in the natural, pastoral setting of the garden where Cano is taken to practise his signature. When his nurse leaves his side he shifts the pen she gave him from his paralysed right hand to his functional left and begins to draw circles; as he does so, the barely audible bird sounds that accompanied the first part of the scene rise on the soundtrack, as various calls by different species join to form an exuberant cacophony. The other instance derives from an unidentified interior space, an apparently abandoned warehouse filled with idle machinery that is presented twice in the film, in the opening credit sequence and a brief, narratively unsituated, segment later in the film that shows Antonio Cano walking through the room. In both scenes, as the camera pans slowly over the hulking machines, a pulsating hum rises on the soundtrack. Over approximately two minutes, we hear variations in pitch, rhythmic intensity and duration, that, while clearly approximating mechanical noises, take on a life of their own that belies their would-be source in the silent turbines, boilers and pistons that occupy the space. These two diametrically opposed sound worlds, natural and mechanical, realized through *musique concrète*, provide complementary representations of the workings of Cano's damaged brain.

Although *Ana y los lobos* is the last Saura film for which de Pablo receives screen credit, he contributed no new composed material for the film. *Ana* pursues and extends still further the principle of musical economy that seems to have governed the Saura–de Pablo collaborations: limited use of music, limited small ensemble scoring for composed material and, here, the 'recycling' of musical cues from earlier films. *Ana*'s three musical themes, only one of which is 'new' to Saura's filmography, are employed as leitmotifs assigned to individual characters and as such work to develop the film's meaning as a darkly allegorical fairy tale. The wolves of the title, three brothers who represent three Spanish institutions – the Church, the military and patriarchy – in the form of sexually predatory males, are allied against the incursions of Ana, the foreign governess who embodies both the threat of modernity and an active, non-Spanish, female sexuality. Thus the 'Ternario' from *El misterio de Elche* is used to characterize Fernando, the would-be hermit and mystic. The new piece, nineteenth-century *zarzuela* composer Federico Chueca's patrotic *pasodoble* 'El dos de mayo', written to celebrate the centenary of the Spanish War of Independence against Napoleon, is identified with José, the family's dominant male and a collector of military memorabilia. The contemporary romantic 'Our Song' which was associated with Teresa in *La madriguera* here accompanies Ana (also played by Geraldine Chaplin). Tellingly, Juan, the sexually obsessed husband, and father of the two daughters Ana is hired to mind, has no music of his own, but shares Ana's theme when he enters her room to fetishistically handle her clothes and belongings, suggesting perhaps an ironic feminization of the would-be 'Don Juan' figure.

Pedro Almodóvar and Alberto Iglesias

The emergence of Alberto Iglesias, and by extension, the figure of the composer as a recognized creative partner in the genesis of a film, reflects a sea-change in attitudes toward the role of music in Spanish cinema on the part of directors, producers and spectators. If the Saura–de Pablo collaborations evince a modernist discomfort with the conventions of the classical film score, played out in an avant-garde aesthetic of 'making strange', Iglesias' work for Almodóvar, in contrast, proposes and brings about a new normativity for film music. Iglesias' compositions respond and contribute to an altered horizon of reception shaped by a conscious recuperation of earlier film music traditions and a discographic rediscovery of classic film composers and scores. Chion identifies a parallel phenomenon in European and American cinema since the early 1980s, an era he cinematically dubs 'back to the future', consisting not in a simple return to traditional musical practices but an opportunity for innovation based in both technical advances in film sound recording and projection, and a dialogue with the symphonic traditions of Herrmann, Korngold, Steiner, Rózsa and others.[25] In interviews Iglesias embraces that common post-Romantic musical inheritance as a 'collective unconsciousness' shared by spectators and composer alike: 'to make film music one needs to rely on that global comprehension [provided by film music traditions] but one can also change, invert and modify'.[26]

Iglesias' identity as a film composer is thus tied to his ability to integrate a range of musical styles and discourses. In his training and compositions, he provides a model of a 'new generation of Spanish composers who bring together a classical formation with contemporary aesthetics'.[27] Born in San Sebastián in 1955, Iglesias first studied piano, guitar, harmony and counterpoint in his home town, and later composition with Francis Schwartz in Paris, and electronic music with Gabriel Brnçic in Barcelona. From 1981 to 1986, a period that coincides with his first excursions into film music, he wrote and performed with fellow composer Javier Navarrete. For Iglesias, then, in contrast to de Pablo and his '*Nueva Música*' group, the issue is not to gain access to the mainstream European avant-garde and its newer currents – that inheritance is already part of their musical formation – but to open avant-garde practices to popular, 'contemporary' influences. And cinema offers a means to do so, as Iglesias observes: 'Twenty years ago, the *avant-garde* composer's path was closed with respect to [popular] music. That attitude is impossible now …. Cinema can take you to regions you hadn't thought of; we live a kind of polystylistics and a string quartet can have rhythm and blues influences without having to disguise itself as rock.'[28]

It is telling that Iglesias' work with Almodóvar begins in the wake of the director's avowedly less than satisfactory collaborations with established film composers Ryuchi Sakamoto and Ennio Morricone.[29] Almodóvar reports that he rejected half of the music composed by Morricone for *Atame* because the 'music [was] much more conventional than … the film. This is a problem I almost always encounter when I commission original music from a composer.' Morricone, he goes on to say, like many film composers, tended to repeat himself, whereas for Almodóvar: 'when I go to work on a film, I am confident in producing something new'.[30] This confidence in the ability to innovate and create something new, not through the negation of past film and film music traditions but out of a familiarity with and fluency in the multiple languages of their respective film and musical canons, is a capacity shared by both Almodóvar and Iglesias. As Iglesias tells Roberto Cueto, his own relation to modernist aesthetics is found in the 'utopian idea of finding a new space' of his own devising within the well-trod terrain of standard film music.[31]

Given Almodóvar's views about originally commissioned music, it is tempting to try to evaluate the specific impact of Iglesias' contribution. As Iglesias admits, 'I met [and began to work with] Pedro when the adjective "Almodovarian" already existed. His cinematic world was already well established. I had to immerse myself in that world.'[32] How, then, does the presence and function of Iglesias' music respond to or allow for significant changes in the character of Almodóvar's 'cinematic world'? And can one distinguish an 'Iglesian' musical world or space within the conjunction between sound and image?

Although the composer himself has questioned the existence of a recognizable 'Iglesias style', the listener/spectator of the Almodóvar–Iglesias films comes to identify a number of constants.[33] Iglesias' musical choices reflect his selective adaptation of that global comprehension rooted in the forms of musical and affective meaning expressed and expressable through the already codified language of late- and post-Romantic idioms. While the composer makes use of a range of tonal and melodic gestures, from the Mendelssohnian/Brahmsian to early twentieth-century expressionist modes, in terms of rhythm his work is characterized by the rationality of common-coin accompanimental gestures with clear downbeats and filling-in of the rhythmic space with evenly distributed, regular punctuating chords (this is in contrast to the irrationality of de Pablo's rhythms). Likewise his scoring practices reveal a decided preference for strings, sometimes massed but often soloistic, and in this respect exploiting the rawer sounds of the exposed voices of late Brahms or early Schoenberg quartets – hence the frequent comparisons to Bernard Herrmann – rather than the grand Romantic gestures of lush orchestral music, the almost excessive expressiveness of Tchaikovsky and early Richard Strauss which also forms a central, one might say *the* central, strand in 'classic' film music.

If one were to characterize in one word the function of Iglesias' score for *La flor de mi secreto* (*The Flower of My Secret*, 1995), the composer's first collaboration with Almodóvar, the key metaphor would be the notion of the bridge, both in the sense of providing a link or transition between different spaces, times and narrative strands and also with respect to its function of lifting the traveller above the ground she or he traverses. The first musical cue (after the opening credit theme) follows a prologue sequence depicting a rehearsal among medical personnel of techniques for soliciting organ donation from the grieving family of an accident victim, which cuts away to a video camera filming the scene. That self-referential gesture prompts the opening phrase of '*Casa con ventanas y libros*', a string quartet rooted in the nineteenth-century idioms of Brahms and Mendelssohn. As its title suggests, the music provides a point of entry to a new space and a new character, the film's protagonist Leo, as the camera glides over her sleeping form and face, pausing to allow us to read the titles of the books piled on her night table. As the music continues, the camera cuts from one shot to another, closing in on the page of a book by Djuna Barnes as we hear Leo's voice citing a line from the novel. The next shots show Leo at her typewriter and the clattering keys accompany the music's fade-out.

While clearly providing a bridge or access point to the story to be told, the conjunction of image and music in this scene also offers us a frame for witnessing the encounter between the artistic 'worlds' of director and composer. The visuals beckon us into familiar Almodóvar territory. The camera tracking along the sleeping body of Leo evokes the opening of *Mujeres al borde de un ataque de nervios* and similar shots of Pepa (Carmen Maura). The typewriter and clacking keys recall *Ley del deseo* (*Law of Desire*) and its writer/director protagonist Pablo. While Iglesias' music is new to the spectator/listener in this context, the musical cue provides an introduction to key tendencies in Iglesias' music for Almodóvar's films.[34] The adoption of a tonal idiom gives rise to certain musical gestures, including in this instance a 'classic' simultaneous manipulation of action and inaction, a chromatically descending melody accompanied by a static bass line. These techniques can be used to create and resolve often slow-moving tensions, instead of constantly being on the edge (the case with more atonal music), and thus serve as a bridge, providing easily understood musical continuity over a span of time while the visual action is variable. In terms of scoring, the string quartet evokes a sense of contained intimacy: traditionally, the quartet, partly because of the clarity of each individual line, is understood to be the most personal and intimate of genres. It provides a glimpse into the private world of the composer – and in this case the character, Leo – while at the same time circumscribing affective range through its monochromaticism. As such the quartet struggles against its inherent intimacy, indeed it sometimes stands in the way of excessive intimacy and never completely imposes or forces an emotional colour.

Over the course of the film, then, the music also provides a kind of bridging-over or distancing effect that allows us to see the characters and their situation with sympathy but without indulging in melodramatic over-identification. Leo, a writer of romantic novels, finds herself in a professional and personal crisis brought on by the collapse of her marriage. While music is tellingly absent from the scenes of her final break-up with her husband, his departure, marked by the sound of a closing door, triggers a musical response. Leo's acts are depicted in fragmented close-ups: of her red cross-shaped medicine chest, a bottle of pills, the pills on a tray and in her hands, then brought to her mouth. The visual images situate us at a distance from the character's deliberate but dramatic acts. In the absence of dialogue, music does the talking, even claiming priority in structuring the sequence as the actions we see appear to be accompanying the music rather than the other way around.

Almodóvar and Iglesias' next collaboration, *Carne trémula* (*Live Flesh*, 1997), moves from the generic universe of the melodrama to the *noir* thriller, although as in all the director's films, such references are never served up straight but act as catalysts in combination with other plot elements. *Carne trémula* is characterized by a number of narratively complex sequences that shift between action and introspection, threatening violence and lyrical longing, and Iglesias' music is central to navigating those changes. One especially charged scene occurs some twenty minutes into the film. Víctor, the naively romantic son of a prostitute (his birth twenty years earlier on Christmas Eve on a Madrid city bus forms the film's opening) has gone to see Elena, the world-weary, drug addict daughter of an Italian diplomat whom he met a week earlier at a Madrid night club. After inadvertently letting him into her luxurious flat – she thought he was her drug pusher – a struggle with her father's gun attracts the arrival of two police officers, the older, alcoholic Sancho and his younger colleague David. As Sancho and David climb the stairs the musical cue, a quiet chordal background punctuated by non-tonal percussive piano notes, evokes tension and danger. The *noir* atmosphere in a minor key is maintained as they enter Elena's flat, guns drawn, and are met by the gun held by the panicked Víctor. David attempts to defuse the situation, ultimately turning on his drunken colleague Sancho whose gun he takes in return for Víctor lowering his. In the middle of the tense negotiations, David and Elena exchange glances and the harmonically fraught *noir* music is interrupted by a lyrical love theme. The momentary shift from action to romance would be imperceptible on the level of the visuals alone. Almodóvar and Iglesias deploy the 'collective unconscious' of musical genre identities to introduce plot complications and predict future character relations as the action continues unbroken. The music returns to a minor key, David reaches for Víctor's gun and removes Elena from the line of fire, Sancho lunges for the gun and he and Víctor wrestle on the floor. The disjuntive shifts in the music find their echo in the camera work: unsteady hand-held camera to communicate David's point of view of the struggle for the gun and slow-motion images of Elena's flight down the stairs. A gun shot, shown in close-up, rings out and David falls to the floor.

Following an ellipsis that finds Víctor sentenced to and released from prison for shooting David, and the paraplegic David and drug-free Elena married, a later scene playfully questions the role of those same genre conventions as a source of reliable knowledge. While visiting his mother's grave Víctor rediscovers Elena at her father's funeral. Apprised of Víctor's reappearance, David denounces the young man to Elena as a psychopath. The next image shows Víctor standing before the daycare centre run by Elena while the music – a series of long-held chromatic chords, rhythmically asymmetrical and harmonically adrift, untethered from traditional, stable tonal harmony, in short, unbalanced – works to confirm David's diagnosis of the ex-convict as a dangerous stalker. But that certainty is soon undercut by the character's actions as well as the musical accompaniment which corrects or normalizes itself as tonal, innocently major to the point of evoking music for children, as Víctor looks through the window of the centre, exchanging a complict smile with a little girl inside. As Elena herself moves into view, the music blossoms into a full lyricism, paralleling the initial David–Elena love theme. When the camera cuts to a shot of David, the *noirish* theme returns to effect a role-reversal, as David is shown watching and waiting outside Víctor's home.

One well-known aspect of the 'pre-Iglesias' Almodóvar cinematic world that persists and enriches the overall musical landscape of these films is the presence of popular songs: boleros sung by Chavela Vargas and Bola de Nieve, the Flamenco-flavoured '*Ay, mi perro*' and '*Rosario de mi madre*'. While Iglesias' scores do not seek to approximate this corpus on a formal level, his music does incorporate a broad range of popular idioms: tango, jazz and certain folkloric effects. Nevertheless, in his tangos and other 'folk' pieces Iglesias uses setting and scoring to achieve a kind of defamiliarization or distancing effect. His '*Tango de Parla*' in *La flor* uses the sophisticated expression of urban Buenos Aires as a bridge between Leo's cosmopolitan solitude and a visit to her mother and sister's home in the unromantic working-class Madrid suburb of Parla. The music that accompanies Víctor's return to his abandoned childhood home in the shadow of Madrid's KIO towers deploys mandolin and clarinet in a folk-accented melody that deliberately eludes any recognizable national or regional stylings.

As Almodóvar pursues increasingly complex and elliptical forms of narration in *Todo sobre mi madre* (*All About My Mother*, 1999) and *Hable con ella* (*Talk to Her*, 2002), Iglesias' music frequently takes on the role of what Chion calls 'a space–time machine'.[35] In *Todo sobre mi madre*, when her son Esteban is left brain-dead after being hit by a car, Manuela, an organ transplant nurse, gives permission for his organs to be donated. As in *La flor*, music is absent from the most emotionally wrenching scenes. Here the score returns to give coherence to an extended montage covering hours of time and a series of journeys as Esteban's heart travels beyond his body from an operating room in Madrid, in a plastic cooler up and down hospital corridors and on helicopters and planes to its new recipient in Coruña in northwest Spain. Against a traditional, accompanimental-style background – solid downbeat bass notes and regularly spaced chords – a solo violin, clarinet and piano give out a more chromatic, less stable melody with few resting points and phrase elisions suggestive of action and motion (rather like de Pablo's music for *La caza*).

Some thirty minutes later, the same theme returns as Manuela watches a performance of *A Streetcar Named Desire* in Barcelona. There is a clear allusion to the scene of Esteban's death, following a birthday trip with his mother to see *Streetcar* in Madrid after which he ran into the street pursuing an autograph from the actress who played Blanche Dubois. In its new setting the recurring musical theme highlights a further repetition as Blanche, on stage, cries out, 'where is my heart?', an evocation of the journey of Esteban's bodily organ to its new host in Coruña and a musical leitmotif linked less to a specific character than to the exemplary nature of Manuela's own journeys over the course of the film as the bearer and instigator of heart-felt and life-giving bonds between people. Iglesias' understanding and use of leitmotifs – he describes them as 'axes for memorization and elements used to divide and structure the general time of the film'[36] – echo Chion's idea while explicitly acknowledging their role in guiding the spectator's construction of meaning beyond the more linear unwinding of visual narrative.

While Iglesias' score for *Hable con ella* likewise enables the film's temporally and spatially fluid narrative with its extended flashbacks and repetitions, both Almodóvar's and Iglesias' artistic virtuosity and knowing relation to film and film music history are most notably on display in the silent film-within-the-film, *El amante menguante* (*The Shrinking Lover*), that plays such a central role in the story's unexpected denouement. The male nurse Benigno, in his total devotion to his comatose patient Alicia, has taken to following her cultural interests – dance and silent film – about which he reports to her in lengthy detail. The silent film is thus first introduced in Benigno's recounting of the plot to Alicia as he undresses and applies lotion to her recumbent body. He confesses that he found the film disturbing and he also makes clear his identification with the male lead, Alfredo. As his words continue we are presented with scenes from the film, the story of the beautiful young woman scientist Amparo and her fiancé Alfredo. Amparo has invented a revolutionary diet concoction and when she laments she has no way to test its efficacy Alfredo offers himself as a human guinea pig. The potion causes Alfredo to shrink and he subsequently flees from Amparo, taking refuge with his mother. After years of searching, Amparo finds Alfredo who is now so tiny she is able to smuggle him out of his mother's house in her purse. The final scene finds the two reunited in bed, the naked Amparo sleeping beside the diminutive Alfredo who is shown exploring the hills and valleys of his beloved's body.

Visually, *El amante* is a loving pastiche of the conventions of silent cinema. Shot in luminous black and white, it offers us the exaggerated acting style, comically accelerated character movements, and intertitles to indicate dialogue that contemporary audiences associate with the form. Iglesias' score represents a similar tour de force: a string quartet 'suite' that echoes the characteristic musical gestures of silent film music. The musical accompaniment to *El amante* shifts with the narrative among three types of material: a love theme marked by a soulful cello line, a more rapid and forward-moving action section, and a reactive component reflective of so-called 'mickey-mousing' where the stops and starts in the music mirror the characters' actions. In its antiquarian perfection *El amante* lures us in, preparing us for a conclusion undreamed of within the narrative conventions of silent (or any) cinema. Arguably, it is the music that first alerts us to the serious stakes of this love story in miniature. For while the gestures largely mimic silent film standards, the fraught, post-tonal harmonic language suggests a deeply ambivalent knowledge attached to Alfredo's final act, his entry into the cave-like opening of Amparo's vagina. Although we spectators will not discover the fact until later in *Hable con ella*, the silent film scene stands in for Benigno's rape of Alicia. The music plays a dual role, alluding to Benigno's guilty awareness while anticipating the viewers' own moral dilemma. By distancing or distracting us from the unreality of the penetration scene (we 'know' that the giant vagina is in fact a movie construction), Iglesias' score – then at its most sublime in the recurring, elegiac motif so evocative of Samuel Barber's *Adagio for Strings* – allows us to believe in the transcendent nature of Alfredo's action and perhaps complicates our understanding of Benigno.

Iglesias explicitly considers this last function of film music in an interview with Walter Silva, remarking on the paradox that music, 'the most abstract of the arts, … faced with the unbelievability of cinema … promotes [film's] credibility'.[37] Expanding from the strictly textual level, the composer goes on to address the demand for music in Spanish cinema: 'The [Spanish] film industry needs true or authentic music to achieve this effect of credibility and in order to make Spanish films compatible with their European and American counterparts.'[38] What we have argued in this chapter is that, within their very different historical and cultural moments, both de Pablo and Iglesias – and their collaborators Saura and Almodóvar – have worked to bring about a new credibility and legibility for Spanish cinema beyond the borders of its homeland.

Notes

1. Chion, M. *La musique au cinéma*, Paris: Fayard, 1995, 295. All translations from French or Spanish are our own.
2. Following his instrumental score for *¿Qué he hecho yo para merecer esto?* (*What Have I Done to Deserve This?*, 1983) Bonezzi would go on to work as a composer with a number of other Spanish directors.
3. For Saura, see the articles by Insdorf, A. '*Soñar con tus ojos*: Carlos Saura's Melodic Cinema', *Quarterly Review of Film Studies*, **8** (2), Spring 1983, 49–53; and Vernon, K.M. 'The Language of Memory in the Films of Carlos Saura', in F. Brown, M.A Compitello, V.M. Howard and R.A. Martin (eds) *Critical Essays on the Literature of the Spanish Civil War*, East Lansing: Michigan State University Press, 1989, 125–42; and the interviews with the filmmaker collected in Willem, L. (ed.) *Carlos Saura: Interviews*, Jackson: University of Mississippi Press, 2003. Almodóvar makes numerous references to film music, both in his films and in general terms, in the

interviews with Vidal and Strauss. Colón Perales et al. deem Almodóvar 'the Spanish director – together with Víctor Erice and Julio Medem – with the most creative ideas regarding the use of music in film' (see Colón Perales, C., Infante del Rosal, F. and Lombardo Ortega, M. (eds) *Historia y teoría de la música en el cine: Presencias afectivas*, Seville: Alfar, 1997, 103).

4. Insdorf, A. '*Soñar con tus ojos*', 49.
5. As well as Colón Perales, et al. *Historia y teoría de la música en el cine*, see: Alvares, R. *La harmonía que rompe el silencio: Conversaciones con José Nieto*, Valladolid: Semana Internacional de Cine, 1996; Pachón Ramirez, A. *La música contemporánea en el cine*, Badajoz, Diputación Provincial de Badajoz, 1992; and Padrol, J. (ed.) *Evolución de la banda sonora en España: Carmelo Bernaola*, Alcalá de Henares: 16 Festival de Cine de Alcalá de Henares, 1986.
6. ECAM = *Escuela de Cinematografía y del Audiovisual de la Comunidad de Madrid* (Cinematography and Audiovisual Community School of Madrid).
7. On Nieto, see Alvares, R. *La harmonía* and the composer's own textbook on film composition, *Música para la imagen: La influencia secreta*, Madrid: SGAE, 1996, as well as the recordings of Nieto's orchestral performances of the works of composers Quintero, García Leoz and Parada, reissued by Fundación Autor.
8. SGAE = *Sociedad General de Autores y Editores* (General Society of Authors and Editors); Cueto, R. *El lenguaje invisible Entrevistas con compositores del cine español*, Alcalá de Henares: Festival de Cine de Alcalá de Henares, 2003, 25–6; see also Alvares, R. *La harmonía*, 189–91.
9. Cueto, R. *El lenguaje invisible*, 24; Colón Perales, C. et al. *Historia y teoría de la música en el cine*, 83.
10. Cueto, R. *El lenguaje invisible*, 30.
11. Alvares, R. *La harmonía*, 194.
12. Cueto, R. *El lenguaje invisible*, 31.
13. In addition to Cueto's collections of interviews with new composers, see the online review of recent releases of Spanish film scores by Steven Kennedy. http://www.filmscoremonthly.com/articles/2001/2_May---Film_Scores_from_ Spain.asp (accessed 2 August 2004).
14. Cited in Colón Perales, C. et al., *Historia y teoría de la música en el cine*, 93.
15. Tosi, D. and Tosi, M. 'Luis de Pablo: una audición panorámica de su obra', in J.L. García del Busto (ed.), *Escritos sobre Luis de Pablo*, Madrid: Taurus, 1987, 249. The authors also discuss the parallel emergence of a Spanish avant-garde in painting and the visual arts and situate both the new music and art with respect to Francoist political and cultural policies and practices in the 1950s and 1960s (see 238–9). Their introduction notably compares de Pablo to Saura as Spanish artists who express their Spanish identity through an implacable critical eye, or ear, toward their home country (221).
16. Our source is the extended entry for de Pablo in the *Diccionario de la Música Española e Hispanoamericana*; see García del Busto, J.L. 'Luis de Pablo', in Casares Rodicio, E. (Director and Coordinator) *Diccionario de la música española e hispanoamericana*, Madrid: SGAE, 2001, 319–31.
17. *Música concreta* or *musique concrète* is an experimental technique of musical composition using recorded sounds as raw material. The technique was developed in 1948 by the French radio producer Pierre Schaeffer and his associates in the ORTF studios. Angulo, J. 'Entrevista con Antxon Eceiza', in C. Heredero and J.E. Monterde (eds) *Los 'nuevos cines' en España*, Valencia: Institut Valencia de Cinematografia, 2003, 276.
18. Chion, M. *La musique au cinéma*, 147–8.

19. Gorbman, C. *Unheard Melodies: Narrative Film Music*, Bloomington: Indiana University Press, 1987, 153–4.
20. The terms 'compiled' versus 'composed' scores are proposed by Kassabian, A. *Hearing Film: Tracking Identifications in Contemporary Hollywood Film Music*, New York: Routledge, 2001.
21. Chion, M. *La musique au cinéma*, 229.
22. Kinder, M. 'Violence American Style: The Narrative Orchestration of Violent Attractions', in J. Slocum (ed.) *Violence and American Cinema*, New York: Routledge, 2001, 61–5.
23. The selection from *El misterio de Elche* included in *Peppermint frappé* (and in *Ana y los lobos*) is taken from the 1924 reconstruction and later recording of the two-act vocal work written in old Valencian supervised by Oscar Esplá (Musical Heritage Society 3118/19). The '*Ternario*' is described in Esplá's liner note as follows: 'the first choral section sung in the annual representation [the *Misterio* is traditonally performed at the Basilica of Santa María de Elche on the feast of the Assumption of the Virgin Mary] is the "*Ternario*", a motet for three voices (hence its name). There are other choral sections for three voices in the "Mystery" but none equals this in interest and beauty. It is hard to find a match for its expressive intensity in any musical creation of the entire polyphonic era.'
24. Compiled music includes a selection from Prokofiev's *Alexander Nevsky* and the Spanish medieval piece '*Fis y verays*'.
25. Chion, M. *La musique au cinéma*, 152–4.
26. Regueira, J. 'Los espacios sonoros de Alberto Iglesias', *Alberto Iglesias: Film Works 1990–2000*, Nuba Records JMB SP 503–4, 2000, 9. Another signal difference between the de Pablo and Iglesias eras in Spanish film music is found in the many interviews with Iglesias and articles on his work in contrast to the almost total critical silence on de Pablo's film music (as opposed to his concert works).
27. Sáenz de Tejada, N. 'El ojo que escucha', *El País*, 30 May, 1994.
28. Ibid.
29. Strauss, F. *Conversaciones con Pedro Almodóvar*, trans. P. Jimeno Barrera, Madrid: Ediciones Akal, 2001, 104; 106.
30. Ibid., 106.
31. Cueto, R. *El lenguaje invisible*, 253.
32. Ibid., 267. One recurring topic in the interviews with Iglesias is the difference between the composer's work with Almodóvar and with Julio Medem. Iglesias himself tends to characterize his work for Medem's films as more challenging (less melodic, tonal, immediate) than that for Almodóvar's (more popular, song-like). These contrasts and comparisons clearly merit further study.
33. Ibid., 253.
34. At one point in the commentary for the US DVD release of *Hable con ella* Almodóvar calls Iglesias 'the master of the string quartet'.
35. Chion, M. *La musique au cinema*, 189.
36. Regueira, J. 'Los espacios sonoros de Alberto Iglesias', 22.
37. Silva, W. 'La música debe tener la apariencia del decir', *Babab*, **2** (1), March, 2000. www.babab.com/no01/alberto_iglesias.htm (accessed 17 July 2004).
38. Ibid.

Chapter 4

Music as a satirical device in the Ealing Comedies

Kate Daubney

The Ealing Comedies, the group of films generally agreed to begin with *Passport to Pimlico* (1949) and end with *The Ladykillers* (1955), are scored sparingly when compared with other British films of the same period, and with their Hollywood counterparts.[1] Although renowned composers such as Georges Auric, Benjamin Frankel and Tristram Cary were brought in by Ealing to score the films, perpetuating the relationship between the concert hall and British cinema established by Ralph Vaughan Williams and William Walton, the film scores they wrote are notably succinct and not structurally complex.[2] They avoid the grand thematic designs of contemporaneous Hollywood scores, and so do not have the integrated narrative function typical of much film scoring. In that sense, the scores for the Ealing Comedies have extricated themselves from the debate about the extent to which British film scoring was influenced by Hollywood models, and as a consequence their understated simplicity is as definitive as the films which they accompany.

Critical examination of the Ealing Comedies reveals that they are much more than simply comedic and, although there are plentiful neat visual jokes, the humorous vein in the films is a powerful blend of sharp satire and essential innocence. Traditionally, composers and directors had compromised on the role of music in visual comedy as being one of punctuation of the rhythms of physical movement, but humour which relies on verbal subtlety or the extended playing-out of a double-edged plot cannot draw on the immediate explanations of quirky instrumentation or spirited motifs. It should not be overlooked that there are some inherently funny, rather than satirical, moments which involve music in the Ealing Comedies. The eponymous criminals in *The Ladykillers* are hilarious as they pretend to be a string quintet, as is Louis Mazzini's father singing operatically while he dries the dishes in *Kind Hearts and Coronets* (1949). Yet moments where music is used comedically in its own right are rare in the films. In his discussion of film music humour, Miguel Mera proposes that the Boccherini String Quintet played by the *Ladykillers* 'is funny only by association. ... any number of pieces from this era ... would create a strong incongruity when compared to the loutish *Ladykillers*'.[3] This is part of Mera's overall conclusion that it is very difficult for music to be funny, and that humour derived from music's use in film usually relies on other frameworks, such as parody, cultural expectation, or unexpected diegetic transgressions. Such is the nature of the challenge presented to the composers by the Ealing Comedies whose narratives satirize large ideas in small contexts.

In the Ealing Comedies both the satire and the way of life under scrutiny are essentially British. Although the period context of *Kind Hearts and Coronets* sets it apart from the contemporary settings of the other films, each of the comedies considers aspects of the compact institutional attitudes and way of life that emerged in Britain in the post-war years, highlighting resourcefulness, innovation and difference as means of breaking out of these customs of behaviour and perception. Humour and narrative positioning are used to legitimize not only the intellectual debate, but also morally dubious activities: the criminal endeavours which form the basis of many of the films are satirized painlessly for the viewer and we might even feel nostalgic for the characters' almost successful attempts to break out of the conventions which stifle them. The message of these films is subtle yet the mood is, in almost all cases, light-hearted.[4]

However, despite the realistic roots of the satire, an additional element which differentiates these films from mainstream comedy is the quasi-fantasy premises on which many of the narratives are constructed. Charles Barr, in his study of Ealing Studios, suggests that the first few post-war Ealing films are dogged by a 'failure, or at least loss of drive' which hampered Ealing's head of production, Michael Balcon, in his plans to progress British filmmaking.[5] The solution, dramatically and diversely demonstrated in the first Ealing Comedies of 1949 – *Passport to Pimlico*, *Whisky Galore!* and *Kind Hearts and Coronets* – was, Barr argues, found by embracing the fantasies which many film characters only dream of. He goes on to suggest that *Passport to Pimlico* established a blend of fantasy and realism in a believable but liberating combination, which facilitated the confrontation and satirization of problematic issues in all the films.[6] These films are therefore not standard comedy, and have a critical purpose as powerful as the fictional coverage of war which preceded them.

Where the wartime films presented more unified views of heroism and purpose, the Ealing Comedies are diverse and subversive in their message. Their narratives do not rely on emotion, and are not structured on the traditional dramatic themes of love, war or loss. Instead they handle ideas within ideas, offsetting innocent narrative events against more profound social arguments. *Passport to Pimlico* uses the post-war ambitions for social and financial betterment as a context for a larger critique about the isolation of communities from each other and from government. Conversely the islanders of *Whisky Galore!* relish their isolation and simple way of life and go to considerable lengths to protect it against a moral code imposed from outside. Progress is similarly questioned in *The Man in the White Suit* (1951), where the conventional battle for control between factory owners and factory workers becomes redefined by the new threat of science. The entire credibility of Louis Mazzini's behaviour in *Kind Hearts and Coronets* is settled on the premise that murder is a legitimate form of advancement for the socially repressed. These sound like serious issues, and they remain so, yet setting the films in geographical and social microcosms prevents them from being weighty and unwieldy. The compactness of the narrative spaces in which most of the films take place – the island of Todday in *Whisky Galore!*, the square in *Pimlico*, Mrs Wilberforce's house round the back of St Pancras in *Ladykillers*, even Louis Mazzini's autobiographical voiceover from his jail cell – provides the physical frame for the personal and social ambitions of the characters to break out of their restrictions and it is this intimate aspect on the larger issues which keeps the subject matter light and manageable.

These definitive narrative elements do not provide an obvious pattern for music to set itself against. Despite the traditional frames of characterization and geographical location which make these films memorable to us, the composers have incorporated very little of these into the score structures. With the exception of the Scottish islanders in *Whisky Galore!*, we do not hear any of the groups of Ealing characters identified collectively through original non-diegetic music, and none of them has themes in the classical Hollywood sense. Furthermore, the repetition of musical material is infrequent, largely because there is so little music in the films. Cues are short, often as little as ten seconds, and in none of the seven films is there a cue longer than four minutes. Even the musical gestures which respond to comic movement are short, mickey-mousing sound effects or physical action in a minimal fashion. So, despite the stylistic and functional unity which has been imposed on the films retrospectively, the scores apparently demonstrate little of the same coherence.

One explanation for this might lie in the number of different composers used by Ealing Studios for these films. It is posterity which has labelled and analysed the Comedies collectively and certainly the music does not own the same sense of authorship that has defined the films by screenplay or production values. Georges Auric's score for *The Titfield Thunderbolt* (1952), for example, eschews music for scene transitions and moments of drama in such a way that the film becomes a virtual documentary at times, while by comparison Ernest Irving's score for *Whisky Galore!* seems positively lush with its expansive seascapes and emotive expressions of anxiety in the community. Yet each Ealing composer has in some way grasped the satirical quality of the films and used music to reinforce it, developing in the process a subtler role for music in comedy than had been heard previously.

Music in the Ealing Comedies is effective because it allows the other complex satirical constructions in the films to be appreciated without overwhelming them. Instead of imposing a layer of interpretation, music plays a bit part in the story, yet like any minor character it has distinct roles. First, music is used to epitomize the way of life being satirized in the film, by defining the subject matter in some form. Secondly, the music captures the alternative visions for society which satirize the original way of life. Finally, and perhaps least conspicuously, the music emphasizes the satire as it occurs in dialogue or physical gesture, occasionally employing a mickey-mousing function.

Music epitomizes the subject matter

Traditionally, the music heard during the opening titles plays a key role in establishing the mood of a film and the geographical or cultural context of the action. This function is particularly key in a film where that context is to be challenged in some way: in almost all the Comedies, music heard early in the film plays a role in defining the context to be satirized. In three of the films, originally composed title music assumes this function: *The Titfield Thunderbolt*, *The Lavender Hill Mob* (1951) and *Whisky Galore!*. Georges Auric wastes no time in evoking the railway setting during the titles of *The Titfield Thunderbolt*, using fast regular rhythms to imitate the sounds of a train and overlaying them with pastoral woodwind and horns. Music is sparsely employed in this film, and the title sequence and opening section are a case in point: music accompanies the simple line-drawn title cards that evoke a bygone age, but the first scenes of the film, of trains crossing the idyllic countryside, remain unaccompanied. This is striking to the sophisticated and experienced listener, but in restraining music's participation in setting the scene, Auric has managed not to over-emphasize the profound irony of the story, that the characters should be fighting to preserve the old-fashioned yet undeniably 'industrialized' train service over the expansion of the bus route. He sets the scene quickly and effectively, then lets the images and the dialogue speak for themselves.

Ernest Irving also refers to the rural idyll in the opening music for *Whisky Galore!*, though here the cultural coding is more complex. The music begins with strong brass tones but this instrumental colour is soon absorbed by energetic and distinctively Scottish melodies which prevail in the title sequence. This balance of material evokes the English–Scottish relationship which will emerge during the film's story, where the single-minded English Home Guard military presence in the form of Captain Waggett is completely overcome by the will of the Scottish islanders. Immediately after the title sequence a voiceover begins, explaining the way of life on the island: Irving plays it straight with muted yet expansive orchestral gestures that match the images of striking landscapes, but counterpoint the faintly tongue-in-cheek narration of frugal island life. In the cue sheet for the film (see Table 4.1) Irving labels this cue 'Barra: seascapes', marking it as 'Descriptive', the only cue in all the scores to be attributed with such a function.[7]

Auric captures a different culture in the opening to *The Lavender Hill Mob* where the countryside is exchanged for the steps of the Bank of England. Against a sequence of virtual stills of City of London imagery – buildings, buses, businessmen – brass instruments chime out a canon in evocation of this timeless British institution. The pompous, regally traditional mood and the canonic

Table 4.1 First page of music cue sheet from *Whisky Galore!* (1949), score by Ernest Irving.
Data reproduced by kind permission of Canal+ Image UK Ltd.

SOUND FILM: WHISKY GALORE

NOTIFICATION OF WORKS

EALING STUDIOS LTD

No.	Title of work	Description	Instrument or combination	Duration of performance: Mins. Sec.	Composer of the music	Author of the words	Arranger of the music	Publisher (if in manuscript state in "M.S.")	Feature or background state (F or B)
	Gong Title	No music	–	0.08	–	–	–	–	–
1	Main Titles	–	Orch.	1.37	Ernest Irving	–	Ernest Irving	M.S.	B
2	Barra: seascapes	Descriptive	Orch.	1.35	Ernest Irving	–	Ernest Irving	M.S.	B
3	Calamity	Melos	Orch.	0.20	Ernest Irving	–	Ernest Irving	M.S.	B
4	No whisky	Melos	Orch.	0.49	Ernest Irving	–	Ernest Irving	M.S.	B
5	Arrival of ship	Melos	Orch.	0.16	Ernest Irving	–	Ernest Irving	M.S.	B
6	1st Love Scene	Melos	Orch.	0.09	Ernest Irving	–	Ernest Irving	M.S.	B
7	2nd Love Scene	Melos	Orch.	0.20	Ernest Irving	–	Ernest Irving	M.S.	B
8	Shipwreck	Melos	Orch.	0.08	Ernest Irving	–	Ernest Irving	M.S.	B
9	Spreading the news	Melos	Orch.	1.37	Ernest Irving	–	Ernest Irving	M.S.	B
10	"Morning of the Sabbath"	Melos	Orch.	0.27	Ernest Irving	–	Ernest Irving	M.S.	B
11	Dies Irae	Church Organ	Organ	0.27	Trad.	–	Ernest Irving	M.S.	F
12	Romance	Radio	Orch.	0.47	Rubinstein	–	Ernest Irving	M.S.	F
13	Midnight	Melos	Orch.	0.36	Ernest Irving	–	Ernest Irving	M.S.	B
14	Treasure trove	Passacaglia	Orch.	3.21	Ernest Irving	–	Ernest Irving	M.S.	B
15	Ship sinking	Melos	Orch.	0.44	Ernest Irving	–	Ernest Irving	M.S.	B
16	Biffer in hold	Melos	Orch.	0.15	Ernest Irving	–	Ernest Irving	M.S.	B

structure then subtly contextualize Holland's exaggeration of the repetitive reliability of his job managing the weekly bullion run in the film's early scenes. This secondary application of broad cultural coding to celebrate the social situation of individual characters also occurs in *The Titfield Thunderbolt*. When the villagers must face up to the responsibility of running the railway for themselves, Auric extols their admission of being 'amateurs' by re-using the pastoral light woodwind, horns and scalic violins to reflect the characters' innocent enthusiasm for their project. This is little England facing up to and relishing its challenges.

The delineation of small communities as a setting for the stories is a crucial element in almost all the Comedies, and the opening of *The Ladykillers* uses music succinctly to frame both the physical and metaphorical space of the story. Terry Gilliam describes how the dilapidated home of Mrs Wilberforce is first seen: '[r]ight from the first shot you know you're in a magic world ... because there's a top shot looking down on the street with the terraced houses on the side and that odd little house at the end of it and the railway lines behind it.'[8] Composer Tristram Cary uses a polyphon,[9] playing *Last Rose of Summer* to create a musical-box effect, miniaturizing the house as though within a glass snowshaker. The house is at the centre of the story and, as all the Ladykillers will meet their doom in and around the house, their mercenary ambition becomes retrospectively a fantasy played out in this harmless setting. The musical-box effect also extends to the reassuring familiarity of the local streets near Mrs Wilberforce's home, along which she can walk and greet by name local shopkeepers and other residents. This safe haven is, as with the other films, presented as an idyll into which disruptive interlopers will blunder with their destructive aspirations to break out of their own situations.

It would be an over-simplification to consider these scoring strategies as epitomizing Britishness, but the features that music is used to capture are key to the way the British perceived their surroundings and their identity in the post-war period: environment, institutions, home and hearth. In fact, the strategies evoke the same signifiers as many of their Hollywood counterparts: the pastoral idyll equates to the wide prairie of the early Westerns; the Bank of England is as iconic to British audiences as an East Coast metropolis skyline to Americans; even the visual construction of diegetic environment found in modern stylized dramas such as *American Beauty* (1999), echoes the suburban focus of *The Ladykillers*. In the more compact social environment of post-war Britain, however, these features were celebrated and criticized in equal parts within a process of social redefinition that renounced the romanticization that music often brought to the Hollywood equivalents. The British penchant for setting someone up for a fall, the lovable failure, the charming rogue, all fuse harsh criticism with genuine fondness in a recognizable context, but subtly and without the hard-edged darkness of equivalent critical movements in Hollywood, such as *film noir*. Even *The Man in the White Suit*, the closest of the Comedies to outright *noirish* criticism, relies on the friendly, almost avuncular qualities of the industrial North to inure the audience to the prospect of a technological revolution: the opening titles of *The Man in the White Suit* begin with a brassy fanfare that once again evokes a familiar institution, in this case the factory. Although the main title theme is perhaps the most angular and unsettling of all the Comedies' title themes, its rattling rhythms picked up from the footage of a mechanized loom, there is a newsreel energy to the sequence which is enhanced by the intimate, revelatory voiceover that opens the film's narrative. Music in all these title sequences draws us right into the setting of the stories, for we must be comfortable with the subject matter before the satire can become effective.

There is a substantial exception to this particular employment of music, however, in the score for *Kind Hearts and Coronets*, and it is an exception that is echoed to a degree in the use of music in *The Ladykillers*. While each of the Comedies is in some way concerned with aspiration – to better status, more money, or just the restoration of how things used to be – *Kind Hearts* explores all three of these ambitions combined in a more ruthless context. Furthermore, where most of the Comedies are situated firmly in one way of life, with the alternative a real or imagined juxtaposition, the central character of *Kind Hearts* finds his body in one context and his heart and mind in the other.

Music delineates the alternative

With the narrative of *Kind Hearts* set in the Edwardian period, already distanced by two world wars from the contemporary audience, its subject matter of social elevation and birthright remains superficially remote to most of that audience. However, the satire on that material is more savage than most of the other Comedies, and in the social reassessment that followed the war, its symbolic arguments are profound. As Charles Barr suggests, the d'Ascoyne family were 'caricatures of a whole patriarchal culture, of an aristocratic English arrogance';[10] these are qualities found in limited quantities in the other films, yet they dominate the whole world of *Kind Hearts*. Musically speaking, composer Ernest Irving accommodates this distanced satire by using the aria '*Il mio tesoro intanto*' from Mozart's opera *Don Giovanni* as the key thematic subject and opening title music of the film's score.

Like the other title themes, the music plays a role in establishing context, but in this case it is highly personal to Louis Mazzini, the film's anti-hero, and becomes his 'theme song' in more than one way. The aria is narratively pivotal in the meeting of his parents, but its text translates as the promise he makes to his mother on her deathbed:

> Go in the meantime and comfort my love,
> Try to dry the tears from her lovely eyes.

> Tell her that I go to avenge her injustices,
> I mean to return only to announce death and destruction.[11]

The music is, however, borrowed by Louis and by Ernest Irving and this contributes to the separation of the film from its audience when compared to the other Comedies: its value to the film relies not only on the audience's immediate identification of it as opera, and therefore more generically specific than any of the other Ealing scores, but also on the significance it brings with it from its original context. If only some of the meaning is identified by the audience, the effect is less incisive, but at whatever level of audience identification this is not simply film music in the background.

The music also frames aspiration far more explicitly than in the other films, in this case social aspiration. Its diegetic use as the means by which Louis' mother and father meet at a private concert is troublesome to the social equilibrium. For the d'Ascoyne family to have an opera singer performing live in the home is a mark of social status, yet the singer is seen as no better than a servant, and compounds the flaws in his status by being foreign also. The aristocratic classes confirm their superior standing with musical taste, yet the actual purveyor of this standing is next seen singing the same aria in a suburban kitchen while drying the dishes, recontextualizing the same performance in a different home. Thus this music and the social status it represents are both subverted from the outset, and yet both Louis' mother and Louis himself still aspire to the class from which they have become removed. Through the aria, Louis is attempting to regain that which was rightly his and yet it was also the means to demote him in the first place. Furthermore, it is difficult to ignore a central irony within the satire which is itself never entirely explicit: Louis' continual ambition to retain his birthright is motivated often by his own satirization of those who currently obstruct his path to his rights. It is as contradictory as the role of the aria.

Once widowed, Mrs Mazzini, Louis' mother, plays Mozart in the home on the piano, to authenticate the sense of cultural value which her son has inherited from each side of the family, practitioner and audience.[12] Louis revisits that sense of familial identity when he sees the whole family gathered in the church for Henry d'Ascoyne's funeral, and Irving reimposes the Mozart aria onto the scene. By now, with two murders complete, it has become fully identified with Louis' ambition to revenge the ostracism suffered by his mother and become the Tenth Duke of Chalfont, and this role is enhanced by comparison with the popular musical culture that Louis has experienced from living in Sibella's family home. Irving gives us originally-composed Edwardian piano waltzes for Sibella's family party, and Joseph Gungl's *Amoretten Tanz*[13] for Sibella's dancing in the nursery, underpinning Louis' comment to her that she should dance through life. Linking the popular music to Sibella advances Louis in their race for social escalation: after the family party when Louis proposes, Sibella refuses him on the grounds that her fiancé Lionel will be very rich some day, while he baits her with the likelihood of his becoming the Duke of Chalfont. When Louis then decides to visit the Chalfont ancestral home, Irving uses Mozart again to reinforce this high-art/low-art distinction in the vastly differing domestic spaces. This separation between Louis and Sibella is further emphasized by the terms on which Louis appreciates Edith d'Ascoyne, widow of Henry, one of his early victims. Sibella is damningly described by Louis near the end of the film as 'suburban'[14] while he has already admired Edith for her poise. She has absorbed the Mozart connotation during the funeral scene, and the similarities to his own mother in grace and bearing under the demands of social difficulty appeal profoundly to Louis.

There is considerable complexity in how the Mozart aria symbolizes Louis' ambition and ultimate success. Audiences would not have been expected to know the meaning of the Italian text to the aria, and so a layer of narrative significance might already have been lost. The aria also plays a role in dignifying behaviour which is otherwise brutal and scandalous: this is, after all, a tale of serial murder, offset by a genteel period backdrop, and by the comic brilliance of Alec Guinness' performance as all the members of the d'Ascoyne family. The use of the aria is therefore part of a mechanism to render the satire both sharper and more distant to the audience, and to epitomize both the society to which Louis is born, and that to which he aspires.

Borrowed classical music is a quite different shield for aspiration in *The Ladykillers*. Five assorted villains masquerade as a string quintet playing the 'Menuetto' from Boccherini's *Quintet* Op. 11 no. 5, while they plot to steal a huge amount of money near St Pancras railway station. The masquerade is superficially a means by which they can gather without suspicion to make plans, but in the context of Mrs Wilberforce's home it becomes a smokescreen of cultural respectability, reinforced by her fond recollection of the Boccherini being played at her twenty-first birthday party over fifty years before. Alec Guinness' character, Professor Marcus, tells Mrs Wilberforce in advance that he will be rehearsing music with his friends, and she is delighted at the prospect of music in the house once more. She even invites her friends round to hear the music and barely contains her desire to witness the performance at first hand by constantly interrupting the gang with offers of tea. Her aspiration to enjoy their skill creates a fragmentation in their 'performance': just as she infrequently allows them to rehearse uninterrupted, so the collective ambition in the group to steal the money begins to dysfunction almost immediately. Furthermore, as with Louis and the d'Ascoyne family in *Kind Hearts*, a piece of pre-composed diegetic music assumes the function of identifying the group of characters collectively. Although each of the Comedies concerns a community and an outsider, none but these two scores interprets the narrative in that way, although the Scots are musically separated from the English in *Whisky Galore!* by means of more general diegetic and non-diegetic Scottish music. In *Ladykillers*, just as in *Kind Hearts*, the characters need the music to lend authenticity to their group identity, although unlike Louis Mazzini it does not represent their ambition, but simply disguises it.

Ladykillers composer, Tristram Cary, cleverly incorporates Mrs Wilberforce into the gang with music just as she is unwittingly brought into the scheme to steal the money. Professor Marcus has asked her to collect his trunk from St Pancras station, thus effecting an innocent-looking exit from the scene of the crime for the stolen money, and Cary inveigles her into Marcus' criminal quintet by accompanying her in the taxi with a twinkling musical-box version of the Boccherini theme. Although the instrumentation (first celeste, then light woodwind and pizzicato violins) is not the same as the polyphon of the film's opening shots, the effect is the same, reminding us of Mrs Wilberforce's innocence of events around her. She appears as small in the back of the taxi as her house does against the backdrop of St Pancras, and it is the instrumentation which reinforces her blissful ignorance while the melodic material gives purpose to her actions. The decency Professor Marcus borrows from Boccherini as a shield for his intentions already belongs to Mrs Wilberforce, and by abusing that loan of age-old dignity of which Mrs Wilberforce is so fond, the fate of the gang is perhaps sealed in advance.

Just as the gang use Boccherini to generate a façade of respectability, so more exotic diegetic music is used to establish the expanding cultural ambitions of characters in other films. In the opening scenes of *Passport to Pimlico*, Latin *rhumba* rhythms echo around the diegetic spaces, notably from beneath an umbrella and across an inflatable lilo on which a slender sunbather rests: these illusions of hot foreign climes are gradually pulled into focus much closer to home as the beach is revealed as a rooftop terrace and the radio music is attributed to 'Les Norman and his Bethnal Green Bambinos'.[15] For the inhabitants of Pimlico, the ongoing heatwave is as foreign as the music they listen to, and both elements foreshadow the story of the borough becoming part of French Burgundy. Despite the plot, however, this is the limit of Georges Auric's reference to foreign music in the film, and the other uses of diegetic music are distinctly 'British' with snatches of song by comic actor Charles Hawtrey and the extended newsreel sequence.

The juxtaposition of foreign and British is similarly emphasized in the opening scenes of *The Lavender Hill Mob*, during which Alec Guinness' character, Holland, is introduced as a conspicuously wealthy Englishman living in South America. Diegetic *rhumba* rhythms emphasize the exotic setting established by the palm trees and parrot of the opening shot. In this film, however, the very symbol of continental exoticism, the Eiffel Tower, is the means to the disposal of the stolen bullion, converting Bank of England treasure to French tourist gifts, ironically not made in France. Composer Auric fuses the French coding of Offenbach's 'Can-can' motif with the twinkling tones of Pendlebury's musical Eiffel Tower paperweight to articulate Holland's realization of how to smuggle the gold abroad.[16] Once in France, however, the music abandons any reference to Frenchness, perhaps emphasizing that the Mob's business on the continent will go badly. Finally, Auric reminds us of Holland's original ambition, using the film's opening *rhumba* non-diegetically while Holland runs up and down the steps of the Underground to escape from the police in London. Holland says, '[I]nstead of changing as usual at Charing Cross I came straight to Rio de Janeiro', showing how easily he exchanged one home for another.

Music and physical gesture

There are few cues in any of the scores in which music directly imitates physical features of the narrative. Auric's capture of the energy of the train in *The Titfield Thunderbolt* is a striking gesture, and in *The Lavender Hill Mob* he conveys the cumulative obsequiousness of the bank staff as they move from office to office by catching not Holland's steps, but his neat sliding sidesteps around his more senior colleagues. Auric is equally subtle later in the same film, using falling scalic motifs sparingly as Holland and Pendlebury run down the stairs of the Eiffel Tower, spinning and circling hysterically. In the opening sequence of *Whisky Galore!* Ernest Irving comes close to parody in his capture of the shock and panic among the islanders at the whisky drought. He moves the music from its descriptive non-diegetic function behind the seascape images to a quasi-diegetic punctuation of the voiceover: 'disaster overcame this little island. ... not the hordes of an invading army but something far [chord] far [two chords] worse [loud shrieking chord]. There is no whisky!'

For *The Man in the White Suit*, Benjamin Frankel creates a musical texture which verges on imitative 'mickey-mousing' while retaining the satirical function of music in the narrative. Sidney Stratton, again played by Guinness, is a scientist utterly misunderstood by almost all those around him. His aims are manipulated by bosses and co-workers, and few individuals appreciate the scientific complexity of what he is proposing. He wishes to be separate from the other scientists in the research facilities, pursuing his own technical dream; his intellectual, and increasingly his ethical position, isolate him further. Frankel creates highly textural material evoking the sound of bubbles moving through glass, the music of chemistry, industry made art. Just as this material has pitch and rhythm, yet is not quite music either in the context of the score or more broadly, so Sidney's fabric is not quite what it seems to its manufacturer or later to those who fear it, and thus Sidney becomes identified with and separated by this 'music'.

In his discussion of *Kind Hearts and Coronets*, Charles Barr refers to the restraint in the dialogue of the film: '[l]ittle is spoken, much is understood .... There is always a tension, a holding-back, a sense of things *not* expressed beneath the restrained elegant forms of social life.'[17] In many respects this applies also to the way the Ealing Comedies are scored. In none of the films has the composer over-expressed the narrative, either in quality of language or quantity of cues and their duration. The composers seem collectively to have perceived the films' narratives as elegant social commentaries which do not need undignified superfluity in musical observation. There is much, particularly in *Kind Hearts* and in *The Titfield Thunderbolt*, which goes unremarked on, yet there is plenty in the films to express. The scores do match the satire of the films, however, being pertinent and well-directed. Their gestures can be as audible as the humour in the films is apparent but, just as the satirical commentary on post-war Britain is most clearly seen in each film as a whole, so the understated participation of music is often neglected because it is so succinct.

This is exemplified by what is perhaps the cleverest musical joke in any of the scores, from *The Ladykillers*. In the absence of Professor Marcus, the remaining four criminals 'rehearse' the Boccherini quintet. One by one they are called downstairs to aid Mrs Wilberforce in the pursuit of her parrot, yet last man Harvey, described by Marcus as the 'temperamental' one of the quintet, continues to play the record as though all five of them were present, displaying his musical ignorance and dogged adherence to the pretence. If noticed, this sequence delights in its ludicrous illogic, but its satirical punchline is almost invisible: frustrated by the record getting stuck, Harvey grabs it from the turntable and smashes it over his knee. In the Ealing Comedies, the aspiration of the individual to disregard the social and moral code is just as easily manipulated.

Notes

1. There is some debate about whether the 1947 Ealing film *Hue and Cry* belongs to the Ealing Comedies, given its production two years before *Passport to Pimlico* and its less enthusiastic critical reception than the other films. Charles Barr remarks that it was *Passport* which 'inaugurated [a] new cycle of comedy' and therefore *Hue and Cry* is excluded from this discussion. Barr, C. *Ealing Studios*, New York: Overlook Press, 1977, 82.
2. Muir Mathieson, conductor and musical director, established this distinctively British approach to the recruitment of composers to work in film after becoming musical director at London Films in 1934. In contrast to the Hollywood model, where a studio maintained a core of composers and orchestrators on staff, British studios in the 1940s and 1950s engaged independent composers, often from the concert hall, for individual film projects. Mathieson's first engagement was Arthur Bliss to score *Things to Come* (1935).
3. Mera, M. 'Is Funny Music Funny? Contexts and Case Studies of Film Music Humor', *Journal of Popular Music Studies*, **14** (2), 2002, 101.
4. *The Man in the White Suit* (1951) is significantly less carefree than the other films.
5. Barr, C. *Ealing Studios,* 80.
6. Ibid., 81.
7. Cue sheet for *Whisky Galore!* Special Collections, British Film Institute. The data in Table 4.1 is reproduced from a copy of the cue sheet provided by John Herron, Manager of the Film Library, Canal+ Image UK Ltd.
8. Terry Gilliam interviewed for *Forever Ealing*, television documentary broadcast on Channel 4, December 2002.
9. The polyphon is the name given to a form of musical box, first invented in the late

1880s, which produced sound by playing steel discs. The cue sheet notes the use of a 'polyphone' but this appears to be a misspelling. For a fuller explanation of the polyphon, see the entry in S. Sadie (ed.) *The New Grove Dictionary of Music and Musicians*, 2nd edition, vol. 20, London: Macmillan, 2001, 74.

10.   Barr, C. *Ealing Studios*, 127.
11.   English version used by kind permission of the translator, Kenneth Chalmers. Louis' voiceover for the scene at his mother's deathbed tallies closely with this translation: 'I made an oath I would revenge the wrongs her family had done her.'
12.   Dennis Price, the actor playing Louis Mazzini, also plays the role of Louis' father in the film. In his study of the film, Michael Newton notes, 'the song [*Il mio tesoro intanto*] alludes to both roles that Dennis Price plays, uniting in an instant both son and father'. Newton, M. *Kind Hearts and Coronets*, London: BFI Publishing, 2003, 65.
13.   Cue sheet for *Kind Hearts and Coronets*, Special Collections, British Film Institute.
14.   Louis remarks, 'Sibella was pretty enough in her suburban way.' This is the barometer by which he has measured her all along: her father was a doctor, and she was married to 'the most boring man in London'.
15.   Bethnal Green is a district in London's East End. The piece played is 'La Guajira' by Oresischd and Mendivil. Cue sheet for *Passport to Pimlico*, Special Collections, British Film Institute.
16.   A further encoding of humour in the score might be found if Offenbach's *Underworld* is interpreted socially rather than mythologically. Holland reads from an American gangster novel to Mrs Chalk in the Balmoral private hotel, and he refers to a 'gang' when first exploring his ambition with Pendlebury. There is also the eponymous 'Mob' of the film's title.
17.   Barr, C. *Ealing Studios*, 123.

Chapter 5

Screen playing: cinematic representations of classical music performance and European identity

Janet K. Halfyard

From the earliest days of the so-called 'silent' film, music has always been associated with the cinema. Musical performance itself has also had a long history of representation on screen, even in films such as Abel Gance's *Napoléon* (1927), where the composer of the French national anthem arrives in Paris with his composition and Danton proceeds to teach it to the assembled multitude – a remarkable feat for a film with no integral soundtrack.

Classical musicians are not frequently the subjects of films other than in biographies of composers, most of which have been made in Europe. However, when they do occur, fictional classical performers are to be found as frequently in Hollywood films as in European ones. This chapter examines the differences between how these two cinematic traditions represent performers and what these differences reveal both about attitudes towards classical music performance and issues of identify in relation to classical music.

Gender and the representation of performers

One immediate difference between Hollywood and European films lies in the gender and status of the performers. In general, where there are two of different genders, in American films the male performer will be older and have higher musical status, which often indicates a didactic aspect to the relationship. One notable exception is *The Hunger* (Tony Scott, 1983) where Miriam (Catherine Deneuve) clearly outranks and is older than John (David Bowie), but the more usual positioning is seen in the relationship of Max (Alexander Gudunov) and Anna (Shelley Long) in *The Money Pit* (Richard Benjamin, 1986); of Herbert (Jeroen Krabbe) and his young accompanist Monique (Sandy Rowe) in *The Prince of Tides* (Barbra Streisand, 1991); of Lestat (Tom Cruise) and Claudia (Kirsten Dunst) in *Interview with the Vampire* (Neil Jordan, 1994); and of Daryl van Horne (Jack Nicholson) and Jane (Susan Sarandon) in *The Witches of Eastwick* (George Miller, 1987). Carl Dupea (Ralph Waite) is both older than and treated as the highest-ranking musician by his sister Partita (Lois Smith) and fiancée Catherine (Susan Anspach) in *Five Easy Pieces* (Bob Rafelson, 1970). These representative examples parallel observations made by Richard Leppert on the nineteenth-century 'duet genre' of painting, which 'presumed the inequality of the partners, an older male teacher, and a younger female student, whose relation mirrors perfectly the domestic rank of husband to wife, and father to daughter'.[1] The teacher/pupil relationship is implied in *The Money Pit* and *The Prince of Tides*, and is explicit in the other films mentioned above.

The slightly unusual gender positioning in *The Hunger* is closer to the situation normally found in European films. Here, when there is more than one performer among the main characters, they generally fail to reproduce the male teacher/female pupil 'duet genre' positioning. In *The Piano Teacher* (Michael Haneke, 2001) for example, Erika (Isabelle Huppert) is clearly older than and senior within the conservatoire environment to Walter (Benoît Magimel), the young man who pursues her, while in *L'Accompagnatrice* (Claude Miller, 1992) both the performers are female, although again it is the older woman who has the higher status. The function of the older character as teacher is also affected by the change in gender. In *The Piano Teacher*, Erika resists teaching Walter, due to the sexual tension between them; and in *L'Accompagnatrice*, Irene (Elena Safonova) may want to educate Sophie (Romane Bohringer), but not in anything particularly musical – she entertains herself by introducing Sophie to her glamorous world, at the same time treating her as a cross between a pet and a servant. Meanwhile, in *Kolya* (Jan Sverák, 1996) the subtext of the duet genre becomes the text itself: Louka (Zdenek Sverák), a former orchestral cellist reduced to teaching and playing at funerals, uses the slightly tarnished glamour of his status as a musician to seduce women.

However, one of the most striking differences between Hollywood and European films is that when Hollywood films cast American characters as classical musicians, we very rarely see them play classical music at all, as if resisting it at some level. In *The Money Pit*, Anna is seen briefly beginning or ending rehearsals with the orchestra, and on the one occasion she plays solo, we only watch her tuning: as soon as she begins to play, the camera cuts away from her and her playing is used as underscore to other, comic action. In *What Lies Beneath* (Robert Zemeckis, 2000), Claire (Michelle Pfeiffer) is seen playing a single short, unidentifiable phrase on her cello; in *Wilder Napalm* (Glenn Gordon Caron, 1993), Vida (Debra Winger) is seen playing her cello only once and she plays a blues rather than classical repertoire; and in *The Man with One Red Shoe* (Stan Dragoti, 1995), Richard (Tom Hanks) finds himself unable to play the violin solo in Rimsky-Korsakov's *Scheherazade* and lapses into his own composition, which owes far more to light music than classical repertoire. In fact, there appears to be only one condition under which American characters may be seen playing classical music in a Hollywood film, and that is when the character is corrupt or being corrupted. Diane Tremayne, the sociopathic pianist of *Angel Face* (Otto Preminger, 1952) and Madison Bell, the equally sociopathic cellist of *Swimfan* (John Polson, 2002) are two prime examples of the former, alongside Tom Ripley (*The Talented Mr Ripley*, Anthony Minghella, 1999) and Hannibal Lecter (*Hannibal*, Ridley Scott, 2001).

In terms of characters being corrupted, Monique, a very minor character in *The Prince of Tides*, is having an affair with Herbert, a married man, although the implication is that she is naive rather than wicked, and Herbert has seduced her. Jane plays her cello in *The Witches of Eastwick* to what turns out to be the Devil, who uses music itself as a means to seduce her: her cello explodes into flames, such is the strength of the passion he arouses in her. In *The Money Pit*, Anna's career as an orchestral viola player directly threatens her relationship with Walter, as the orchestra's conductor attempts to seduce her away from him; and when the teenager Alice (Beth Ehlers) plays classical trios with Miriam and John in *The Hunger*, we know that she is being groomed as Miriam's next vampiric companion. Similarly, in *Interview with the Vampire*, Claudia has already been vampirized by Lestat when we see her taking keyboard lessons with him and then using her status as 'child prodigy' to assist him in gaining access to people's homes as one of their hunting tactics.

In all these examples, classical music lays a female American character open to physical possession through either sex or the supernatural; and in each case, the person who poses that threat is usually male and, by implication, European. Both Max and Herbert are played by European actors speaking with clearly accented English; likewise, Deneuve and Bowie in *The Hunger* are Europeans playing European – or, at least, non-American – vampires, and Lestat is positioned as French in both Anne Rice's book and screenplay. In *The Witches of Eastwick*, although the Devil has an obviously American accent, the three women who accidentally summon him ask for a foreign prince. The name he adopts has a European inference – Daryl van Horne – and one of the first things we learn about him is that he bought the local mansion because he needed the space for his pianos, so connecting his status as foreigner and outsider to the Eastwick community with the idea of him as a musician. Only in *Five Easy Pieces* are there no designated European characters but, as in *The Witches of Eastwick*, European identity is again signalled in the names of the musical characters, Catherine van Oost and the three Dupea children, Robert Eroica, Carl Fidelio and Partita, names connecting them unequivocally to European classical musical history and heritage, referencing Beethoven and Bach. In the same vein, Tom Ripley and Hannibal Lecter have pretensions towards European classical culture manifested by the characters settling in Italy, attending the opera and playing Bach on the piano – Hannibal plays the *Goldberg Variations* while Tom plays the *Italian Concerto*.

Music as threat in Hollywood cinema

The Money Pit, a comedy, and *The Prince of Tides*, a drama, are two films from Hollywood's recent history that demonstrate the way in which European identity and classical music are regularly elided in Hollywood films and are then positioned as being fundamentally threatening to the American characters and values. In both films, the villain is a European musician of international standing who is also married, or has been married, to the film's leading lady: Max is Anna's ex-husband, Herbert is currently still married to Susan (Barbra Streisand). Likewise, in both films, European identity and classical music are positioned in direct opposition to American popular culture, which is associated with the film's hero. In *The Money Pit*, Walter (Tom Hanks) is a lawyer who acts for popular musicians, and his character is represented as an American Everyman, with an unselfconscious and slightly adolescent boy-next-door charm. This is then contrasted with the European Max's self-assured, supremely arrogant sophistication. Although the film's popular musicians are not portrayed particularly sympathetically, nonetheless, Walter's association with popular music helps construct the opposition between him and the corrupting influence of Max and his classical music.

In *The Prince of Tides*, the antagonism between Tom (Nick Nolte) and Herbert is played out as a war for the affections of both Susan and her teenage son Bernard, who finds himself torn between being his father's son – playing the violin and going to the Tanglewood summer school – and being Tom's surrogate son. Tom is a football coach and agrees to coach him for a place on the school football team. The result is a fairly straightforward confrontation between America, football and Tom on the one hand and Europe, classical music and Herbert on the other, with Bernard caught between the two.

Tom, however, comes out as the moral superior while Herbert's moral integrity is continually questioned. He invites Tom to a dinner party at which he plays his violin – a million-dollar Stradivarius. He makes an unrelentingly continuous attempt to humiliate Tom, patronizing him for being a Southerner, which he does in several ways including musically. His rendition of 'Dixie', the song of the Confederate South, becomes an almost physical attack. They stand abnormally close to each other so that Herbert's final extravagant gesture with the bow causes Tom to flinch back as if he has been struck.

Herbert continues to be outspokenly rude to first Tom and then Susan. In retaliation, Tom dangles Herbert's Stradivarius over the balcony of the skyscraper apartment, refusing to give it back until Herbert apologizes to his wife. Herbert calls his bluff: he apparently cannot believe that anyone would seriously threaten an object of such monetary and cultural value. Tom throws the violin high in the air, at which point Herbert screams an apology, never talking his eyes off the instrument. Tom catches it, but there is no doubt that Herbert's apology was insincere, only given to retrieve the instrument, revealing that it is of greater value to him than his wife's feelings. He places more value on the violin and, by extension, on his music and, by further extension, on himself as the performer of that music than he does on his wife or his marriage. His dedication to his music is effectively positioned in this film as a form of moral and emotional bankruptcy, and it is symptomatic of someone who stands outside the American system of values that Tom Wingo represents.

Five Easy Pieces also sets up an opposition between American popular culture and European classical music: Robert Dupea (Jack Nicholson) moves between these two worlds in the film, unable to settle in either. In his American world, he is Bobby, with his girlfriend Rayette, who both listens to country music and sings it beautifully. In the highly cultured world of his family, from which he attempts to exclude her, classical music is heard being played almost constantly, in a house with three pianos and several violins scattered around. Here, he is Robert and, in the absence of Rayette, he finds himself drawn to the pianist, Catherine. His life with Rayette frustrates him for being too limiting, but neither can he be happy in the quasi-European world of his family, which seems cold and oppressive. He rejects his classical music upbringing, but it appears that this has nonetheless rendered him unfit for life as a normal American.

Two ideas, then, can be seen associated with playing classical music in Hollywood cinema. First, there is a clear connection to European-identified characters who are positioned as supremely gifted musicians but also often as the villains or anti-heroes of their narratives. Secondly, there is the idea that playing classical music may represent a threat to an American character, seducing him or – more usually – her away from American values.

Classical music and musicians in European cinema

In contrast to Hollywood, European films present a very different idea of the relationship between characters and the act of musical performance. One of the most immediate differences is that there is no specific association between classical music and villains or anti-heroes: in fact, quite the reverse. The practising musicians of *Un Coeur en Hiver* (Claude Sautet, 1992) and *Diva* (Jean-Jacques Beineix, 1981) are beautiful, talented, sympathetic and intelligent, although somewhat enigmatic. They are not arrogant, nor are they a bad influence on those around them, but their connection with music gives them an almost mystical dimension that can leave them seeming, on one level, distanced from the real world and its practical concerns and, on another level, idealistic to the point of naivety.

Even when the musician is unsympathetic, performance seems to be exempt from this characterization. In *The Piano Teacher*, where both the principal characters are musicians and neither is particularly likeable, it is only when they play that their idiosyncrasies – Erika's unsmiling, annoyed demeanour, Walter's arrogance – are in abeyance. In *L'Accompagnatrice*, set during World War II, Irene is both self-centred and self-deluding, refusing to admit that she is ethically compromised by performing to German audiences in occupied Paris. It would be easy for Irene to be represented as an unsympathetic character but, again, there is no clear condemnation of her evident in the film's direction.

Another obvious difference between European and Hollywood narratives is that confrontational juxtaposition of high culture and popular culture is largely absent. However, the relationship of the two is by no means a topic that European films concerned with classical music avoid. In *Diva*, both popular music and 'new age' culture exist alongside and complementary to classical music and high art, although the central musical character is deeply conflicted about her own relationship with the world of commercial music and the recording industry. Cynthia (Wilhelmenia Wiggins Fernandez) is – ironically – an American opera singer who has never allowed her voice to be recorded. Her main reason for this is that she considers a performance to be a unique moment, an experience shared by performer and audience. A recording removes her from that experience, leaving only the trace of her voice. Cynthia, one suspects, has been reading Walter Benjamin. She attempts to preserve classical music performance as a pre-recording era practice, concerned that the act of mechanical reproduction will threaten the authenticity of her art.

In *Un Coeur en Hiver*, a dinner party scene revolves around a discussion among the intellectuals and musicians present on the potentially antagonistic relationship of high art and popular culture. Daniel (Jean-Luc Bideau) is troubled by the democratization of culture that gives equal value to 'a pop video, a Claudel play … a Ravel sonata and Madame Amet's apple pie'. Their host affectionately tells Daniel that he represents 'an anxious elite in a world threatened by democratic excess', whilst the violinist Camille (Emmanuelle Béart) argues that culture is still a privilege, but one that is no longer reserved for quite so few. Stéphane (Daniel Auteuil) comments that her argument is still ultimately elitist, in that she conceives of art as being able to speak to some – 'the sensitive individual in the blind masses' – but not all. As in *Diva*, one hears in this discussion echoes of another text, Pierre Bourdieu's social critique of the judgement of taste:

> Intellectuals and artists are thus divided between their interest in cultural proselytism … which inclines them to favour popularization, and concern for cultural distinction … and their relationship to everything concerned with the 'democratization of culture' is marked by a deep ambivalence.[2]

The very fact that this conversation, with its allusions to Bourdieu, occurs within the film itself points out some cultural distinctions between Hollywood cinema and the European films under discussion here, all of which are essentially art-house films, although *Diva* has some obviously mainstream elements. As art-house films, Bourdieu's research would indicate that their audiences will tend to have higher levels of educational and social capital, and resultingly higher levels of cultural competence for high art, in comparison to the general population. As such, they will value art works, including films and classical music itself, which demand a higher degree of intellectual engagement in order to be appreciated than would generally be expected in the appreciation of the products of popular culture. Being products of the same culture that values classical music, it is unsurprising that most of the representations of classical performers in art-house films are positive. Similarly, given that the Hollywood films under discussion here are more firmly situated in popular culture, it is equally unsurprising that popular cultural products and practices are looked on more favourably than the products and practices of high art. Given that most high cultural practices historically originated in Europe, and most commercial and popular cultural practices originated in America, again, it should perhaps not surprise us that Hollywood films demonize the European classical musician and elevate the American popular cultural hero.

Music as narrative

Films on both sides of the Atlantic often focus on just one piece of music. In Hollywood cinema, it is relatively unusual for pieces of music to be identified, but in European cinema, the music is generally identified by both composer and title and the music's own programmatic meanings are frequently central to an understanding of the narrative and the musical characters.

This narrative significance can be observed in a group of British films from the 1940s. All of them involve love-triangles and create a situation in which the composers find themselves faced with a choice, and invariably make the choice involving greatest personal sacrifice, which is usually rewarded at the very end of the film. At least part of the narrative will be set during World War II, and the plot is constructed around the composition of a musical work that comes to symbolize the ideas of both love and sacrifice. This can be seen, with greater or lesser variation, in *Dangerous Moonlight* (Brian Desmond Hurst, 1941) where the two loves are occupied Poland and the composer's wife, and for which Richard Adinsell wrote the *Warsaw Concerto*; in *Love Story* (Leslie Arliss, 1944) where the composer is a woman who finds herself in competition for the love of an RAF pilot as she writes her *Cornish Rhapsody*; and in *The Glass Mountain* (Edoardo Anton and Henry Cass, 1949) where the composition is an opera of the same name, and in which a married English composer falls in love with an Italian girl after his RAF bomber crashes in the Italian Alps. *Brief Encounter* (David Lean, 1945) is also arguably part of this group: it has a similar love-triangle plot, the unselfish sacrifice, and it also has a piano concerto, although there is no putative composer in the narrative and the music, Rachmaninoff's *Piano Concerto No. 2*, remains largely in the underscore.

The idea of the musician as an altruist appears to be unique to this group of British films: none of the characters in the other films, European or American, could be described as altruists. Generally, they behave badly, naively and enigmatically, but not altruistically; and few of the musician-protagonists of recent European films are men, whereas they are more likely to be male in the 1940s. Two American films from the same period, *Deception* (Irving Rapper, 1946) and *The Great Lie* (Edmund Goulding, 1941), also have the love-triangle plot but, consistent with more recent Hollywood films, the musicians are not portrayed in a particularly flattering light. Rather than making altruistic sacrifices, they are involved in various kinds of deceptive and vindictive acts, seeking to promote their own interests.

With the obvious exception of *Three Colours: Blue* (Krysztof Kieslowski, 1993) the majority of European films since 1980 featuring classical musicians focus on performers rather than composers. Here, the choice of music often acts as a commentary on the narrative and sometimes actively participates in its development in a way similar to the music of the fictional composers. In *The Piano Teacher*, the recurring music is Schubert's '*Im Dorfe*' from *Winterreisse* and, although Erika's student Anna (Anna Segalevitch) plays it more often, it nonetheless comes to represent Erika. The last time it is played it is one of a set of events that turns Erika away from her path of passive resistance.

First, Anna is upset and Walter talks to her and makes her laugh. Erika observes this from a distance, her face bearing its usual, impassive expression. Secondly, as Anna begins to play, Erika's attention is drawn to her. Again, her expression is hard to read, but the fact that Anna's playing attracts her attention implies that she is playing well. Schubert is Erika's composer: she is very protective of his music, and that Anna might be playing well directly threatens Erika's ownership of and identification with it, compounding the threat Anna poses by potentially usurping Walter's affections. Thirdly, as the singer enters, the words appear to speak directly to Erika of her own situation, of a life in which pleasures have only existed as fantasies, a situation the singer rejects, wanting to grasp life itself rather than be satisfied with illusions:

> Dogs are barking, chains are rattling;
> People are sleeping in their beds,
> Dreaming of things they don't have,
> Refreshing themselves in good and bad
> [...]
> I am finished with all my dreams.
> Why should I linger among the sleepers?

Erika, listening to this song, is suddenly on the edge of tears, and it is this moment that marks her transition from repression and resistance to action. Her first act is to sabotage Anna's coat-pockets with broken glass, reclaiming Schubert for herself by preventing Anna from playing; her next act is to stop denying herself the thing she wants by beginning her disastrous attempt at an affair with Walter.

In *Diva*, the piece of music most closely identified with Cynthia is '*Ebben?…
ne andro lontano*' from Catalani's *La Wally*. Again, there is a direct connection
between the aria and Cynthia's fear of being recorded. The lyrics – 'I will go far
away … you will see me no more' – run in parallel to Cynthia's anxiety over not
being present when the listener hears her voice. This is the aria we hear every time
Jules' bootleg recording of her concert is played and it is both a statement of the
situation – Cynthia is far away and cannot be seen – and as the plot progresses and
her relationship with Jules develops, it also becomes a threat. When she finds out
that it was he who made the illicit recording, he may lose her forever.

Music embodied

In the 'concerto films' of the 1940s, the music is a manifestation of the
composer's desires and experiences and so can be read as representing the
composer. However, in films since 1980, performers – specifically female
performers – are often positioned as embodiments of music itself. In this reading,
their desires and experiences cannot be separated from the music they perform or
from the act of performing it: music is not something the performer does but
something she is. This representation is nothing new: music has been embodied as
a woman since Euterpe. Male gods may be musicians, but music itself is a woman
who, like other women, offers 'a promise of male pleasure'.[3]

This is most directly represented in the way that the camera and other
characters look at the musician as she performs. The concept of the male,
heterosexual gaze directed at the female character is one both long-established
and well-discussed among film theorists but it is particularly overt in European
films concerning classical music performance.[4] The gaze directed at musicians by
other characters is always possessive: the gazer signals the extent to which they
covet the performer as the embodiment of music. In *Diva*, the opening scene
shows Jules at the concert where he secretly records Cynthia's voice. His
unblinking gaze signals his fixation on her at the same time that this desire drives
him to 'steal' her voice and, later, her dress. Likewise, in *L'Accompagnatrice*, the
first scene shows Sophie going to her first meeting with Irene and hearing the end
of her concert. As Irene sings, we see Sophie, standing in the darkness in her dark
clothing, gazing as if stunned by Irene who, by contrast, stands in the light, a
shining figure in a white dress framed by the camera in a head and shoulders shot.
This is not Sophie's view – she is seeing Irene from high up at the back of the
theatre – but it represents Sophie's idealized vision of Irene as music embodied.

Even though, as a female pianist, Sophie might expect to be regarded in a
fashion not unlike Irene, as a quasi-mystical embodiment of music, she is
constantly sidelined. In their first concert, the dark/light positioning is reiterated,
with Sophie in an unflattering black dress, and Irene in her elegant white. Sophie's

voiceover demonstrates that she knows which of them is 'music', the rightful object of the gaze: 'She doesn't even look at you. She sings, the glory is hers. So is the happiness ... and you, the accompanist. The concert is her concert, not yours.' The camera focuses on Sophie as she plays but she, in turn, is fixedly gazing at Irene: we too are, paradoxically, looking at Irene, even though we cannot see her, overwhelmed by the subjectivity of Sophie's gaze. At the end of the scene, the image fades to black, obliterating Sophie. Throughout the film, people fail to recognize her or cannot remember her name, which is covered over on posters. As one character says goodbye to her, he tells her 'not to disappear', but Irene's embodiment of music leaves Sophie, the other female musician, in constant danger of disappearing, of disembodiment. Both Irene and *Diva*'s Cynthia actively want to be looked at: Cynthia's horror of recording is the fear that she will disappear from her own performance, which is exactly Sophie's fate.

Another aspect of the gaze is that gazing and physical contact become mutually exclusive. If the gaze is sexual and possessive, then physical sex renders it redundant. Irene is heterosexual and so there is no opportunity for Sophie to move beyond gazing, although her obsession with Irene makes a sexual relationship with Benoît (Julien Rassam) impossible. In *Diva*, the most physically intimate moment between Cynthia and Jules is when they listen to the recording of her disembodied voice. At the point at which she ceases to embody music, Jules embraces her for the first time. Stéphane, in *Un Coeur en Hiver*, gazes at Camille as she plays, and she thrives on his gaze when he comes to the recording studio. The flaw in their relationship is that he never wants to take it beyond that point: he loves her as music but is not able to love her as a person.

In *The Piano Teacher*, Walter falls in love with Erika whilst watching her play the piano. She, likewise, begins to desire him when she hears him play: and after their relationship becomes physical, we never see her play again. Having gained access to her body, Walter does not merely want to look anymore and he is frustrated that she still watches him play in their piano lesson, wanting to leave music-making behind and concentrate on physical intimacy.

By contrast, in the same way that we rarely see 'good' American characters play classical music, when listening to performances in Hollywood cinema, characters are likely to close their eyes. When Vida attends a concert in *Wilder Napalm*, she listens with her eyes closed, effectively negating the fact that there is a live string quartet in front of her; and in *The Prince of Tides*, Susan also listens to Herbert playing with her eyes closed. In playing, the musician is the only active character present: listeners are generally passive, and the music therefore gives the performer power over the audience. In European films, the gaze challenges the musician, objectifying her in the very gesture that acknowledges her power. However, in American cinema, women are more likely to play in domestic settings, while men dominate the professional arena, listened to by women, and so the power relationship is differently balanced. By closing their eyes, Vida and Susan resist the player's power, rendering the music an acousmatic experience, eliminating the performer's visual presence and reclaiming the music for themselves by internalizing it, much as Cynthia fears in *Diva*. In *The Prince of Tides*, during the recital scene, Monique's eyes are open and she is seduced by the force of Herbert's musical presence. Susan's are closed, signalling her resistance and rebellion against her husband.

Truly Madly Deeply

Truly Madly Deeply (1991) is probably the best known of recent films to feature classical music performance and it can be read as mediating the distance between the Hollywood and European positions. First, it is a European film, but closer to the commercial market position of a typical Hollywood film than art-house cinema, combining ideas of comedy, tragedy and a ghost story. It also situates itself quite self-consciously in relation to other films concerned with classical music, as several of the videos the ghosts watch reference it: *Brief Encounter*, *Five Easy Pieces*, *Fitzcarraldo* (Werner Herzog, 1982) and *To Forget Venice* (Franco Brusati, 1979).

Some of Robynn Stilwell's observations in her comprehensive account of how music and acts of performance function in *Truly Madly Deeply* highlight the way in which its representation of classical musicians takes elements from both Hollywood and European cinema. Like Hollywood, the film combines both popular culture and high culture within its diegesis, but rather than using these as a symbol for the confrontation between opposing characters, both popular and classical music are used to explore and establish the depth and intimacy of Jamie and Nina's relationship. The various musics represent a significant aspect of how their relationship is constructed and, as Stilwell observes, is crucial to how the characters are identified and understood.[5]

Again, like many Hollywood films, the man in the relationship is the senior musician, but he is senior by implication only. We assume that Jamie is a professional cellist, but it is never stated, although it is obvious that Nina is not a professional pianist. His cello, like Herbert's violin, is worth a lot of money, and he is evidently a highly competent player, but while there may have been an intention to present Jamie as a professional, there is no unequivocal evidence for it in the film. In fact, the reason we assume Jamie is a professional is because, in the same way that European films tend to embody music in a particular character, Jamie embodies music here. The unusual aspect is that he is man and this is perhaps the clearest point of mediation between the Hollywood figure of the senior male musician and European figure of music embodied as a (female) performer.

Jamie's association with music is present from the title sequence of the film, as the black-and-white sequence of him playing freezes into a photograph, capturing him in the moment of music-making and preserving him there. We also watch

Nina play the same piece by Bach. However, when we do, she is recreating Jamie's musical voice, singing in his cello part as she accompanies herself on the piano. Jamie is thus musically present even when he is physically absent from the film. Nina's grief-stricken attempt to keep him symbolically alive through music is ultimately successful – it is whilst playing the Bach sonata that she quite literally re-embodies him. After he returns, Nina never plays classical music again, no longer needing to once she has Jamie instead: Jamie and classical music are functionally interchangeable. There is also an explicit association between Jamie and his cello, to the extent that Nina at one point declares that 'it *is* him'. The cello is frequently present in scenes, visible behind her or being embraced by her; when he returns, it is through playing the cello that he first announces his presence; and after he leaves, Nina's moment of closure is signalled by her placing the cello in its case for the first time in the film and closing the lid, symbolically putting Jamie's body in its coffin.

Although much more sympathetically represented, Jamie also displays some of the arrogance of his Hollywood counterparts: he has a tendency to be controlling and overbearing, chiding Nina for being untidy and disorganized, taking over her home and then turning her objections back on her to make her feel guilty and ungrateful. However, this American model is also mediated by an idea drawn from the European one, in particular the way that the concerto films of the 1940s consistently represent the central, often male, musician as altruistic. In the same way that these characters make a choice that involves great personal sacrifice, at the end of *Truly Madly Deeply* it is revealed that Jamie's return and subsequent behaviour have also been altruistically motivated by a decision to help Nina, to make her 'realize that, literally or figuratively, she cannot live with a ghost' and must go on living her own life without him.[6] That this is a choice that causes Jamie himself to suffer is seen at the end: there are tears in his eyes when his ghost-companions ask 'is it time?' and in the very final scene, as Nina walks away with her new lover and the ghosts wave goodbye from the living room window, Jamie wipes a tear from his eye and the others comfort and congratulate him on the successful completion of his mission. His return and his second departure are both sacrifices he has made for her sake.

Conclusion

The way that music functions in the films discussed in this chapter demonstrates a range of representations of classical music performers and performance, frequently coloured by ideas of European identity. In Hollywood cinema, this is often a negative representation, with European-ness, classical music, high culture and antipathetic characterization being conflated as part of a binary construct that positions this against American-ness, popular music, popular culture and heroic characterizations. In European cinema itself, classical music is on its home territory and is frequently located in films that are fundamentally sympathetic to high culture, which in turn leads to a more sympathetic representation of the performer. *Truly Madly Deeply* is possibly unique in synthesizing elements from both cinemas to create an unconventional, but nonetheless central, heroic male character who is also a classical musician. This balances some of the distortions in the representation of classical musicians in other films. Despite the fact that there are in reality many talented and internationally successful American classical performers, the representation of classical musicians in Hollywood films frequently positions them as outsiders and as a corrupt or corrupting 'other'. In Europe, although representations are more positive, the female performers often have a slightly tenuous grip on reality, sometimes resulting in them becoming mentally unbalanced. *Truly Madly Deeply* plays with all these representations at numerous levels and from them creates a narrative that represents classical musical performers – even when dead – as fundamentally normal, heroic and compassionate.

Notes

1. Leppert, R. *The Sight of Sound: Music, Representation and the History of the Body*, London and Berkeley: University of California Press, 1993, 161.
2. Bourdieu, P. *Distinction: A Social Critique of the Judgement of Taste*, trans. R. Nice, Cambridge, MA: Harvard University Press, 1984, 229.
3. Leppert, *The Sight of Sound*, 60.
4. See, for example Mulvey, L. 'Visual Pleasure and Narrative Cinema', *Screen*, **16** (3), Autumn 1975, 6–18; Silverman, K. 'Masochism and Subjectivity', *Framework*, **12**, 1980, 2–9; Kaplan, E.A. *Women and Film: Both Sides of the Camera*, New York: Methuen, 1983; Stacey, J. 'Desperately Seeking Audience', in J. Caughie, A. Kuhn, and M. Merck (eds) *The Sexual Subject: A* Screen *Reader in Sexuality*, London: Routledge, 1992, 244–57.
5. Stilwell, R. 'Symbol, Narrative and the Musics of *Truly Madly Deeply*', *Screen*, **38** (1), Spring 1997, 75.
6. Ibid., 63.

Chapter 6

Outing the synch: music and space in the French heritage film

Phil Powrie

At the beginning of *Le Colonel Chabert* (Yves Angelo, 1994) we see a battlefield with scavengers stripping Napoleon's dead soldiers of clothes and jewellery, corpses being carted away and tipped into pits. There is no diegetic sound, only the *Largo* from Beethoven's Trio, Opus 71 'The Ghost', fittingly enough given that the story, which most of the French audience would have been aware of, is that of a soldier given up for dead, but who returns like a ghost to claim his inheritance. The music matches what we see: Beethoven fits the period, the Trio's title fits the story. But the fact that we hear chamber music when we might have expected full orchestra, and even more the fact that we hear only the music, is unsettling and, for a heritage film, unusual.

The purpose of this chapter is to begin an investigation into the complexity of the music track in French heritage cinema, and more particularly the way in which music can unsettle. The music track does not always work in concert with the image track to create unproblematic pseudo-historical spectacle; Miguel Mera has pointed out that 'representing accurate historical eras musically in film music is much less important than achieving an appropriate dramatic narrative'.[1] However, I wish to argue here that music in the French heritage film can also be incongruous, rather than working to support historical accuracy or dramatic narrative. It can, on the contrary, problematize what we see.

I shall first discuss the basic issue of historical authenticity, but then move on to explore what might lie beyond this simplistic conceptualization of music's function in the heritage film. Such a conceptualization takes no account of the variety of musical idioms in the French heritage cinema: some films have 'classical-sounding' music by contemporary film composers, some adapt classical music, some incorporate 'ethnic' or folk music into their overall scheme, while others are straight compilations of classical pieces with no original score. Nor does it take account of music's relationship with space. In what follows we shall see how one (admittedly loose) concept can be used to link these lines of enquiry, that of 'narrowness'. To underpin my analysis I shall call upon Foucault's notion of heterotopia, Bhabha's 'third space', and, finally, Deleuze and Guattari's concepts of lines of flight and deterritorialization, showing how these concepts can illuminate compositional practice.

The corpus

Heritage cinema emerged both in the UK and in France during the 1980s. Ginette Vincendeau, in a recent *Sight and Sound* anthology devoted to literary adaptations and heritage films, defines them as films which 'are shot with high budgets and production values by A-list directors and they use stars, polished lighting and camerawork, many changes of décor and extras, well-researched interior designs, and classical or classical-inspired music'.[2] The difference between French heritage films and the French costume dramas which preceded them (and of which some are remakes[3]) is that 'there is a change of emphasis from narrative to setting'.[4] In France, as in the UK, heritage cinema covers a variety of films and periods. In the UK there has been some debate about whether heritage cinema is a genre, and what films should be included in that remit. Andrew Higson's recent monograph on the British heritage cinema usefully summarizes these debates, and posits some basic guidelines for definition (which I am adopting here), such as the use of literary texts or the biographies of historical figures,[5] and a cut-off date at the Second World War.[6] Higson's work is also useful in its thorough exploration of the ideology of the British heritage cinema. As he points out, the debates about heritage cinema have revolved around two basic positions: the first, broadly left-leaning position is that they are regressively nostalgic, and a celebration of (abhorrent) conservative values; the second, broadly postmodern and feminist position, is that they are less conservative than they appear, not so much celebrations as ironic questionings of those values; and linked to this second position is the recognition of the many pleasures associated with popular cinema.

In France, heritage cinema began, arguably, with adaptations of novels and plays by Marcel Pagnol set in the first half of the twentieth century, although they can range very widely in historical terms.[7] They can be set in the sixteenth century, as is the case with *La Reine Margot* (Patrice Chéreau, 1994), based on the novel by Alexandre Dumas. They can be set in the seventeenth century, such as *Tous les matins du monde* (Alain Corneau, 1991), or the very popular *Cyrano de Bergerac* (Jean-Paul Rappeneau, 1990). They can be set in the eighteenth century, such as *Beaumarchais, l'insolent* (Edouard Molinaro, 1996, based on a play by playwright and film director Sacha Guitry) or *Ridicule* (Patrice Leconte, 1996), or *Le Bossu* (Philippe De Broca, 1996). Many of them are set in the nineteenth century, based on well-known texts: *Le Colonel Chabert* (Yves Angelo, 1994), based on the Balzac short story; *Le Hussard sur le toit* (Jean-Paul Rappeneau, 1995), based on the twentieth-century novel by Jean Giono; and *Germinal* (Claude Berri, 1993), based on the late nineteenth-century novel by Émile Zola. Such films can also be based on well-known artistic or historical characters, such as *Les Enfants du siècle* (Diane Kurys, 1999), an account of the tempestuous relationship between Georges Sand and Alfred de Musset; or, moving to the turn of the twentieth century, *Camille Claudel* (Bruno Nuttyens, 1988), based on the equally tempestuous relationship between the eponymous heroine and the sculptor Rodin; and, finally, the story of the Resistance fighter, *Lucie Aubrac* (Claude Berri, 1997).

Music and history

Music's prime function in the French heritage film seems to be the 'authentication' of period. Starting in the furthest historical period, *Tous les matins du monde* recounts the relationship between two musicians, Marin Marais and his reclusive teacher Sainte-Colombe. The subject matter naturalizes the compiled score with music by Marais, Sainte-Colombe, Lully and Couperin, music which obsessively grounds the film in its period. A similar procedure occurs in *Le Colonel Chabert*, directed by the photographer of *Tous les matins du monde*, Yves Angelo, where the score is an entirely classical compilation, very roughly contemporaneous with the film's period stretching from the French Revolution to the 1820s (Mozart, Schubert, Schumann and Beethoven).

Much more frequent, however, is the 'historically informed' composed score with classical references, often with interpolated classical pieces. Starting with early historical periods, Goran Bregovic's score for *La Reine Margot*, set in the sixteenth century, uses a mixture of Renaissance folk dance and choral music. As can be seen from Table 6.1 (which lists the main French heritage films since their recognition as a genre in the mid-1980s to the end of the 1990s), Jean-Claude Petit is often called upon for heritage scores. *Cyrano de Bergerac*, although an adaptation of a nineteenth-century play written in 1897, is set in the seventeenth century (Cyrano lived 1619–55). Petit's score has baroque touches; the overture, for example, is structured slow-fast-slow, as were Lully's overtures in the seventeenth century (Lully lived 1632–87), and Cyrano's theme is in *sarabande* style with a solo trumpet. For *Le Hussard sur le toit*, set in 1832, Petit calls upon Schumann and Brahms, including the *Intermezzo* no. 6 from Brahms' late piano *Fantasy* Opus 116 in the final sequence to underline the musical affiliations (the mismatch between the date of the action and the music is something I shall return to). Jean-Louis Roques' score for *Germinal*, set in 1865, is in the late Romantic idiom of Saint-Saëns, whose main orchestral compositions date from the 1850s. Gabriel Yared's tortured score for *Camille Claudel*, set in the period 1880–1913, uses a string orchestra in the style of Mahler and Bruckner, with touches of Schoenberg's *Verklärte Nacht* of 1899.

It is worth looking at one film in a little more detail to see how authenticity is sought. Luis Bacalov's score for *Les Enfants du siècle*, which recounts the affair between Georges Sand and Alfred de Musset in Venice in 1833–34, corresponds to the period of early Romanticism. Bacalov explained how it had not been easy to find 'a good harmonic rapport between the music [he] was to compose and that of the great nineteenth-century composers (Schumann, Schubert, Liszt)' which the director, Diane Kurys, had insisted on.[8] There are a variety of classical pieces

Table 6.1   French heritage films from the 1980s to the end of the 1990s

Year released	Title	Director	Author of original texts	Period set	Major stars	Spectators* (millions)	Position**	Composer
1986	*Jean de Florette*	Berri	Pagnol	20th c.	Depardieu, Montand, Auteuil	7.2	1	Jean-Claude Petit
1986	*Manon des sources*	Berri	Pagnol	20th c.	Montand, Auteuil	6.7	2	Jean-Claude Petit
1988	*Camille Claudel*	Nuttyens		20th c.	Adjani, Depardieu	2.7		Gabriel Yared
1990	*La Gloire de mon père*	Robert	Pagnol	20th c.	Roussel	6.3	1	Vladimir Cosma
1990	*Le Château de ma mère*	Robert	Pagnol	20th c.	Roussel	4.7	3	Vladimir Cosma
1990	*Uranus*	Berri	Aymé	WWII	Depardieu	2.6	6	Jean-Claude Petit
1990	*Cyrano de Bergerac*	Rappeneau	Rostand	17th c	Depardieu	4.7	2	Jean-Claude Petit
1991	*Tous les matins du monde*	Corneau		17th c.	Depardieu	2.1	1	Classical compilation
1992	*Indochine*	Wargnier		20th c.	Deneuve			Patrick Doyle
1993	*Germinal*	Berri	Zola	19th c.	Depardieu	6.1	2	Jean-Louis Roques
1994	*Le Colonel Chabert*	Angelo	Balzac	19th c.	Depardieu, Ardant	1.7	7	Classical compilation
1994	*La Reine Margot*	Chéreau	Dumas	16th c.	Adjani	2.0	6	Goran Bregovic
1995	*Le Hussard sur le toit*	Rappeneau	Giono	19th c.	Binoche	2.4	6	Jean-Claude Petit
1996	*Ridicule*	Leconte		18th c.	Ardant			Antoine Duhamel
1996	*Beaumarchais, l'insolent*	Molinaro	Guitry	18th c.	Luchini			Max Gazzola, Bernard Gérard
1997	*Lucie Aubrac*	Berri	Aubrac	WWII	Bouquet, Auteuil			Philippe Sarde
1997	*Le Bossu*	De Broca	Féval	18th c.	Auteuil	2.3	7	Philippe Sarde
1999	*Les Enfants du siècle*	Kurys	Musset	19th c.	Binoche			Luis Bacalov

*   The number of spectators in France in millions
**   The position of the film in the best-selling French films of the year of release

ranging from Schumann's *Carnival* and *Arabesque*, to Bruckner's motet *Christus factus est* from 1884, and Allegri's *Miserere*. But there are also pieces inserted as much for historical authenticity as anything else. So, for example, we see Paris high society dance to a waltz, *Flüchtige Lust*, by Joseph Lanner (1801–43); we see Liszt playing one of his romances at a soirée, the characters commenting on the fact that he had trained to be a priest when younger (a real historical fact); Sand plays a Liszt transcription of Schubert's lied *Der Müller und der Bach*, leading to a lively exchange between Sand and Musset, who jealously thinks she has been seeing Liszt. Finally, Musset goes to the opera in Venice while an aria from Bellini's opera *Beatrice di tenda* is being performed; it premiered in Venice on 16 March 1833, whereas Sand and Musset only arrived in Venice in December 1833, but they both knew Bellini in the mid-1830s in Paris.

Music therefore functions, one might argue, rather like costume or props to ensure a nostalgic experience of the past, as explained by Jameson, who points out how the simulacrum effect negates history:

> Nostalgia films restructure the whole issue of pastiche and project it onto a collective and social level, where the desperate attempt to appropriate a missing past is now refracted through the iron law of fashion change and the emergent ideology of the generation ... Faced with these ultimate objects – our social, historical, and existential present, and the past as 'referent' – the incompatibility of a postmodernist 'nostalgia' art language with genuine historicity becomes dramatically apparent.[9]

Unlike the costume dramas of the 1950s, the modern French heritage film is dependent on a museum aesthetic. As we have seen, the composed scores (by far the most frequent type of score) mimic musical styles so as to ground the narrative in a recognizable period. Music seems to act as a guarantee of authenticity as much as the image, something which the compiled score consisting of period music attempts to do even more forcefully, especially 'when the music is actually embedded within the narrative events of the story'.[10]

However, music complicates the issue of the loss of affect which Jameson sees as the inevitable corollary of the museum aesthetic. Music provides the 'emotional depth not verbally representable'[11] in film dialogue, and is 'first and foremost ... a signifier of emotion itself';[12] it therefore reintroduces affect into the spectacular, 'emotionalizing' history in considerably more striking ways than costume or props. Emotion arguably rearticulates the return to the past as a return to the maternal origin, a well-rehearsed psychoanalytical argument.[13] The visual track and the soundtrack may well work in concert to frame the narrative; but the narrative, conversely, acts as a frame for the music as origin, capturing it, as it were, so that the lost past, the utopia of pre-Oedipal fusion with the mother, can be recovered. I shall explore this function briefly – because it is the least interesting from my perspective in this chapter – in its relationship to landscape, before moving on to more relevant functions which have to do with dystopia, such as we saw in the opening sequence of *Le Colonel Chabert*.

Music, landscape and utopian openness

The equivalent of the British heritage cinema's obsession with the English country house in French heritage cinema is landscape. The obsession with landscape functions rather as it does in the American Western. The Wild West has connotations of freedom and authenticity, contrasted both with urban corruption (the saloon) and with the effeminizing and urbanized 'East'; so too the French heritage film contrasts landscape with townscape. The ideological value attached to the land is historically linked to France's pre-Second World War rural economy. It is not a coincidence that the heritage cinema emerged in the mid-1980s. In the period 1945–74, French society changed dramatically with economic growth, and massive urbanization through the rural exodus. The 1974 oil crisis was followed in the early 1980s by serious social problems, such as rioting in the major cities. The land, then, represents a purer pre-Second World War past, an Arcadian non-urban paradise, the reason indeed why Jean in *Jean de Florette*, a city-dweller, returns to his native village, to 'cultivate the authentic', as he puts it. Pagnol's own film *Manon des sources* was made in 1952; he then novelized it in 1962, the novel being the source for Berri's diptych; the 1950s and even more the 1960s, were the high period of France's shift from the rural to the urban.

The music used in conjunction with landscape shots is, unsurprisingly, typically broad-sweep *tutti*. This is the case, for example, in the opening sequences of *Jean de Florette*, or the frequent 'galloping hero' shots of *Le Hussard sur le toit*; both of these films are set in the South of France, and both are scored by Jean-Claude Petit. It is also the case with Vladimir Cosma's rather more sentimental orchestrations for the Pagnol follow-up diptych, *La Gloire de mon père/Le Château de ma mère* (Yves Robert, 1990). The music in these films does not just *support* the setting as an 'unheard melody', to reprise Gorbman's terminology; it does much more than this. In such French heritage films where landscape plays a vital role, music *draws attention* to the landscape, puts it on display, its lush orchestration working with crane shots and panning shots to articulate the epiphanic emotion of the return to origins. Even with a considerably darker film set in Northern France – *Germinal*, dominated not by sunny mountain tops but by dark mines – the opening and closing credits are long crane shots of the landscape. These shots bookend the hell of the mines with the open space of the nomad (whether the hero Étienne or Souvarine the anarchist) and freedom from oppression.

The 'openness' articulated by the music and extreme long shots of landscape is emphasized by other framing techniques, as we stand with the hero at the window looking out. When Jean (Depardieu) and his family arrive in their *bastide* in *Jean de Florette* they fling open the windows, the camera pulls forward through the frame of the window to focus on the 'paradise' below, as Jean walks away from the window. When he returns to join his wife (played by Depardieu's real-life wife, Elizabeth Depardieu) he is playing the film's signature theme from Verdi's *La*

Forza del destino on his harmonica, and she accompanies him singing, their lips joining at the end of the phrase. The use of the harmonica as a demotic instrument 'humanizes' and democratizes the music which might otherwise have suggested the impersonal workings of fate.[14] Jean and his wife therefore form a very human but utopian family in a utopian location, Adam and Eve in Eden, their emotion at 'returning to the land' doubly voiced, and framed by the window which anchors them in epiphanic openness. Moreover, in the second film, it is Jean's daughter who will play the harmonica, and who will control the flow of water from the underground spring; music, water and 'Mother Earth' all come together.

It is all far too good to be true, however, as we know from the opening credits and their signature tune with its connotations of tragic destiny, restated here. Windows are liminal spaces, both outside and inside. Jean's bedroom window may open out onto paradise, but it also frames the characters, as is emphasized by the reverse shot of Ugolin, who will eventually do so much harm to them, here spying on them as they perform their duet at the window. The harmonica may well humanize and democratize, but in so doing it also underlines Jean's frailty, written on his body in the form of his hunchback. Much more significant than what I shall call the 'utopian openness' typically associated with heritage film music as outlined in the previous paragraphs, is the 'dystopian enclosure', more prevalent in the films studied, which narrows and constrains that openness. It does so in two ways.

Music and dystopian enclosure

The first of these is the use of chamber music which, in contrast to the *tutti* of the symphony orchestra associated with wide-open spaces or action sequences, seems to narrow down both space and action, tending to connote a sense of confinement. We have just seen how this works in relation to the use of the duet at the window in *Jean de Florette*. *Lucie Aubrac* has a chamber score, composed by Philippe Sarde,[15] consisting of piano, flute, clarinet and cello, with full orchestra intervening on only a handful of occasions. Most of the time, the score consists of only two or three of the instruments, mainly piano and clarinet, but also cello and clarinet, or all three. The austerity of the score matches the austerities experienced under Nazi occupation, of course; but the effect is more to suggest imprisonment within very specific spaces, that of the home for Lucie, and the prison for her husband, and to narrow the narrative focus onto the couple's relationship and the domestic spaces they inhabit (their child is often in evidence in these spaces). Spectacular action sequences – such as the derailing of the train at the beginning of the film, or the hijacking of the Nazi convoy taking Raymond off to be shot – where one might well have expected full orchestra, have ambient sounds (explosions, gunshots) without dialogue, music only intervening in subsequent domestic scenes.

The second way in which music narrows space is the use of classical compilation, either of occasional pieces within a composed score, or a score made up entirely of compiled classical pieces. Here, as in *Lucie Aubrac*, chamber pieces are the key. I have already mentioned the opposition in *Tous les matins du monde* between spiritual solo pieces and worldly orchestral pieces, as also the Brahms' piano fantasy in the final sequence of *Le Hussard sur le toit*; the latter film also ostentatiously interpolates Mozart's *German Dances*. On the first occasion Angelo and Pauline are sleeping rough, and the music floats across 'from the other side of the valley', he says; she recognizes the music. The second time, we see a clarinettist playing them in the convent where the couple are quarantined. Angelo remembers the composer and tells Pauline that the musician is from Marseille; like them, he has been 'on the road'; the inmates used to complain, he tells her, but now they need the music to get to sleep. The music very clearly signifies the loss experienced by the displaced and the imprisoned, and its progression in the film from the outside (the camp fire, the distant, 'free' music) to the inside (the prison, the body of the imprisoned clarinettist seen in medium shot) demonstrates just as clearly the point I am making about the narrowing of space through music. Music makes the point certainly as clearly as the patterns set up in the *mise-en-scène*; arguably it does so more clearly than the sight of two contrasting spaces (valley, prison) lost in the welter of spaces we see in the film. As Deleuze and Guattari point out when comparing the respective power of music and painting, 'colors do not move a people'.[16]

In *Le Colonel Chabert*, as is the case with *Tous les matins du monde* and *Lucie Aubrac*, the mainly Romantic chamber pieces by Schubert, Schumann and Beethoven emphasize the domestic drama, the personal contrasted with the political and the public, as well as the different types of spatial confinement of the characters: the Countess is confined to the domestic role while her husband plays politics, Chabert is confined in his poverty, emphasized by his cramped and dirty quarters, and subsequently in his resigned misanthropy.

Such pieces have the function which Deleuze ascribes to the ritornello: 'the raising or falling back of pasts which are preserved.'[17] As a group they constitute a refrain, as well as often individually being calqued on the ritornello (the *German Dances*, for example). The rhythmical return of classical pieces (or of classical-inspired pieces) functions to establish both a time (the 'Natal', as Deleuze and Guattari call it), contrasting it with the 'innate';[18] and a place (the Territory) anchored in pastness: 'We call a refrain any aggregate of matters of expression that draws a territory and develops into territorial motifs and landscapes.'[19] We shall see in the next section how music in the heritage film, although it serves to narrow time and space to *locate* the fantasied past, can also *dislocate*, assuming a deterritorializing function.

So far in this section, I have shown how classical or classical-inspired music in the heritage film is often chamber music, and that this functions to narrow space and what space represents. The use of chamber music limits action to the domestic, it limits freedom of movement, and it creates moments of nostalgia and loss within wider historical frescos. Before moving on to my final type, it is worth pausing to consider the theoretical implications of these findings. Music in the heritage cinema not only narrows space, but also narrows musical possibilities by excluding or minimizing the surprises which unfamiliar original scoring may bring. For example, in *Tous les matins du monde*, once the initial shock is over at a film whose score is almost entirely a baroque music compilation, there are not many surprises; music is put at the service of the key opposition between the spiritual (authentic emotion) and the worldly (inauthentic emotion). This is a version of the conservative or regressive function of background scoring, the way in which 'functional music' creates 'an *untroublesome social subject*'.[20]

Moreover, the music here functions less as music and more as language. It is not allowed to have the breadth and flexibility implied by Kassabian, with the surprise of unexpected connotations, because it works as metaphor for enclosure, rather than as an artefact in its own right. The referential opacity normally associated with music, which legitimizes its association with the complexity of emotion, is therefore narrowed even further, the element of surprise carefully erased in the orchestration of dystopian emotion. It is the element of surprise which will form the focus of the final section.

Third space music: heterotopia and lines of flight

In this section, I will consider the alternative to the binary utopia (figured by the mountain) versus dystopia (figured by the house or prison) on which the preceding analysis is based. This immediately brings to mind the first of three concepts I would like to mention so as to define this alternative, Foucault's 'heterotopia', a term he uses to identify 'counter-sites, a kind of effectively enacted utopia in which the real sites, all the other real sites that can be found within the culture, are simultaneously represented, contested, and inverted'.[21] What would heterotopic music consist of? In this alternative space, elements from the binary utopia/dystopia form part of a range of strategies whose function is not to 'open' or 'close' musical and diegetic space, but to fissure it, to lateralize it (as in 'lateral thinking') in a different opening. It is signalled by musical signs which are unexpected. Foucault's term refers to real topological spaces, however, whereas the concept I am now elaborating is not topologically locatable, unlike the open and closed spaces discussed above where spaces we see are linked to musical forms.

A second concept is Deleuze and Guattari's notion of deterritorialization and lines of flight. Deleuze and Guattari oppose aborescent structures to rhizomatic structures; the tree is hierarchical, the rhizome is a nomadic, flexible and ever-changing network which undermines any notion of fixed territory, and of duality, such as the utopian/dystopian structure argued above. They assert:

> There is a rupture in the rhizome whenever segmentary lines explode into a line of flight, but the line of flight is part of a rhizome. These lines always tie back to one another. That is why one can never posit a dualism or a dichotomy, even in the rudimentary form of the good and the bad.[22]

They point out how music naturally deconstructs itself as it constructs itself: 'Music has always sent out lines of flight, like so many "transformational multiplicities", even overturning the very codes that structure or arborify it'.[23] Indeed, we might argue that film music is especially rhizomatic, in that it rarely accompanies what we see continuously, as in a musical piece performed in the concert hall; it surfaces occasionally, rather like mushrooms out of the mycelium. It is precisely because music is always already 'rhizomatic' that we need to find another term to suggest what eludes the binary utopia/dystopia within the rhizomatic structure of music. Terms such as 'lines of flight music' or 'flight music' are too ambiguous, even if the concept is the closest to what I wish to explore.

I shall therefore call this space 'third space music', following Homi Bhabha's use of the term to indicate fluidity and hybridization. This has the virtue of suggesting both a different type of heterotopic space, musical and diegetic, and of being related to a moment of deterritorialization by its insistence on hybridity and new types of formation, and by its association with radical politics:

> The importance of hybridity is not to be able to trace two original moments from which the third emerges, rather hybridity to me is the 'third space' which enables other positions to emerge. This third space displaces the histories that constitute it, and sets up new structures of authority, new political initiatives, which are inadequately understood through the received wisdom … The process of cultural hybridity gives rise to something different, something new and unrecognisable, a new area of negotiation of meaning and representation.[24]

Third space music creates that space of negotiation where different, alternative, subversive meanings emerge. To return to the window, this time as metaphor, audiences receptive to third space music are neither inside nor outside the window, but poised liminally on the window-ledge, always ready to jump out of the film-structure, shuttling nomadically across the boundaries of the willing suspension of disbelief. There are a range of strategies employed in third space music.

If we assume that French heritage cinema works towards congruence of music, image and period, as we have demonstrated above, then unexpected musical idioms upset period authenticity, creating fissures or spatio-temporal dislocations. For example, we might have expected Petit's score for *Le Hussard sur le toit*, set very specifically in July 1832 (as we are told at the start in a title), to refer to early Romanticism. More specifically still, given the tempestuous hero and his associations with Italy (he is a colonel in the Italian Hussars, fighting for liberation from the Austrians who rule Italy), a French audience might well have expected an idiom related to the best-known French composer of the early nineteenth century, Hector Berlioz, associated with the Romantic movement by his music and his memoirs, and very present in the French cultural imagination for these reasons. Berlioz completed the work which brought him success, the *Symphonie fantastique*, in 1830, and is linked to Italy in several ways: he dreamt of winning the Prix de Rome, went to Italy, and composed *Harold in Italy*. Petit's music is late Romantic, however, midway between Schumann and Brahms, emphasized by the inclusion of the Brahms *Intermezzo* mentioned above.

A related example is the use of 'ethnic' Balkan music in *La Reine Margot*, the score being composed by the Sarajevo-born ex-rock star Goran Bregovic, best-known for his collaborations with the director Emir Kusturica.[25] The film's period is the sixteenth century, and we might have expected Renaissance music comprised of folk dances with appropriate period instruments on the one hand (tambourines, hand drums, recorders), and Gregorian chant on the other. These are indeed the types of music used, as pointed out above; the idiom, however, is not Western European, but Central European. The folk music has pronounced gypsy inflections (for example in the opening and closing piece, 'Elo Hi'), and uses geographically and culturally coded instruments such as the zither. The choral music used for the Massacre of Saint Bartholomew and for Margot's wedding to Henri de Navarre has Orthodox inflections. The music is more raw than expected, and its undermining of expectations causes productive discomfort. As Robynn Stilwell points out, 'when there is a discrepancy between screen and score, the emotional truth is almost always in the music'.[26] The music in this film *dislocates* the action, taking the audience in a line of flight away from France geographically, nomadizing (literally through the connection with gypsy music) the narrative, as image-track (France) and music-track (Balkans) work with and against each other. The dislocation crucially encourages a metaphorical reading of the film. The music tells us that this is as much about Serbs and Croats as it is about Protestants and Huguenots, as was made clear by the director and star on the release of the film.[27] The Balkan conflict arguably acts as a further displaced metaphor for the deterioration of the socialist dream in France as Mitterrand's government gradually shifted from socialism to social democracy, and became rife with corruption.

A third strategy is the use of an unfamiliar instrument within the context of the music. For *Les Enfants du siècle* Bacalov explains how he substituted the guitar for the piano as a solo instrument – not an instrument associated with the dominant compiled music by Schumann, Schubert, and Liszt – in his composed score: 'This took me away from a more clichéd conception of Romanticism, with its predominant use of solo piano.'[28] The effect is to make those scenes where the guitar plays more intimate, thereby lessening the distance between high literary characters and the audience. More interesting is the use of the accordion in Roques' music for *Germinal*, integrated within a score which constantly echoes Saint-Saëns. We see the accordion in the long central utopian sequence of the miners' festival; it is heard but not seen in the credit sequences at the start and the end of the film. Saint-Saëns is fissured by this musical embodiment of the miners, an apparently radicalizing move. However, the accordion as embodiment of popular pleasure is repressed by the very same manifestations. Festive proletarian fun is framed and contained in the central sequence, just as Jean's harmonica was framed by the window. The accordion we hear in the credit sequences is fleeting, overwhelmed by the rest of the orchestration; it appears to be merely a gesture of local colour.

The final strategy I shall cover in detail complicates this view, however. The accordion is associated not just with popular culture, but also with the *chansonnier* Renaud, who plays the lead role, and with whom the film's composer, Roques, an accordion player, has frequently collaborated. The strategy here is to create a third space by incorporating a well-known singer into the fabric of the film,[29] forcefully raising the issue of how Renaud's star-image intersects with his role as Étienne Lantier in the film, given that *Germinal* is the only film in which Renaud has acted. Renaud's persona as a singer is that of 'a working-class Parisian, a revolutionary anarchist who identifies with popular culture';[30] but, crucially, as Hawkins points out, this remains very much a persona, given Renaud's middle-class origins, a persona he parodies in much of his work. Indeed, his work more generally relies on pastiche and parody of other *chansonniers*, to such an extent that 'the layers of quotation and derision are multiple, and at times one is not sure where the real Renaud lies, if a real Renaud exists as such'.[31] The character he plays is someone who cannot really settle down. Rather like the mysterious and charismatic Visitor (Terence Stamp) in Pasolini's *Teorema* (*Theorem*, 1968) who changes each member of the bourgeois family, so too Lantier (Renaud) changes forever the mining community by encouraging them to go on strike, as a result of which the mine is eventually destroyed, the soldiers brought in, and several members of the mining family he has stayed with die. Lantier, the nomad, packs his bags, and moves on. Renaud never sings in the film; on the contrary, our impression of him is that he spends much of his time watching other people, speaking in clipped phrases, neither his appearance nor his voice being particularly charismatic (in contrast, say, to the histrionics of Depardieu as the salt-of-the-earth Maheu). His role in the film therefore intersects with his persona as observer and satirist with anarchist leanings. It is no surprise that the film begins with his arrival and ends with his departure: he is not really part of this community, and does not share their worldview, he is just passing through, like the accordion which 'stands in' for the singing voice we never hear.

Conclusion

This chapter has explored how music in the French heritage film is used in a number of highly complex ways. There are other strategies used for third space music, such as the self-reflexive foregrounding of music by the dialogue, or the temporary abandonment of the leitmotif which supports particular characters in the narrative. These strategies will have to be explored in future work, not least because they raise a new set of questions which have to do with music and gender. I hope to have shown how music in the French heritage film functions in three distinct but related ways. First, it supports the visual track by its utopian connotations of 'open' maternal landscapes; second, it uses chamber music and classical compilation to narrow space down in dystopia; finally, it creates what I have called a third space, a heterotopic space of displacement, whose lines of flight fissure and fracture the utopia/dystopia binary, creating a nomadic, indeterminate and constantly fluctuating space. Third space music opens space out laterally through temporal or idiomatic mismatch, or the introduction of 'foreign bodies' which question the notion of continuity between the image-track and the music-track. In that respect, third space music undermines what Michel Chion calls synchresis, the fusion between the image-track and the music-track (formed on the two words synchronism and synthesis). Third space music is asynchretic; it outs the synch.[32]

Notes

1. Mera, M. 'Representing the Baroque: The Portrayal of Historical Period in Film Music', *The Consort: The Journal of the Dolmetsch Foundation*, **57**, Summer 2001, 19.
2. Vincendeau, G. (ed.) *Film/Literature/Heritage: A Sight and Sound Reader*, London: BFI, 2001, xviii.
3. *Le Colonel Chabert* (René Le Hénaff, 1943); *Le Bossu* (Jean Delannoy, 1944; André Hunebelle, 1960); *La Reine Margot* (Jean Dréville, 1954); *Germinal* (Yves Allégret, 1963).
4. Vincendeau, G. (ed.), *Film/Literature/Heritage*, xix.
5. Higson, A. *English Heritage, English Cinema: Costume Drama Since 1980*, Oxford: Oxford University Press, 2003, 20.
6. Ibid., 10.
7. See Table 6.1.
8. Bacalov, L. 'Composer's Notes', *Les Enfants du siècle*, http://www.deccaclassics. com/music/soundtracks/enfants.html (accessed 1 March 2004).
9. Jameson, F. *Postmodernism or The Cultural Logic of Late Capitalism*, Durham, NC: Duke University Press, 1991, 19.
10. Mera, M. 'Representing the Baroque', 17. Mera cites *Tous les matins du monde*, to which I have already alluded. This does not exclude other uses, of course, whether of the composed or the compiled score. Robynn Stilwell explores the way in which Patrick Doyle's 'Classical' piano composition played by Marianne in *Sense and Sensibility* (Ang Lee, 1995) uses the sonata form 'to fit the dramatic demands of the sequence, as well as using them to inflect the drama itself'; Stilwell, R.J. '*Sense and Sensibility*: Form, Genre and Function in the Film Score', *Acta Musicologica*, **LXXII**, 2000, 219–40.
11. Gorbman, C. *Unheard Melodies: Narrative Film Music*, London: BFI; Bloomington and Indianapolis: Indiana University Press, 1987, 67.

12. Ibid., 73.
13. See ibid., 62–3.
14. See Powrie, P. '"I'm Only Here for the Beer": post-tourism and the recycling of French heritage films', in D. Crouch, F. Thompson and R. Jackson (eds) *The Media and the Tourist Imagination*, London: Routledge, 2005, 143–53.
15. He has almost 200 film scores to his credit, beginning in 1969.
16. Deleuze, G. and Guattari, F. *A Thousand Plateaus: Capitalism and Schizophrenia*, trans. B. Massumi. London: Athlone, 1987, 348.
17. Deleuze, G. *Cinema 2: The Time Image*, trans. H. Tomlinson and R. Galeta, London: Athlone, 1989, 93.
18. See Deleuze, G. and Guattari, F. *A Thousand Plateaus*, 332–3.
19. Ibid., 323.
20. Gorbman, C. *Unheard Melodies*, 57 (her emphasis). The view I am putting here, it should be said, runs counter to Anahid Kassabian's view that compiled scores, unlike composed scores, create a sense of openness because of 'histories forged outside the film scene'; Kassabian, A. *Hearing Film: Tracking Identifications in Contemporary Hollywood Film Music*, New York and London: Routledge, 2000, 3.
21. Foucault, M. 'Of Other Spaces', http://foucault.info/documents/heteroTopia/foucault. heteroTopia.en.html (accessed 9 January 2004). Originally published as 'Des espaces autres', *Architecture/Mouvement/Continuité*, **5**, October 1984, 46–9. Amongst his examples are spaces where deviants are placed, such as psychiatric hospitals and prisons; spaces of juxtaposed spaces (cinemas, gardens); sacred spaces (cemeteries); spaces of accumulated time (museums, libraries); spaces of transitory time (festivals, fairgrounds, holiday cottages); spaces of illusion which critique quotidian space (brothels); spaces of attempted perfection (the colonies).
22. Deleuze, G. and Guattari, F. *A Thousand Plateaus*, 9.
23. Ibid., 11–12.
24. Bhabha, H.K. *The Location of Culture*, London: Routledge, 1994, 211.
25. *Dom za vesanje/Time of the Gypsies* (1988) and *Arizona Dream* (1993). After the break-up of Yugoslavia, Bregovic worked in France, scoring a film starring Adjani – *Toxic Affair* (Philomène Esposito, 1993) – before working with her again in *La Reine Margot*.
26. Stilwell, R.J. '*Sense and Sensibility*', 228.
27. See Austin, G. *Contemporary French Cinema: An Introduction*, Manchester: Manchester University Press, 1996, 168.
28. Bacalov, L. 'Composer's Notes'.
29. Renaud is not the only popular singer to have starred in films in the 1980s and 1990s. Patrick Bruel has appeared in 30 films since 1979; Johnny Hallyday, already an Elvis-clone star during the *yé-yé* era in the 1960s has starred in ten; and Alain Souchon a similar number. I have discussed the way rock stars are 'always "out of place", disjointed, disarticulated' in an article on Sting/Gordon Sumner; see Powrie, P. 'The Sting in the Tale', in I. Inglis (ed.) *Popular Music and Film*, London: Wallflower Press, 2003, 39–59.
30. Hawkins, P. *Chanson: The French Singer-songwriter from Aristide Bruant to the Present Day*, Aldershot: Ashgate, 2000, 178.
31. Ibid., 178.
32. I am grateful to Robynn Stilwell, Miguel Mera and David Burnand for their perceptive comments on an earlier draft of this chapter.

Chapter 7

Seán Ó Riada and Irish post-colonial film music: George Morrison's *Mise Éire*

David Cooper

George Morrison's 1959 documentary film *Mise Éire* (*I am Ireland*), which considers the period leading up to Irish independence, takes its title from a short poem by the writer and educationalist Pádraig Pearse, one of the leaders of the abortive 1916 Easter Rising against British rule. Pearse personifies Ireland as a mother who has given birth to greatness, but has been betrayed by her own offspring:

> I am Ireland:
> I am older than the Old Woman of Beare.
>
> Great my glory
> I that bore Cuchulainn the valiant.
>
> Great my shame:
> My own children that sold their mother.
>
> I am Ireland:
> I am lonelier than the Old Woman of Beare.[1]

In this allusion to the Hag of Beare, the goddess of sovereignty and the subject of the anonymous Gaelic poem '*Aithbe dam bés mora*' ('The Lament of the Old Woman of Beare') written around the turn of the ninth century, Pearse draws on one of the most ancient and potent Irish literary images of woman as virgin, mother and crone. Such maternal tropes are found in much later Irish song and literature, a characteristic that is, perhaps, unsurprising in a culture in which the Catholic church has exerted such an important influence, and in which emigration has been so widespread.[2] Pearse advocated the cleansing and sanctifying function of blood sacrifice, and his highly charged and pietistic poem 'A Mother Speaks', written in Arbour Hill Detention Barracks in 1916, shortly before his execution for treason, identified his own impending death with the crucifixion of Christ:

Dear Mary, that didst see thy first-born Son
Go forth to die amid the scorn of men
For whom He died,
Receive my first-born son into thy arms,
Who also hath gone out to die for men,
And keep him by thee till I come to him.
Dear Mary I have shared thy sorrow,
And soon shall share thy joy.[3]

For Edna Longley, 'Pearse's appetite for martyrdom marks the point of elision between his Nationalism and his Catholicism', and she remarks that 'Pearse organising his Pietá resembles a suicide who thinks he will be able to watch everyone being sorry watching him'.[4] The Easter Rising, largely co-ordinated by idealistic artists such as Pearse, was a military failure and was greeted in Ireland at the time with public apathy if not open hostility, at least according to some historical assessments. However, mainly as a result of the overreaction of the British government, it soon took on enormous symbolic importance, preparing the way for the formation of the Irish Free State in 1922, and creating heroes and martyrs of its leaders.

Morrison's *Mise Éire*

Morrison's *Mise Éire*,[5] is a feature-length documentary that presents the history of Irish independence from the 1890s, through the 1916 rising, up to the 1918 General Election. It employs actuality film stock and a soundtrack combining Irish language narration (written by Morrison and Seán MacReamoinn), sound effects, and a non-diegetic orchestral score composed by Seán Ó Riada.[6] Morrison, who was profoundly influenced by the Brazilian filmmaker Alberto de Almeida Cavalcanti's survey of British documentaries, *Film and Reality* (1942),[7] had been working on a catalogue of Irish film since 1952, and had indexed some 300,000 feet of film by 1959, the vast majority of which was discovered outside Ireland.[8] It was this stock, along with rostrum camerawork of photographs, cartoons, newspaper articles and other materials, that formed the source both of *Mise Éire* and the subsequent *Saoirse?* (*Freedom?*) produced in 1961, the first two parts of a projected trilogy that was never completed.[9]

Louis Marcus, one of the film's assistant editors, maintains that 'the material has been treated with the greatest of respect; it has not been slanted politically or in any other way'.[10] However, as Kevin Rockett notes, there is 'a general lack of critical distance in the film from the events portrayed', and this is particularly the case in relation to its representation of Ulster Unionism.[11] In Harvey O'Brien's analysis, 'the impression one takes from them [*Mise Éire* and *Saoirse?*] is an attempt to fashion an orthodox mythology of the state suited to the ideological needs of the time in which they were made'.[12] Morrison hinted at the stance adopted in *Mise Éire* himself by declaring that *Saoirse?* – a film that considered the later fractured period leading up to Civil War and did not achieve anything like the popular success in Ireland of *Mise Éire* – made 'no concessions to romantic nationalism'.[13]

For the non-Gaelic speaker it is difficult on the basis of the images alone to comprehend the film's ideological position, and the absence of a version dubbed in English or with English subtitles has undoubtedly complicated its reception. In point of fact, the tenor of the narration is ambivalent: at one moment it adopts the neutral tone of the newsreader, and at another, often in extravagantly metaphorical language, it openly declares its political leanings in statements such as 'In this building ... Ireland began to regain her soul', 'unwittingly they have lighted a living fire' and 'There is no cold like the cold of spring. But this cold lasts until the summer. It is a cold outcome to a heroic bid for freedom.'[14] O'Brien remarks that:

> *Mise Éire* and *Saoirse?* pandered to the Irish obsession with recent history embodied in the teachings at school and the idolatry practised through commemorative public monuments and plaques since the establishment of the Republic, and provided ample material for national self-definition. They offered a credible mythology of Ireland's past which shielded the Irish people from the ravages of change during the subsequent traumatic period of social and economic re-definition ... . Their focus on the role of change in the formation of the state ironically served to reinforce the self-satisfaction with achievement which inhibits further action.[15]

Mise Éire owed much of its popular success to the score written by Seán Ó Riada, and it is probably because of his music, as much as the film itself, that it has retained its reputation as a seminal document in Irish film history.

Seán Ó Riada and the score for *Mise Éire*

Although Seán Ó Riada (1931–71) is now best known as the instigator of an innovative style of performance of Irish traditional music, particularly through his formation of the band *Ceoltóirí Cualann* (the precursor of *The Chieftains*) in the 1960s, he was still principally regarded as a 'serious' composer in the 1950s. Gerard Victory remarks that *Mise Éire* 'changed him from a musician respected and admired by musical connoisseurs into a truly national figure',[16] and it is tempting to argue that this score marks the turning point in his compositional style from one drawing largely on characteristics of European high modernism, to one attempting to be congruent with the aspirations of the Irish state through the invocation of tradition by means of 'folk music'.

The composer and director first met in 1958. Ó Riada had by this stage Gaelicized his name from John Reidy, an act of some cultural and political moment.[17] Morrison (who declared himself more interested in European than American cinema) regarded music as 'one of the most essential features in almost every type of film', and took the opportunity to show Ó Riada as much material as he could to support this view.[18] One of the films the pair examined was Harry Watt and Basil Wright's 1936 documentary *Night Mail*, made for the GPO Film Unit, with a score by Benjamin Britten. Although Morrison felt that Britten's score was among the finest examples of British film music, there is little in Ó Riada's approach to *Mise Éire* that can be seen to bear its direct imprint. The issues that the pair discussed during this exploratory period seem to have been wide ranging, and included Japanese Kabuki theatre, which according to Morrison exerted an influence on Ó Riada's approach, though he does not explain where or how this is revealed.[19] Morrison was particularly concerned that music did not 'compete for attention or fill in gaps but entered positively and diminished naturally into an appropriate "field" of sound, whether effects or voice'.[20] A discussion of the subtlety of interaction between music, dialogue and effects in the soundtrack is outside the scope of this chapter.

Ó Riada makes use of several traditional Irish airs in his score for *Mise Éire*, in particular '*Róisín Dubh*' ('Dark Haired Rose'), a melody associated with a love song that, at least since James Hardiman's version of the text published in *Irish Minstrelsy* in 1831, has been widely regarded as a political allegory in which *Róisín Dubh* represents Ireland. Ó Riada's orchestral setting of this (and several other traditional melodies linked with lyrics which express nationalist sentiments) is striking for its allusion to Irish *sean-nós* (old-style traditional or 'folk') performance techniques, despite being performed by orchestral rather than 'traditional' instruments. However, other cues reveal Ó Riada's fascination with European musical modernism, and I would suggest that the musical disjunction that results from what Harry White has called the 'anguished irreconcilability' of these two aesthetic standpoints, complicates the film's reception as a piece of simple nationalist propaganda.[21] In White's estimation, Ó Riada failed to live up to the promise of his early, modernist works (which include the series of pieces entitled *Nomos* or 'rule'), and his later career was a 'downward curve towards self-indulgence and silence which ended with the composer's death in October 1971'.[22] With his effective rejection of European modernism, White argues that 'he silenced the claim of original art music as a tenable voice in the Irish cultural matrix: he silenced it too in its address upon the Irish mind. In its stead, he advanced the claim not of original composition but of the ethnic repertory itself.'[23] The film scores, and especially *Mise Éire*, are a particular focus of White's criticism, and he notes that while they have similar conceptual underpinnings to the 'original' works, they have distinctly different vocabularies and styles. Furthermore, he remarks that 'the music of *Mise Éire* is confined to projections and rhapsodic variations of the ethnic corpus of melody'.[24] Jeremy Dibble makes a similar point by suggesting that 'with its rather conservative and derivative idiom, no claim would be made for it as highly original music'.[25]

A survey of the soundtrack to *Mise Éire* indicates that Ó Riada's approach is perhaps more complex than White and Dibble allow.[26] Six types of musical material are found: settings of traditional melodies with strong nationalist associations, principally '*Róisín Dubh*', '*Sliabh na mBan*' and '*Boolavogue*'; original cues written in the style of traditional melodies; parodies or arrangements of popular songs or tunes ('Keep the Home Fires Burning', 'The Eton Boating Song', 'The Red Flag', 'It's a Long Way to Tipperary', 'Garryowen' and the British National Anthem); military fanfares and sidedrum calls; original material that evokes the musical language of art-music composers such as Vaughan Williams, Mahler and Sibelius; and original cues with more overtly modernist characteristics, similar in style to the *Nomos* series of works. Such eclecticism is, of course, by no means unusual in film scores, whether American or European in origin, but Ó Riada's art music of the time also displays a considerable degree of stylistic diversity. For instance, *Hercules Dux Ferrariæ* (*Nomos No. 1*) for string orchestra, premiered in 1957, is simultaneously based on the solmization of the vowel sounds of the name Hercules Dux Ferrarie (Hercules, Duke of Ferrara) – a process borrowed from the Renaissance composer Josquin's eponymous mass – and on two serial rows.[27] Of the eight movements of this work, the second, third, fifth and seventh adopt a more severely expressionist character (the second and seventh particularly seem to demonstrate the influence of Webern), while the others rely to a greater or lesser extent on tonal models and the application of neo-classical contrapuntal technique. It is illuminating to compare *Nomos No. 1* with another work first performed in 1957, which also alludes to early music practices, Peter Maxwell Davies' *Alma Redemptoris Mater*. While Davies' score draws on the developments of the 1950s European avant-garde, both in terms of complexity of notation and compositional technique (and it is notable that the plainchant melody on which the third movement of this work is based is scarcely perceptible in performance), Ó Riada's work is marked by clarity and simplicity, and harks back to an earlier generation of European composers. There is certainly little in it that is more radical than might be found, for example, in the works of Bartók's American period.

Nomos No. 4 for piano and orchestra, composed between November 1957 and March 1958, and the concert work written immediately before *Mise Éire*, further exemplifies Ó Riada's desire to write contemporary art music in an accessible mode. In this piece, as is the case with most of his serial works, the note row is primarily employed as a melodic matrix, and rows often suggest tonal practice in their internal organization. He is judicious in his use of material and only relatively simple manipulations of the row are found (he was certainly not drawn to the total serialism which was developing in Europe in the 1950s). Equally, his compositions tend to be rhythmically simple, and structurally regular and clear-cut, with frequent employment of repetition and ostinato (both of which were anathema to the 1950s avant-garde).[28] While the serial works are undoubtedly stylistically coherent, they are able to admit external influences, whether in terms of the direct quotation of, or allusion to, other composers' styles or musical ideas.

Although traditional material is suggested or even brought into play in several works of the 1950s (particularly *The Banks of Sullane* and *Seoladh na nGamhan* [*sic*]), it does not appear explicitly in the *Nomos* cycle, and in general Ó Riada does not attempt to assimilate it into his 'art-music' style, as for example, Bartók does. As Dibble notes:

> When Ó Riada died in 1971, after several years of deep depression, he had come no further in establishing elements of a national identity within his home music, and his activities within traditional music still remained only a form of parallel interest. No serious attempt was made to integrate or fuse them, and it is quite likely that he could find no way of doing so intellectually.[29]

The score for *Mise Éire* and post-colonialism

Post-colonial theory concerns itself with the interactions between colonizer and colonized, from the point of colonization through to liberation and beyond. The cultural artefacts of a colony or former colony, including its music, bear witness to these exchanges through the inscription upon them of strategies of appropriation and abrogation of elements of the colonial culture, and of the development of hybridized forms of expression.[30] It should be noted here that the treatment of Ireland in the general run of post-colonial theory is not entirely unproblematic, for although Ireland can be seen as England's first colony, organized colonization was part of a more complex pattern of resettlement across the British Isles.[31] The Irish Roman Catholic Church was itself involved in what could be considered to be quasi-imperial strategies through its missionary work in places such as Africa, Asia, North and South America and Australia; and many 'native' Irish men and women sustained the British colonial project overseas.[32] It is more difficult in the Irish context to draw sharp distinctions between colonizer and colonized in simple ethnic or racial terms than it is, say, in French North Africa or British India; and religion and class can be seen as more significant drivers in the colonial relationship between Britain and Ireland. However, as Malik has pointed out, common characteristics have been identified between the people of Ireland and India since as early as the eighteenth century.[33]

The attempt to demonstrate (or establish) a distinctly 'Irish' culture that differed in significant ways from that of mainland Britain was a key thread in the events leading to the independence of the larger part of Ireland in 1922. The assemblage, throughout the nineteenth century, of relics from earlier periods of Irish history (including the collections of 'ancient music' of Bunting and Petrie), the work of Young Ireland (active between 1843 and 1848) and *Conradh na Gaeilge* (the Gaelic League, established in 1893 to promote the Irish language); and of writers such as Moore, Ferguson, Lady Gregory and Yeats, were all important in this process of the abrogation of the language of the centre. *Mise Éire*, which was produced eleven years after the final declaration of the Irish Republic and Ireland's withdrawal from the Commonwealth in 1948, is a manifestation of the later stages of this process.

The film's opening shots can be taken to symbolize, through the cut between a long-held image of the Irish flag with the words 'Irish Republic' superposed in English, and the tide wiping out footprints in the sand, the erasure of 'the stain of colonial occupation'.[34] Ó Riada places an orchestral setting of the *sean-nós* ('old style') air '*Róisín Dubh*' against the first of these images, a solo horn playing the melody with subtle harmonization (often with a single change of harmony per bar and a restricted harmonic palette) provided by a miasma of tremolando strings. This melody is associated with a complex of texts including a seventeenth-century Gaelic love song and a series of translations of it by Thomas Furlong, Samuel Ferguson and, most significantly in terms of nationalist rhetoric, James Clarence Mangan. In the final verse of Mangan's 'Dark Rosaleen' the protagonist expresses the immortality of his lover in language that takes on an overtly political significance:

> Oh! the Erne shall run red
>   With redundance of blood;
> The earth shall rock beneath our tread,
>   And flames wrap hill and wood;
> And gun-peal and slogan-cry
>   Wake many a glen serene,
> Ere you shall fade, ere you shall die,
>   My Dark Rosaleen!
>   My own Rosaleen!
> The Judgement Hour must first be nigh
> Ere you can fade, ere you can die,
>   My Dark Rosaleen![35]

A version of the melody of '*Róisín Dubh*' appears in *Ár gCeol Féinig* (*Our Own Song and Music*) by Fr. Patrick Walsh (Pádraig Breathnach), whose collections of Gaelic-language folksongs in tonic sol-fa notation were published in the second and third decades of the twentieth century and used as a teaching resource in Irish schools.[36] *Ár gCeol Féinig* and *Ceol ár Sinnsear* (*Music/Song of Our Ancestors*) are still widely used by *sean-nós* singers in Munster[37] and the titles of these books, published in the period depicted in *Mise Éire*, underline the approach taken by the Gaelic League in abrogating the language of England.

Example 7.1   Opening of the melody '*Róisín Dubh*'

Ó Riada's music supports the ideological implications of the title sequence and opening credits – the abrogation of English culture and language – by drawing on a number of musical tropes. The *sean-nós* melody (see Example 7.1), as an artefact derived from the Gaelic tradition, connotes 'authentic native culture', but equally it suggests the notion of freedom itself, through its exploitation of melisma and rubato. However, the use of a western classical orchestra rather than a 'traditional' ensemble of 'Irish' instruments locates the score within the mainstream of European and American art- and film-music, and arguably also confers upon it the bourgeois respectability of the concert hall. Within the conventions of the western art-music tradition, the assignment of '*Róisín Dubh*' to the French horn conjures up standard intracultural musical signifiers of nature, nobility and power.[38]

The opening pitches of the melody form an arpeggiation of an A♭ major triad ($E\flat_4$–C_4–$E\flat_4$–$A\flat_3$), a figure which is fundamentally tonally stable in western art-music terms, and might be taken to intimate strength and fulfilment, or even, if Deryck Cooke's model of musical semantics is allowed, of 'having come home'.[39] The subsequent melodic overshooting of the upper A♭ of the rising arpeggio onto B♭ (see Example 7.1, bar 2), and the elaborate deferral of the resolution of the appoggiatura that results from the extended and rhythmically free inverted turn, intensifies this instant of delayed gratification. While the emphasis placed on this figure, which appears in various permutations six times in the course of the melody, and could be seen in rhetorical terms to connote desire, adds to the almost erotic quality of the cue, Ó Riada's setting of '*Róisín Dubh*' reaches its climax with a IV–I structure that betokens spiritual validation through the invocation of a plagal cadence. The final gesture is a brief quotation from the opening of the air '*Sliabh na mBan*' ('Mountain of the Women'), also played by a solo horn (see Example 7.2). By conjoining these two similarly arpeggiated melodies, Ó Riada draws attention to their musical (as well as political) consanguinity.

Example 7.2   Opening figure from the melody '*Sliabh na mBan*'

Perhaps most importantly, the entire cue provides an overtly *emotional* underpinning to the image of the flag, and suggests to the viewer that what is to follow will be a tale of epic proportions rather than a neutral historical document. It must be remembered that the melody, and its significance as a covert symbol of Ireland, was well known by its audience, and indeed it has been seen by some to offer an alternative Irish national anthem.[40] Nine further cues directly derived from '*Róisín Dubh*' are identified in Table 7.1. These articulate key points in the developing narrative, and often involve the intellectual and literary leaders of the nationalist movement, and of the Gaelic League.

Table 7.1   Cues in *Mise Éire* derived from '*Róisín Dubh*'

Cue no.	Cue starts h:m:s	Narrative	Musical characteristics
1	0:6:23	The foundation of the Gaelic League by Eoin Mac Neill and Douglas Hyde.	Scored for strings, the melody is reduced to its first line played first at the original pitch (with a simplification of the resolution of the appoggiatura), then transposed up a fourth (with an elaboration of the resolution);
2	0:11:14	The appointment of Pádraig Pearse as the editor of the Gaelic League's journal, *The Sword of Light* ('not only an editor but a prophet, an evangelist').	This cue is similar to cue no. 1 above.
3	0:20:21	The sailing of the gunrunning boat the *Asgard*, crewed by by Erskine Childers, Darrell Figgis and Máire Spring Rice, which carried German guns for the Irish Volunteers. The narration compares its arrival at Howth with those described in ancient sagas, where the Fianna awaited the ship's arrival on the land.	An extended version of the previous two cues, with solo woodwinds taking the melody. Tremolando strings, sequential writing and prolongation of the dominant combine to suggest an aspirational atmosphere, and fanfares and side drum figures bring the cue to an end on a military note.
4	0:27:23	The cortege and funeral of the nationalist hero O'Donovan Rossa.	A return to the orchestration and much of the character of the title music, though at a slightly slower tempo.
5	0:47:48	Following the execution of the leaders of the rising.	The first line of the melody, now in the minor mode, is played by strings, and accompanied by harp arpeggios based on the pitches D and A.

Table 7.1 *concluded*

Cue no.	Cue starts h:m:s	Narrative	Musical characteristics
6	0:58:15	The opening of the third part of the film 'Summer has come – ushered in by Sinn Féin'.	The cue begins like the title music, but is terminated with a repeat of the first line of '*Róisín Dubh*' rather than '*Sliabh na mBan*'.
7	1:05:44	The funeral of the hunger striker Tomás Ashe.	A funeral march based on the first four pitches of the melody (5–3–5–1) in the minor key.
8	1:08:07	The march of the Volunteers to Smithfield following Ashe's interment.	Like the previous cue, this is initially based on the four-note opening arpeggiation sequentially developed, but now in the major mode. It finishes with an incomplete statement of the first line of the melody in the horn, and an assertive timpani figure.
9	1:23:29	Michael Collins' oratory during the general election and the closing images of the sea.	The climax of an almost Sibelian process of accumulation of energy by repetition of a nine-note figure ($E\flat$–F–$E\flat$/$G\flat$–$E\flat$/$A\flat$–$B\flat$–C/$D\flat$). The melody is scored for full orchestra with a predictable (in terms of nineteenth-century western art music) diatonic harmonization. A massive plagal cadence brings the film to a close on a note of religious finality.

Ó Riada's use of '*Róisín Dubh*' (and the other Irish melodies in the score) may seem indicative of an essentially conservative and conventional approach to the exploitation of traditional material within a western art-music context, not particularly out of line with that of Irish composers from the Protestant and Unionist tradition, such as Stanford and Harty. It is arguable, however, that his selection of a melody whose configuration stems more directly from the vernacular of the *Gaeltacht* (the Gaelic-speaking areas of Ireland) albeit mediated through Walsh, and his generally subtle harmonization, which schematically supports the slow air in line with the type of accompaniment Bartók referred to as 'the mounting of a jewel', locates it as an act of post-colonial appropriation, and thereby perhaps of reinterpretation, even repatriation, of the colonial forms of 'Irish national music' propagated on behalf of the imperial centre by composers who often saw themselves as equally British and Irish.[41] One might also contend that it demonstrates the hybridity that is 'a primary characteristic of all post-colonial texts'.[42]

The film's second cue follows the recitation of a prescient stanza from '*Aithbe dam bés mora*':

> The incoming wave,
> And the retreating wave ebbing.
> The thing that the flowing wave gives you
> The ebbing wave will take from your hand.[43]

It accompanies the image of footsteps in the sand being erased by the tide and photographs of Ireland's early material culture, and sets a markedly different tone. Given the character of the title sequence, it might have been expected that Ó Riada would have continued to underscore these symbols of Ireland's liberty and antiquity with music which, like '*Róisín Dubh*', connotes the 'heroic'; but instead he draws on the modernist language of his art music, and presents a fragmentary, atonal cue that bristles with grating flutter-tonguing in the flutes, brash three-note trumpet figures and abrupt xylophone interjections. It is undoubtedly disturbing and disconcerting music, and makes few concessions to its audience.

Further modernist cues are found in strategic positions throughout the score, often accompanying images of violence or devastation and associated with Ulster Unionism or British rule. If the ones based on traditional music seem to be concerned with simple affirmation, these often appear to express negation and alienation (Table 7.2). Although it might be argued that these cues draw on modernist gestures in much the same way that Hollywood has, since the early days of sound film, used the avant-garde as a source of conventionalized and stereotypical markers for fear, horror, anxiety, power, and so on, here they demonstrate a formal and expressive integrity that sets them apart from the rather cruder examples of musical signification, suggested, for example, by Frank Skinner in his film composition treatise *Underscore*, or more recently by Karlin and Wright in *On the Track* (where they note that 'twelve tone technique … is often used by composers for moments of tangled texture and stress').[44] They were, after all, written in what was Ó Riada's vernacular, and were not simply the application of a technique as a stylistic signifier.[45] Helen Tiffin has remarked that:

> Post-colonial cultures are inevitably hybridised, involving a dialectical relationship between European ontology and epistemology and the impulse to create or recreate independent local identity. Decolonisation is process, not arrival; it invokes an ongoing dialectic between hegemonic centrist systems and peripheral subversion of them; between European or British discourses and their post-colonial dis/mantling

Table 7.2   Modernist cues in *Mise Éire*

Cue no.	Cue starts h:m:s	Narrative	Musical characteristics
1	0:14:31	The Ulster loyalists are described as having 'unwittingly lighted a living fire' by pledging themselves in 'solemn covenant' against home rule.	A figure with an incisive syncopated rhythm gradually builds up through the pitches Ab_4–G_5–Eb_5 | Ab_4–G_5–Eb_5–$F\sharp_5$ | Ab_4–G_5–Eb_5–$F\sharp_5$–B_5, a similar strategy of accumulation to the one Ó Riada exploits in the final section of *Nomos No. 4* (from bar 179 onwards). This figure can be seen to function as the complement to the 'Sibelian' process discussed above in Table 7.1, cue 9.
2	0:17:30	In the scene that precedes the gunrunning activities of the *Asgard*, the narrator describes weapons being brought from Hamburg to the Antrim Port of Larne for use by the Protestant Ulster Volunteer Force.	Material from the cue described in cue 1 above is extended by crosscutting it with a march-like modal idea played by the brass section.
3	0:30:00	Images of the First World War and of the death of Irish men on the battlefields of France.	A searing lament increasingly dominated by non-harmony notes, played by unison violins, supported by a $G\sharp$ minor triad in the brass.
4	0:37:18	The British army takes over the command positions previously held by the Irish Volunteers.	Quiet strings slowly build up an intense, wraithlike chord in high register ($D\sharp_6$–E_6–A_6–$F\sharp_5$–F_5), the piccolo adding emphasis to the top A, a harmonic process that bears comparison with the sixth movement (*lento*) of *Nomos No. 1*. The use of cymbals to articulate sixteen slow regular pulses is a particularly disconcerting and alienating touch.
5	0:39:17	Military rule having been enforced, the narrator comments on the loneliness of	Ó Riada evokes both Webern's orchestral miniatures and Bartók's night music, the

Table 7.2   *concluded*

Cue no.	Cue starts h:m:s	Narrative	Musical characteristics
		the city 'now once again under the domination of her imperial conqueror her citizens driven from the central streets they normally thronged'.	material returning to the spirit of the second cue, and involving the interaction of fragmentary motifs and brief repeating figures. The use of rasping flutter-tonguing in the flutes, incisive punctuation by the xylophone, and sudden shifts of register and dynamic combine to establish a sense of dislocation and disorder.
6	0:43:43	The nadir of the Easter Rising, the execution of its leadership, lying at the centre of the film.	This is one of the longest cues in the film, and draws on material which involves common musical topics for death: for each of the executions, drum rolls and minor triads played by the brass in a funereal dotted rhythm precede the gunshot, and a series of intense rising figures ensues, played by bass instruments echoed by high dissonant tremolandi passages played by upper strings. The model here would seem to be Shostakovich at his most mordant.

[*sic.*]. Since it is not possible to create or recreate national or regional formations wholly independent of their historical implication in the European colonial enterprise, it has been the project of post-colonial writing to interrogate European discourses and discursive strategies from a privileged position within (and between) two worlds.[46]

Seán Ó Riada, as a western art-music composer and academic on one hand, and as a traditional musician on the other, found himself in just such a privileged position within and between the two musical worlds of Europe and Ireland. In his score for *Mise Éire* he does not attempt to integrate or synthesize the traditional Irish and modernist European elements into a seamless whole. Instead, he juxtaposes heterogeneous constituents to form a kind of postmodern patchwork, which challenges as much as reinforces Morrison's unified linear narrative. The constant changes of emotional register that result from the shifts between the different types of musical material simultaneously underline and undermine the film's role as republican propaganda. Indeed the discontinuities in the score could be seen to mirror the ideological tension inherent in the struggle for an independent country that simultaneously looked backward to an idealized and mythologized Gaelic Ireland, and forward to a modern state, and, for at least some of those involved in the Easter Rising a socialist one.[47] In Pádraig Pearse's poem 'Mise Éire', Ireland speaks of her antiquity and former glory, but also of her shame and loneliness – affirmation and repudiation being the two sides of the same coin. Although Ó Riada's score does ultimately support a positive vision, it admits music that equally betokens alienation, ironic detachment and despair. This, I would suggest, mirrors in artistic terms the reality of the post-colonial state: in which absence is as important as presence; in which the modern and the ancient sit together, but not always comfortably; and in which the 'margins' simultaneously dismantle and replicate the processes and norms of the 'centre'.

Notes

1. Pearse, P. *Plays, Stories, Poems*, Dublin: Talbot Press, 1966, 323. Pearse's reference is to the poem 'The Lament of the Old Woman of Beare'. See Meyer, K. *Ancient Irish Poetry*, London: Constable & Company Ltd, 1913, 90–93.
2. The Roman Catholic Church in Ireland is characterized by a distinctly Marianist ethos.
3. Ó Buachalla, S. *The Literary Writings of Patrick Pearse*, Dublin, Cork: The Mercier Press Ltd, 1979, 28.
4. Longley, E. *The Living Stream*, Newcastle upon Tyne: Bloodaxe Books, 1994, 72–3.
5. Pronounced approximately as 'Mishuh Ayruh'.
6. See O'Brien, H. 'Projecting the Past: historical documentary in Ireland', *Historical Journal of Film, Radio and Television*, **20** (3), 2000, 335–50.
7. Cavalcanti moved to England in 1933, and joined John Grierson's unit at the GPO the following year.
8. Rockett, K. 'Documentaries', in Rockett, K., Gibbons, L. and Hill, J. (eds) *Cinema and Ireland*, London: Routledge, 1987, 86.
9. The third part was never commissioned. Harris, B. and Freyer, G. (eds), *Integrating Tradition: The Achievement of Seán Ó Riada*, Terrybaun, Bofeenaun and Ballina: Irish Humanities Centre and Keohanes, 1981, 70. *Saoirse* is approximately pronounced as 'seershuh'.
10. *Irish Times*, 9 April, 1965, 11. Cited by Rocket, K. 'Documentaries', 86–7.
11. Rocket K. 'Documentaries', 87.
12. O'Brien, H. 'Projecting the Past', 336.
13. Morrison, G. 'Film Making', in Harris and Freyer, *Integrating Tradition*, 69.
14. Quotations from *Mise Éire* are all taken from the unpublished and unofficial translation very kindly supplied by Máire Harris of Gael Linn.
15. O'Brien, H. 'Projecting the Past', 336.
16. Victory, G. 'Ó Riada on Radio', in Harris and Freyer, *Integrating Tradition*, 56.
17. In fact, the manuscript of the score of *Nomos No. 4* (1958) gives his name as John Reidy, while the 1959 score of *Seoladh na nGamhan* (*sic*) is signed Seán Ó Riada by the composer. According to Tomás Ó Canainn the Irish version of his name appeared on the Abbey Theatre Christmas pantomimes from 1955. *Seán Ó Riada: His Life and Work*, Wilton: The Collins Press, 2003, 42.

18. This and subsequent information in this paragraph is taken from Morrison, G. 'Film Making', 65–6.
19. The offstage music found in Kabuki has a highly developed semantics and semiotics, and it has been suggested that it is used in an analogous way to film music. See Malm, W.P. 'Kabuki', in *Grove Music Online*, ed. L. Macy, http://www.grovemusic.com (accessed 26 November 2003).
20. Morrison, G. 'Film Making', 66.
21. White, H. *The Keeper's Recital*, Cork: Cork University Press, 1998, 126.
22. Ibid., 148.
23. Ibid., 149. White's use of the expression 'ethnic repertory' has resulted in some criticism.
24. Ibid., 146.
25. Dibble, J. 'Musical Nationalism in Ireland in the Twentieth Century: Complexities and Contradictions', in T. Mäkelä (ed.) *Music and Nationalism in 20th Century Great Britain and Finland*, Hamburg: von Bockel Verlag, 1997, 142.
26. *Mise Éire*, Gael-Linn, CEFCD 080.
27. The tenor in Josquin's mass *Hercules Dux Ferrariæ*, the apparent model for the solmization in this piece, is based on the pitches D–C–D–C–D–F–E–D (vowel sounds from the sequence Re-Ut–Re–Ut–Re–Fa–Mi–Re, Hercules Dux Ferrarie). Presumably for musical reasons Ó Riada reverses the pattern to the solmization of Ferrarie Dux Hercules.
28. It is worth remembering that Ó Riada described the term *Nomos* as 'implying a piece "pledged to a basic scheme and to basic ornaments"'. Bodley, S. 'The Original Compositions', in Harris and Freyer, *Integrating Tradition*, 32.
29. Dibble, J. 'Musical Nationalism in Ireland in the Twentieth Century', 143.
30. For a detailed discussion of post-colonial theory in the context of literature, see Ashcroft, B., Griffiths, G. and Tiffin, H. (eds) *The Empire Writes Back: Theory and Practice in Post-Colonial Literatures*, London: Routledge, 1989.
31. Some anecdotal evidence for this is suggested by a survey published in 2001, in which up to 25 per cent of the population of Great Britain claimed to have some Irish ancestry. See http://news.bbc.co.uk/1/hi/uk/1224611.stm (accessed 22 February 2003).
32. Fintan O'Toole writes of the map of the world which appeared on the back of his Christian Brothers school copybook: 'At the centre of this world was Ireland, and arcing out of Ireland like shooting stars were lines leading to Australia, North America, Argentina, Africa – the contours of a spiritual conquest that had begun in 1802 when Edmund Ignatius Rice founded the Christian Brothers … It was our Empire.' 'Our Boys', in *The Ex-Isle of Erin*, Dublin: New Island Books, 1997, 75. See also Liam O'Dowd's introduction to Memmi, A. *The Colonizer and the Colonized*, trans. H. Greenfeld, London: Earthscan Publications Ltd, 1990, 49.
33. Malik, I.H. 'Ireland Orientalism and South Asia', *Asian Affairs*, **32** (2), 2001, 189–94.
34. O'Brien, H. 'Projecting the Past', 337.
35. *Walton's Treasury of Irish Songs and Ballads*, Dublin: Walton's Musical Instrument Galleries Ltd, 1947, 69.
36. Dublin: Brown & Nolan, 1920. See O'Sullivan, D. *Songs of the Irish*, New York: Bonanza Books, 1960, 194.
37. Lillis Ó Laoire, private email communication.
38. Horn calls or their imitation have been widely used by western art-music composers to reference heroism, a particularly familiar example, which also involves a prominent falling arpeggiation, being Siegfried's horn leitmotif from Wagner's

Siegfried. See my discussion of the theorization of meaning in film scores in *Bernard Herrmann's Vertigo: A Film Score Handbook*, Westport: Greenwood Press, 2001, 61–6.

39. Cooke, D. *The Language of Music*, Oxford: Oxford University Press, 1959, 130. It is significant that Ó Riada did not choose to use one in a more clichéd 'Irish' mode such as the Dorian.

40. This point was made by Lillis Ó Laoire (private communication).

41. Bartók, B. 'The Relationship Between Contemporary Hungarian Art Music and Folk Music' in B. Suchoff (ed.), *Béla Bartók Essays*, Lincoln and London: University of Nebraska Press, 1976, 351.

42. Ashcroft et al., *The Empire Writes Back*, 185.

43. I would like to thanks Lillis Ó Laoire for this translation.

44. Skinner, F. *Underscore*, New York: Criterion Music Corp, 1950. Karlin, F. and Wright, R. *On the Track: A Guide to Contemporary Film Scoring*, New York and London: Schirmer Books, 1990, 228.

45. This is not to suggest that film composers working in Hollywood (for example Leonard Rosenman) were not able to retain their modernist vernaculars.

46. Tiffin, H. 'Post-Colonial Literatures and Counter-Discourse', *Kunapipi*, **9** (3), 1987, 17–34.

47. One of the other leaders of the rising, Scottish-born James Connolly, was a leading Marxist, a trade unionist, and founder of the Irish Socialist Workers Party. Although he was a Catholic, and regarded Protestantism as capitalism in the sphere of religion, he wrote of the co-operation that would exist between workers of all religious persuasions after the overthrow of the capitalist system. See 'Labour, Nationality and Religion' in Berresford Ellis, P. (ed.) *James Connolly: Selected Writings*, Harmondsworth: Penguin Books, 1973, 57–117. The Gaelic League, of which Pearse was a leader, was founded in 1893 by the Protestant Douglas Hyde, with the espoused purpose of de-Anglicizing Ireland through the restoration of, in particular, the Irish language. Of the many Irish artists influenced by the Gaelic League, perhaps the most familiar is W.B. Yeats, another Protestant, Anglo-Irish writer, whose writings drew extensively on Irish mythology.

Chapter 8

Angel of the air: Popol Vuh's music and Werner Herzog's films

K.J. Donnelly

Florian was always able to create music I feel helps audiences visualize something hidden in the images on screen, and in our own souls too. In *Aguirre* I wanted a choir that would sound out of this world, like when I would walk at night as a child, thinking that the stars were singing, so Florian used a very strange instrument called a 'choir-organ' ...[1]

The sleevenotes to one of Popol Vuh's film soundtrack albums suggests that 'it is through the sensual experience of the music that the audience grasps the intentions of the director for the first time'.[2] German group Popol Vuh's music found a fitting place in the films of Werner Herzog, one of the leading lights of the 'New German Cinema' in the 1960s and 1970s. Indeed, Werner Herzog's films betray an intense interest in music more generally. In *Letzte Worte* (*Last Words*, 1967) there is a lyre-playing leper, while in *Fata Morgana* (1971) we hear an electronically enhanced folk song sung by a young girl in a cave. *Land des Schweigens und des Dunkelheit* (*Land of Silence and Darkness*, 1971) includes the cutting-in of some of Hanns Eisler's score for *Nuit et Bruillard* (*Night and Fog*, 1955), while in *Jeder für sich und Gott gegen alle* (*The Enigma of Kaspar Hauser*, 1974) there is music by Lassus, Mozart, Albinoni and Pachelbel. *La Soufrière* (1977) couples Wagner and Rachmaninoff to aerial shots of the volcano, while in *Stroszek* (1977) there is American country music and Bruno S's unique musical performances. *Fitzcarraldo* (1981) opens and closes with opera, while *Wo die grünen Ameisen träumen* (*Where the Green Ants Dream*, 1984) also includes opera and even has a recurring song sung by the Australian Aborigine pilot ('My Baby Does the Hanky-panky').[3] In addition to all these musical moments, Herzog's films have used the highly singular music of German group Popol Vuh to add another dimension to his highly individualized films, and Florian Fricke even appeared on screen in *Lebenszeichen* (*Signs of Life*, 1968) and *Jeder für sich und Gott gegen alle*.

Werner Herzog

During the 1990s, Werner Herzog worked mainly on documentaries although he is still best known for the series of feature films he made during the 1970s and early 1980s. Uniquely, he managed to reach a sizeable public with these films despite their very personal nature. Herzog's feature films often focus on an 'outsider' figure who makes a massive effort to break free from dominant conventions[4] and they pose profound questions concerning achievement, humanity, human nature and cultural difference. Some of these films are set in exotic locations that are problematic for both on-screen characters and the filmmakers. The use of such locations proves Herzog to be one of the primary film directors to have a deep feeling for landscapes. Often foregrounded, the natural settings of his films, including his documentaries, seem to resonate with mythic and philosophical associations. In fact, Herzog's films seem to suggest that we all inhabit private, dream-like worlds connected to our crucial spiritual dimension. This ties his interests to the tradition of German Romanticism. Brigitte Peucker notes that, 'more than any current writer, and certainly more than any current filmmaker, Werner Herzog is the profoundest and most authentic heir of the Romantic tradition at work today'.[5]

Herzog was born in 1942 as Werner Stipetic, assuming the more aristocratic nom de plume (Herzog means duke) when he became a writer and filmmaker. He had something of an exotic life of travel and varied work and study, including television work for NASA and working in a steel mill. However, we should be wary of the stories surrounding Herzog's life, just as we should be wary of the stories about the gargantuan problems encountered during filming for, as Thomas Elsaesser notes, Herzog is the consummate self-publicist.[6]

Herzog's first film was *Fata Morgana* (1968–70), which included a narrator reading from the Popol Vuh (the Guatemalan creation myth), while its soundtrack included an eclectic mix of Handel, Mozart, Leonard Cohen and rock supergroup Blind Faith. Herzog went on to direct *Auch Zwerge haben klein angefangen* (*Even Dwarfs Started Small*, 1970) and *Land des Schweigens und der Dunkelheit* (1971). His first feature film, *Aguirre, der Zorn Gottes* (*Aguirre, Wrath of God*, 1973), starring Klaus Kinski, and *Der grosse Ekstase des Boldschnitzers Steiner* (*The Great Ecstasy of Woodcutter Steiner*, 1973–74) both had music by Popol Vuh. The latter was made as a documentary for German television and used Popol Vuh's evocative music to accompany sequences of Steiner ski-jumping in slow motion. After *Jeder für sich und Gott gegen alle* (1974), starring the highly singular Bruno S, Herzog again returned to Popol Vuh for the music for *Herz aus Glas* (*Heart of Glass*, 1976). After making *Stroszek* (1976–77), which again starred Bruno S, and *Woyzeck* (1978), after a Georg Buechner fragment and starring Kinski, Herzog used Popol Vuh to supply the music for his next three feature films: *Nosferatu – Phantom der Nacht* (*Nosferatu the Vampyre*, 1978), *Fitzcarraldo* (1981), *Wo die grünen Ameisen träumen* (1984) and *Cobra Verde* (1987). All apart from *Wo die grünen Ameisen träumen* starred Klaus Kinski, with whom Herzog had a fruitful yet fraught relationship, as illustrated by his documentary film *Mein liebster Feind – Klaus Kinski* (*My Best Fiend*, 1999).

Popol Vuh

Recording artists Popol Vuh were named after the Guatemalan Quiche Mayan Indian holy manuscript. Although the group included significant input from other members, Popol Vuh was led by and cohered around pianist, singer, composer and producer Florian Fricke, who was born at Lake Constance in 1944, and died in 2001. He had received a classical training at Freiburg University, and was taught by Rudolf Hindemith, brother of the more famous Paul. Fricke trained as a pianist but gave up on such a career, and acquired a synthesizer in 1969 after being introduced to electronic music by Eberhard Schoener.[7] Indeed, Fricke was one of the first individual musicians in Europe to have possession of one, a Moog,[8] and it became a central feature of the early Popol Vuh music, played by both Fricke and Frank Fiedler. At the outset, Popol Vuh were informed by late 1960s experimentation and technological developments, and the group's music exhibited a growing influence from diverse music from across the globe, spurred on by Fricke's youthful travels. At this time, German pop and rock music was beginning to carve out a place and identity for itself, and began to be known abroad as 'Krautrock'.[9]

Krautrock might be seen as the pop/rock music equivalent of the developments in German film that are called the 'New German Cinema'. It manifested an attempt to create a localized form of the dominant British-American forms of popular music. As in other European countries, Germany had pop groups and rock bands that played music that owed its whole existence to the internationalized format. Krautrock, on the other hand, took inspiration from and attempted to integrate certain aspects of avant-garde and experimental music, both in classical music as well as jazz. This included an embracing of new technology by synthesizer groups Tangerine Dream, Kraftwerk and Klaus Schulze (the producer of Popol Vuh's *Sei Still, wisse ICH BIN*), the eclecticism of Can, the noise experimentalism of Faust, and other, more rock-based groups like Amon Düül II, Neu! and Ash Ra Tempel. Almost all of these groups had little commercial success, and indeed, few thought in such terms. The groups that assembled under the Krautrock umbrella had little in common apart from the fact that they developed very individual indigenous responses to international rock music.[10]

While Krautrock tended to explore the limits of progressive rock, it had much less of an emphasis on virtuoso musicianship as evinced by British progressive rock groups like Emerson, Lake and Palmer, or Yes. They also eschewed the borrowing and allusions to established classical music evident with these groups, and instead demonstrated an interest in sound and rhythm inspired partially by electronic music and the avant-garde. It is absolutely impossible to disintricate Popol Vuh's film music from their wider *oeuvre*. Their music for films is merely an aspect of the particular developments of their singular musical philosophy. Their overall output includes their film music as an integral aspect, and Table 8.1 lists all their recorded output, noting the soundtrack albums.

Table 8.1   Popul Vuh discography

Year	Title
1970	*Affenstunde*
1971	*In den Gärten Pharaos*
1972	*Hosianna Mantra*
1973	*Seligpreisung*
1974	*Einsjäger & Siebenjäger*
	Aguirre (soundtrack)
1975	*Das Hohelied Salomos*
	Die Erde und Ich Sind Eins (limited edition album, Florian Fricke only)
1976	*Letze Tage – Letze Nächte*
	Yoga
	Herz Aus Glas (soundtrack)
1978	*On the Way to a Little Way – Nosferatu* (soundtrack on Egg records)
	Brüder des Schattens – Söhne des Lichts (*Nosferatu*) (soundtrack on Spalax records)
1979	*Die Nacht Der Seele – Tantric Songs*
1981	*Sei Still, Wisse ICH BIN*
1982	*Fitzcarraldo* (soundtrack)
	Agape – Agape
1985	*Spirit of Peace*
1987	*Cobra Verde* (soundtrack)
1991	*For You and Me*
1995	*City Raga*
1997	*Shepherd's Symphony*
1998	*Messa di Orfeo* (live album)

Some notable characteristics of Popol Vuh's music include a concentration on timbre. While it might be argued that some of their sound derives from western classical music, their instrumentation was not orchestral, nor was it the classic pop/rock band line-up. Fricke played keyboards, often piano, and provided some vocals. The group used a synthesizer very prominently on the first two albums, but afterwards tended to use a selection of more traditional instruments. After the first album, Popol Vuh included a guitarist (at first Conny Veit and then Daniel Fichelscher) as accompaniment for Fricke, sometimes a female singer (Djong Yun, Renate Knaup), sometimes a sitar player (Al[ois] Gromer), and occasional other instruments such as percussion (although not a drum kit) and oboes. The combination of timbres never sounds like pop music, rarely sounds like rock music, and often sounds more like folk music from some far away, exotic but indistinct place.

As well as using the very distinctive and otherwordly sounds of the Moog synthesizer, Popol Vuh also used another keyboard instrument, the Mellotron (what Herzog referred to in the opening quotation as the 'choir-organ'). This had a number of recorded tapes of sounds including strings, choirs and woodwinds, looped and triggered by a conventional keyboard to produce sustained sounds. The Mellotron had first been produced in the late 1940s by small Canadian company called Chamberlin, although it was only with the advent of more adventurous pop/rock music in the late 1960s that its haunting and unexpectedly distinct sound became more prominent. It was featured to great effect on recordings such as The Beatles' 'Strawberry Fields Forever' from 1967 and King Crimson's 'Epitaph' from *In the Court of the Crimson King* (released 1969).[11]

Another notable characteristic of the group's music would be its general lack of drama in favour of more gentle calm serenity. This makes their output highly atmospheric, and engages a spiritual dimension. Consequently, it was particularly suited to films that required an added dimension of feeling, but not music that would provide kinesis and dynamics for the screen action. Indeed, the group's pieces usually tend to have regular rhythmic and temporal structures, being based often upon four beats to the bar and strophes of four, eight or sixteen bars. Again in terms of form, there is little sense of thematic or material development in the music, which is based more on repetition and gradual unfolding. There is equally little sense of alternation of musical material and no evidence of the verse–chorus song formats that have dominated popular music. In reality, Popol Vuh did not really produce songs in the popular music sense; most of their vocal pieces could better be described as chants. This demonstrates how far they were influenced by religious and ritual music and keeps them a firm distance from any connection with the mainstream of pop and rock music.

During the course of the group's development, they went through a number of changes, in philosophy as well as in personnel. On each occasion, Popul Vuh pioneered or at least foreshadowed significant later developments in music. At first, they were a group premised upon the use of synthesizers. Upon Fricke's conversion to Christianity, the use of electronics was halted and a significant influence from choral religious music imported to their style. For example, *Hosianna Mantra* (1972) is religious and acoustic in character. It includes a *Kyrie* and is quietly devotional with Djong Yun's vocals and Fricke's piano to the fore. A number of the 1970s releases were settings of religious texts. Increasingly during the 1970s, Popol Vuh began drawing inspiration from diverse types of folk music, foreshadowing the explosion of interest in 'world music' during the 1980s and 1990s. The sense of calm and serenity in their music made them a precursor to the development of 'new age' and relaxation music from the mid-1980s onwards, testified to by Fricke becoming a member of the Society for Breathing Therapy in the late 1970s. As the group reached old age they showed an influence from electronic dance music, which was the only occasion where they were not the ground-breaker for a particular musical trend, as evidenced on *City Raga* (1995) by the inclusion of a 'Mystic House remix' of the title track.

While it would be wrong to construe Popol Vuh's music as a negative reaction to the Hollywood blueprint of film music, we should see it as an attempt to generate a different type of music for films that have a profoundly different character from mainstream Hollywood feature films. Rather than write music for the rough cut of the film, their film music often consisted of pieces written for the film before and during production, along with remixes and re-recordings of already existing pieces, in both cases cut in concert with the film rather than written to match the exigencies of the film's découpage. Herzog's films exhibit some defining technical aspects. As well as being concerned with dreamy aspects, they also embrace a sense of realism. They are predominantly shot on location and thus privilege a notion of capturing a 'real' profilmic event. This Bazinian position[12] leads to a regime of slow cutting and spectacle (that is thus guaranteed as a 'real' profilmic event), allied to a 'primitive' film style, which matches jagged, and at times seemingly 'amateurish', edits with simple and basic camerawork derived from a more *cinéma verité* documentary-style. Herzog notes that *Aguirre, der Zorn Gottes* moves 'between what is almost documentary-style filming and these highly stylized frozen stills'.[13] Discussing the same film, Holly Rogers notes that what she calls 'musical stills' dominate, and that Popol Vuh's music provides 'an aural elongation of the terrifying static images'.[14]

Through expediency, Herzog's spectacular visual style requires a form of musical accompaniment that will not interfere with the expression of the 'real', or become a functional part of a standardized form of narration, like most film music. Popol Vuh's film scoring, while not requiring the discipline and craft of traditional film music is thus more autonomous, more an object in itself than music that (in theory) can only have integrity when combined with the image for which it was constructed. Like songs imported to films, the musical pieces retain a sense of their own organic unity and inner coherence as recordings that are able to exist outside the confines of the film. They are thus more 'listening' music than 'accompanying' music, which, of course, marks a radical difference from the dominant traditions of music in narrative film established by Hollywood, or, indeed, much other cinema. Popol Vuh and Herzog are indifferent to film music traditions. Popol Vuh's music is not functional in the sense of being matched to action, screen dynamics or providing informational 'cues' for the audience, instead it is wielded precisely for effect, for furnishing thick atmosphere rather than anything else. As such, it is not really structural, and not functional in the sense of developmental film music that retains a consistent presence, but is more a momentary object, entering the foreground and then receding, leaving whole swathes of the film free of musical accompaniment, yet making those sections that contain music into something significant. Thus the music appears almost like a discrete attraction rather than as an integral part of the film. It infuses significant moments with an added dimension of atmosphere and emotion, lifting Herzog's already striking images onto a higher plane of aesthetic contemplation. Indeed, it is most commonly used for sequences of visual spectacle with no dialogue – converting film atavistically into the sort of poetic visual-musical spectacle of some silent cinema that existed before the advent of synchronized recorded sound, particularly the acclaimed film works of directors such as Sergei Eisenstein and Abel Gance.

The feature films

Popol Vuh's music for *Aguirre, der Zorn Gottes* consists simply of the same few pieces cut into the film. Three principal themes dominate: the first is the opening of the track '*Lacrimae di re*', which is known simply as *Aguirre* on some recordings; another is the second section of the same piece; while the third is a quiet guitar-dominated piece. The opening of '*Lacrimae di re*' accompanies the celebrated opening of the film, where a long line of *conquistadores*, Peruvian Indians and llamas snakes slowly across a misty mountain. This is shown in a single take with the camera moving to embrace the whole convoy in both long-shot and close-up. This spectacular scene is accompanied by highly ethereal music. It consists of a Mellotron choral sound playing high-pitched chords, punctuated by an echo-repeat on electric guitar that marks out the second and third beats of each bar of 4/4. There is a *rubato* feeling to the rhythm, where strict time and co-ordination between the instruments is not enforced. The length of the opening sequence is about three and a half minutes with almost no dialogue (only a short voiceover where the volume of music is temporarily reduced) allowing full rein to the combined audiovisual spectacle of the remarkable images and music. This discrete sequence, marked by music finishes with a sudden explosion as a cannon falls into the river. This same piece is simply cut in again later for the sequence where Guzman (who has been dubbed 'King of El Dorado') weeps, literalizing the Latin title of the piece of music.

The second theme appears on recordings as the second section of '*Lacrimae di re*', where there is a *segue*, a rather rough transition, between two pieces of music of distinct character. This consists of deep Mellotron choral chords with aimless and modest guitar improvisations over the top of them, and is of about three minutes' length. This piece appears as an accompaniment for the entourage's movement through the jungle. Near the start of the film, there is a sustained and startling shot of rough waters that is highly static and takes on something of an abstract appearance. This is accompanied by another theme by Popol Vuh, which consists of a lone electric guitar playing a slow improvisatory succession of two- and three-note chords while using a volume pedal/control to remove the attack (and thus the defining quality of the timbre) to each note and chord. This same theme also appears as accompaniment for a scene of the entourage's women at a camp by the river, a sequence where a previously-noble slave talks to Aguirre's daughter, and for scenes with the raft on the river. The ethnic and ethnographic concerns of the film are apparent during a short long-take sequence that simply 'captures' an Indian playing the pan pipes on screen as Aguirre listens. Popol Vuh's music in *Aguirre* marks the film out as very different from mainstream feature films. The opening sequence is stylistically as well as sensually remarkable, premised as it is upon dramatic long takes (including one of over a minute and a half) in long-shot and handheld close-up shots of the entourage walking past the camera. This is moved onto the transcendent plane by Popol Vuh's music, which has a distinctly religious character through sounding like an uncannily defamiliarized church choir.

Herzog and Popol Vuh also worked together on *Die Große Ekstase des Bildschnitzers Steiner* (*The Great Ecstasy of Woodcarver Steiner*, 1974), with their music accompanying the ski-jumping shots, interrupting the silence. William van Wert noted: 'The Popol Vuh score for *Steiner* … seems to shadowbox with the visuals; it drops off when the jumpers soar, it rises in crescendo when they fall.'[15] This suggests something of the individual way that Herzog uses Popol Vuh's music; not to heighten tension in the mainstream sense of film music, but essentially to cut across the image and add a sense of emotional and spiritual depth.

Herz aus Glas[16] alternates Popol Vuh music with historically accurate songs performed by the Studio der Frühen Musik (early music specialists). This alternation is evident in the film's memorable opening (and title) sequence, which runs for seven and a half minutes before any real engagement with the film's narrative. The Studio der Frühen Musik provide an unaccompanied choral song, which includes some short and rather odd yodelling vocalizations. While it is wordless, it has something of the character of a *Sanctus*, based around tonic and dominant harmony. This accompanies a shot of a visionary called Hias. As he sits, we see shots of cows, mountains, mist and clouds (some in fast motion). The music then fades out for a voiceover monologue about 'seeing'. This is just after four minutes of this opening sequence. Then there are shots of a waterfall, quite static, also through muslin/gauze across the camera lens, which furnishes an effect of making the image look like oil painting on canvas. This visual abstraction is reminiscent of the succession of shots of turbulent waters to Popol Vuh's music near the start of *Aguirre*. The waterfall shot is accompanied by Popol Vuh music comprising a sheen of electric guitars that set up a rhythmic and timbral density that is monochordal, without modulation. This is music as texture rather than the more traditional sense of music as melody and harmony. After over a minute of this, the music's volume is turned down for another, shorter monologue voiceover on top of the music. Once this finishes, the music's volume is resumed as it accompanies more mountains and clouds shots, and about thirty seconds after the start of the voiceover a guitar solo over repeated electric guitar backing ensues. However, this is a long way from the sort of melodic, screaming, blues-based electric guitar solo beloved of progressive rock bands at this time.[17] It appears more aimless and refuses to build a melody upon which to provide variations, or to show off instrumental virtuosity. This is less an indication of a musical strategy for use in film than it is a confirmation of Popol Vuh's conscious lack of engagement with popular music tradition more generally. The music's rhythm becomes a much more insistent and swinging 12/8 beat during the guitar solo, while harmony of the repetitious chiming guitar backing alternates between the notes of two chords. This piece is available on disc in a different version as 'Die Umkehr' on the Nosferatu soundtrack album Brüder des Schattens – Söhne des Lichts. The film's opening minutes are an unambiguous instance of Popol Vuh's music being used to express visionary aspects, engaging beyond standard sound and vision, which is precisely how Herzog has exploited Popol Vuh's music in most of his films. The music is not structurally integrated with Herz aus Glas as a whole and merely proves to be a momentary diversion, helping to elevate this sequence onto a poetic level before the film's engagement with dialogue and narrative.

Nosferatu – Phantom der Nacht was Herzog's first big budget feature film, co-produced by Gaumont (France) and distributed by 20th Century Fox. The film recontextualizes some existing pieces, such a Gounod's Sanctus from Messe Solennelle as Jonathan Harker rides into the distance, and Wagner's Rheingold overture as Harker passes through spectacular scenery on the way to the castle, and as Nosferatu first arrives in Bremen. In terms of Popol Vuh music, the film uses a number of pieces, some especially written and others developed from earlier pieces of music already released on disc.

The opening of the film showcases two principal Popol Vuh pieces, both of which appear on Tantric Songs (1979) as well as on soundtrack albums. Nosferatu opens with shots of a mausoleum. This is accompanied by the opening of Brüder des Schattens – Söhne des Lichts (Brothers of Shadow – Sons of Light), comprising medieval chanting based on two notes a tone apart, increasingly supported and overridden by other instruments, most notably oboes and cymbals. There is a conspicuous resonance and emphasis of overtones on the sustained second note. This repetitive opening leads to a more orchestral sounding interlude, led by a melancholy duet of oboes (and sounding medieval, Germanic and vaguely Wagnerian), along with some punctuating by short Mellotron chords and percussion. This is not typical of Popol Vuh in that there is a clear sense of harmonic movement, particularly helped by the deep bottom line of bass notes played by Fricke on the piano. This insistent choral section reappears in the film as Jonathan Harker reaches the Borgo pass, when coffins are put on a river raft, when the ship is on the sea and then for a memorable slow montage sequence that includes a slow-motion shot of a bat; again for Nosferatu on the ship, Harker riding, Lucy in the window and the crewless ship arriving in Bremen harbour. This has the effect of seemingly starting the film again, signifying the onset of the next act of the story in northern Europe. On a more mechanical level, the music unifies a montage sequence of disparate images and different spaces.

Brüder des Schattens – Söhne des Lichts moves from the Gothic choir of the opening to the persistent woodwind section, and then bursts into an extended, repetitive and bright acoustic guitar and piano piece, bolstered with an increasing amount of droning sitar. This section accompanied images of Bremen (actually Delft in Holland), Jonathan with Lucy on the beach and Jonathan riding away on a horse. This is a lengthy piece of music, which is highly repetitive and fairly hypnotic, making little in the way of any notable development. The piano and clean electric guitar make something of a 'groove', a sheen of sound, and the guitar then plays short melodic cells that almost make a melody but certainly never cohere into a lyrical one. It is based on an *ostinato* of two bars' length with a pedal point where the bass hangs a tone below the tonic of the single chord and after a while the melody is joined and supported by oboe. A section then ensues of alternating stasis and movement (where the instruments play a phrase and then leave a corresponding gap for the sound to sustain and ebb away), with piano, guitar and sitar playing a slow melody in unison, before returning to the previous music. This whole structure is repeated again. This is hardly typical of Popol Vuh in that their music tends to develop in itself, organically, rather than being based on a structure of presentation and repetition. Indeed, Popol Vuh's music tends to be more organic than much popular music in that the group often do not follow strict song-based time formats and many pieces seem to develop in an almost improvisatory manner (despite actually being written pieces). With music that is thus conceived, it is easy to see how difficult it might be to twist it into more conventional film music functions, such as emphasizing action and thematic repeats paralleling action thus making for musical coherence across a film.

One notable repeated theme in *Nosferatu* is a synthesizer monody. As Lucy sleepwalks, there is a succession of very resonant single synthesizer notes (played on the monophonic Moog synthesizer). This same piece appears as Lucy enters the warehouse and later as Nosferatu looks from the warehouse window. It is a development from an earlier piece by the group, the title track of *In den Gärten Pharaos* (*In the Gardens of Pharoah*), particularly its opening section. Similarly, as Lucy walks on the beach, we hear the Popol Vuh piece '*Höre der Du Wagst*' ('Listen, He Who Ventures'), as it is named on *On the Way to a Little Way – Nosferatu*. This very calm piece with slow solo downward piano runs was a development of some of Florian Fricke's solo piano work that was recorded as *Spirit of Peace* (part two).[18]

Typically of Herzog and Popol Vuh's collaborations, the music was not written to fit action or screen dynamics, and hence it appears only once or twice under dialogue. The music tends to be used for spectacular sequences that lack dialogue or loud sound effects. This is common in cases where music has not been written for the momentary exigencies of a film but has been written more as mood pieces to accompany more generic scenarios in films. This is perhaps inevitable in that Herzog's process of filmmaking eschews the use of storyboards and tight planning in favour of catching the moment, improvising and fitting the film together later from existing shots. Consequently, music is badly edited in and especially badly edited out, and this is highly evident in *Nosferatu*. On some occasions the music is just cut dead, while on some others it is quickly, and rather unceremoniously, faded out. This is not 'bad technique', but rather an instance of Herzog's insistently 'primitive' film style. There is some confusion surrounding the music for the film in that there were two different soundtrack albums on different record labels: *Brüder des Schattens – Söhne des Lichts* on Spalax records and *On the Way to a Little Way – Nosferatu* on Egg records, both released in 1978. None of the songs from *Brüder des Schattens* is duplicated on *On the Way to a Little Way*, although some appear in different versions. Yet much of the *Brüder des Schattens – Söhne des Lichts* album fails to appear in the film, most notably the abundance of sitar-led pieces. The contents of the two albums suggest a significant amount of music was presented to and then rejected or unused by Herzog in the final cuts of the film.[19]

Fitzcarraldo (1981) tells the story of an Amazon rubber tapper (played by Klaus Kinski) who wishes to build an opera house in the jungle. With the help of a tribe of Indians, he manages to drag a large boat over a hill separating one river from another. The film starts and finishes with opera, the first being Verdi's *Ernani* at the Manaus opera house and the end where Bellini's *I Puritani* is performed on the river by a company of singers and musicians.

The film uses pre-existing pieces by Popol Vuh, three from *Sei still, wisse ICH BIN* (1981) and *Engel der Luft*, sometimes called *Engel der Luft, part I* (*Angel of the Air*) from *Die Nacht der Seele – Tantric Songs* (1979). The opening sequence depicts the jungle and Klaus Kinski with Claudia Cardinale, intercut with opera in Manaus. For the jungle shots we hear the second section of *Wehe Khorazin* (*Woe to Khorazin*). The first part of *Wehe Khorazin* appears when Kinski is sitting on some logs, and then the camera completes a long-shot pan across the misty forest. *Wehe Khorazin* is a choral piece with bass drum punctuation, based on a repeated vocal structure. This leads to a sustained guitar chord and the vocals changing to encompass wordless vocal chanting over clean electric guitar power chords, with piano, bass drum punctuation and some metallic percussion, which almost but never quite becomes a beat. *Engel der Luft, part I* has an essentially different character, comprising solo oboe which is then joined by another, playing a plaintive melody with some punctuation from bass notes on the piano.

Engel der Luft later appears prominently after the boat has crossed the mountain and enters the river listing and smoking in long-shot. A piece called *Im Garten der Gemeinschaft* (*In the Garden of the Community*) appears as Kinski and Cardinale look over the boat and when they work on it. It accompanies a spectacular long take in which the mist hangs over the boat as it rests on the slope, and then we are shown the Indians working the capstan. It is also used when the boat re-enters the water after its trek across the mountain. *Im Garten der Gemeinschaft* consists of bass drum and piano with a solo wordless vocal. Guitar joins as part of the rhythmic mesh in a major mode, creating a looped strophe of four bars of 4/4. Chanting, in a minor mode, then begins over the top of this, imperling a modal character that is also reminiscent of the way that blues creates tension by mixing major and minor scales. This is not the sort of tension that supplies a sense of forward movement, as does dissonance in traditional tonal music, but marks more of a static dialectic, which might be interpreted as a homology of the film's backdrop of interaction between the Indians and the *conquistadores*.

Another piece, ... *Als lebten die Engel auf Erden* (*As If the Angels Lived on Earth*), accompanies the boat on river, then it fades out and subsequently fades back in over images of the town of Iquito. Its harmony is rooted on one chord throughout and it consists of a chorus-effect electric guitar picking short arpeggios, with overdubbed melodic guitar playing. The melody is banal in rhythmic terms and has something of an 'oriental' character. This is borne out by the guitar playing without much sustain and thus sounding something like plucked eastern stringed instruments, such as the Japanese koto or Chinese pipa. This adds a sense of more general exoticism to sections of the film. Rather than allowing the music to depict a specific location, this paints a wash of global, rootless, yet transcendent spirituality to the film. Generally speaking, *Fitzcarraldo* tends to use operatic pieces as indications of dreaming and the cultural incongruities of 'civilization', while the Popol Vuh pieces tend to exemplify the grand scale of endeavours and the sublime of the jungle, river and nature more generally.

Cobra Verde (1987) received rather less acclaim than Herzog's previous feature films. Again it starred Klaus Kinski, this time as a white Brazilian who rises from abject poverty to be the Viceroy of Dahomey during the time of the slave trade. The film uses pieces written especially for the film by Popol Vuh and does not raid their back catalogue. It has its own soundtrack album. The opening piece has similarities with previous pieces by the group, like *Engel der Luft, part II* on *Tantric Songs* (1981); it has a similar harmonic progression based around a plodding, regular diatonic melody. The piece is based on an extended melody that is articulated in a basic rhythmic manner with each note falling on dominant beats of the bar. This gives it something of the character of plainchant and devotional music where rhythm is a matter of the expression of unity, rather than something for variation. On the soundtrack album, *The Death of Cobra Verde* is a different version of this piece, consisting of more prominent (requiem-like) deep male choral vocals over a swinging guitar rhythm. Like Herzog's other features, music is still important in this film, as witnessed by the extraordinary diegetic performance by the singing girls of Zigi Cultural Troupe, which appears less like part of a feature film and more like an ethnomusicological document on film. Here, in these two pieces of music, two of Herzog's principal concerns are apparent: the convincing depiction of a level of reality in a film fantasy, and a persistent interest in the transcendent or religious, and cinema's ability to engage it.

Conclusion

In the wake of his run of feature films with music by Popol Vuh, Herzog went on to direct operas in the 1980s, including Wagner's *Lohengrin* at Bayreuth in 1987. He also made a short (18-minute) film called *Pilgrimage* in 2001 about the feverish devotion of pilgrims at the Basilica of the Virgin in Guadeloupe, Mexico. It was part of the BBC2 'Sound on Film' series, which had been premised upon a close collaboration between a film director and composer, in this case pairing Herzog with British composer John Tavener, an artist similarly interested in transcendence. Herzog has commented,

> An image does not change *per se* when you place music behind it, but … certain qualities and atmospheres in the images … could be seen more clearly when there was certain music playing. The music changes the perspective of the audience; they see things and experience emotions that were not there before.[20]

Herzog's quotation suggests that the music clarified elements of his vision that were already there, yet the sublime and atmospheric music plays an absolutely central role in the definition of key moments in Herzog's films. The character of Popol Vuh's music never really changed to fit the film, it was rather the reverse: that the film had to *accommodate* their music. Popol Vuh's music has had a central role in Werner Herzog's films, even when it makes only occasional appearances; music is integrated with the film in a profoundly different manner from in mainstream Hollywood films. Rather than being written to complement a film that is perceived in production terms as a virtually finished object, Popol Vuh's music is actually part of the artistic vision of Herzog's films, either through inspiring film activity or through exploiting the music as an object to which the visuals can be cut, almost as if they were an accompaniment to the music. The transcendental character of Popol Vuh's music also provides a crucial experiential dimension to the films, marking out the very singular status of Herzog's films as exceptional objects concerned both with philosophy and feeling. This is a 'sensual' cinema, concerned with the materiality of visual and audio aspects more than simply relating a story.

It is striking how opening sequences in Herzog's films showcase music and spectacle, most notably in *Aguirre, Herz aus Glas* and *Cobra Verde*. These constitute an 'overblown' version of the mainstream film title/opening sequences, which also allow some increased scope for film music. Yet in Herzog and Popol Vuh's case these sequences are precise set-pieces that can be seen to emblematize the entire film to follow. Music is not matched or written to fit the action on screen and tends only rarely to be used under dialogue, whereas it comes into its own for spectacle sequences, often showcasing majestic landscapes. Herzog's technical primitivism, most notably in terms of editing, is also highly evident in the way that the music is edited and faded in and out in a most unsophisticated manner.

Popol Vuh were a unique group, setting and inspiring a number of musical trends. They stretched the rubric of 'pop/rock' and were among a number of other German experimental rock groups whose influence is becoming more apparent as time goes on. Indeed, some of the Krautock groups, spearheaded by Popol Vuh, took their experimentation out of the recording studio and into films, which proved most receptive to individualistic music.[21] A concurrent trend, the New German Cinema, marked a rebirth of German national filmmaking.[22] Promoting a very particular character for film, including the rejection of commercial cinema, and cohering around a number of film directors, including Herzog, Rainer-Werner Fassbinder, Alexander Kluge, Hans-Jürgen Syberberg and Volker Schlöndorff. There are distinct parallels between the New German cinema and Krautrock, and perhaps the most important point of convergence between the two was the collaboration of Werner Herzog with Popol Vuh.

Notes

1. Werner Herzog, on Florian Fricke, leader of Popol Vuh. Cronin, P. (ed.) *Herzog on Herzog*, London: Faber & Faber, 2002, 256.
2. Gillig-Degrave, M. Sleevenotes from *Popol Vuh, The Best Soundtracks From Werner Herzog Films*, trans. D. Loos, Bell Records, BLR 84 705 (CD), 1993.
3. Badelt, K. 'Shiver Me Timbres', *Film Score Monthly*, **8** (6), July 2003, 25.
4. Elsaesser, T. *New German Cinema*, Brunswick, NJ: Rutgers University Press, 1989, 218–22.
5. Peucker, B. 'Werner Herzog: In Quest of the Sublime', in K. Philips (ed.) *New German Filmmakers: From Oberhausen Through the 1970s*, New York: Frederick Ungar, 1984, 193.
6. Elsaesser, T. 'An Anthropologist's Eye: Where the Green Ants Dream', in T. Corrigan (ed.) *The Films of Werner Herzog: Between Mirage and History*, New York: Methuen, 1986, 133.
7. Composer Schoener received a degree of acclaim in art music circles, producing eclectic music that derived inspiration from the Far East, spirituality and the capabilities of electronic instruments.
8. These were an early modular synthesizer, based on voltage-controlled oscillators and filters; they were monophonic keyboard-controlled (a significant innovation) and produced startling sounds. Robert Moog developed these and made them available commercially from 1968–69 onwards. These instruments, in the form of Mini Moog, Micro Moog and Polymoog, became a staple of electronic and rock music in the 1970s.
9. Neu! produced a parodic piece of music called *Krautrock*, which was intended to embody the stereotypical aspects expected of Krautrock groups.
10. Indeed, Daniel Fichelscher, Alois Gromer and Renate Knaup had been in Amon Düül II before Popol Vuh.
11. A notable Krautrock example of Mellotron usage was Tangerine Dream's 'Mysterious Semblance at the Strand of Nightmares' from *Phaedra* (1973).
12. Influential French film theorist Andre Bazin declared that the essence of cinema was its 'realism', that it was able to catch something of the reality it photographed. Consequently, cinema that was 'cinematic' should be premised upon long takes

without edits, and a building of the film world through on-screen aspects (*mise-en scène*) rather then through editing.

13. Cronin, P. *Herzog on Herzog*, 256.

14. Rogers, H. 'Fitzcarraldo's Search for Aguirre: Music and Text in the Amazonian Films of Werner Herzog', *Journal of the Royal Musicological Association*, **129** (1), 2004, 77, 85.

15. Van Wert, W. 'Last Words: Observations on a New Language' in T. Corrigan (ed.) *The Films of Werner Herzog*, New York: Methuen, 1986, 70.

16. For which Herzog famously insisted that the whole cast be hypnotized before shooting. Peucker, B. 'Werner Herzog: In Quest of the Sublime', 184.

17. It is vaguely reminiscent of the sound and articulation achieved sometimes by Mike Oldfield, notably on David Bedford's *Instructions for Angels* (1977).

18. This piano solo appears on the Celestial Harmonies release of *In the Garden of Pharao/Aguirre* (released 1983, 13008–2).

19. *Nosferatu* was shot twice, making two final cuts, an English language version and a German language version of the film.

20. Herzog, quoted in Cronin, P. *Herzog on Herzog*, 256

21. It is notable that films had a hold on some Krautrock groups: Can's first two albums were called *Monster Movie* (1969) and *Soundtracks* (1970), while in the late 1990s Faust provided music for F.W. Murnau's silent film *Nosferatu: eine Symphonie des Grauens* (1922), which was released as the album *Faust Wakes Nosferatu* (1998), and included a subsequent screening with a live musical performance at the Royal Festival Hall, London, on 25 October 2000.

22. Elsaesser, T. *New German Cinema*, 2.

Chapter 9

Modernity and a day: the functions of music in the films of Theo Angelopoulos

Miguel Mera

> I take Angelopoulos to be a modernist director – not only a modern one, and almost
> certainly not a postmodernist one (whatever that might be). The ultimate reasons
> derive, of course, from the ways in which his films are put together and the effects
> they aim to achieve.[1]

Bordwell's interpretation of Theo Angelopoulos as a 'second-generation postwar
Euromodernist',[2] is a viewpoint that is shared by many other writers
(Kolocotroni, Jameson, Horton) who discuss the modernist tradition that the
Greek director upholds. Indeed, one volume that examines Angelopoulos' work is
entitled *The Last Modernist*,[3] as if he alone is striving to maintain a dying or dead
form of filmmaking. The director has himself identified with the central pillars of
modernist cinema and acknowledged the influence of many modernist filmmakers
(such as Antonioni, Mizoguchi, Godard and Tarkovsky).[4] A framework such as
this helps us to understand Angelopoulos' recurrent technical and philosophical
approaches to filmmaking; the creation of non-causal narrative structures, muted
emotional expression, an overt reflexivity, ambiguity and open textures. Bordwell
further believes that Angelopoulos shows his affinity with the modernist project
in his 'keen grasp of the director's role in shaping critical appropriation of his
films'.[5] There are numerous interviews, for example, where the filmmaker
provides detailed explanations of the recurrent themes, structures and
philosophies at the heart of his work and how these have changed over time. To
understand Angelopoulos as a modernist filmmaker, then, is to accept that there is
a deliberate attempt to make the reading of the filmic text challenging. This
approach is not designed to render the content or ideas impossible to grasp, but
rather to make the process of decoding itself provocative, so that 'to read is to
work'.[6] It is a strategy that has helped define the look, sound and feel of
Angelopoulos' films.

However, when we come to examine Angelopoulos' work from the 1990s
onwards, for example, in films such as *Eternity and a Day* (1998) we find that this
modernist agenda has softened considerably. The style is much more inviting, is

much more emotionally and psychologically engaging, is much more contemplative, is less bleak and less futile, encourages empathy and has a greater focus on the individual. Many critics observed this new 'tenderness and emotional intensity',[7] which seemed to be at odds with what they expected from the filmmaker. However, as Angelopoulos explains, the journey towards this new approach was one that he had begun as far back as *Taxidi Sta Kithira* (*Voyage to Cythera,* 1983), where he consciously changed his directorial strategy because:

> Art is once again anthropocentric and has far more questions than answers. The world is a chessboard on which man is just another pawn and his chance of an impact on the proceedings negligible. Politics is a cynical game that has turned its back on the commitments of the past. This does not mean that we have to go back to the hero in the primitive sense of the word, but at least to a narrative that puts man in the center. It is not a return to psychology, but a transition from the generalities of the epics to a far more personal cinema, in which the filmmaker is questioning himself and his art.[8]

This statement contains a number of interesting features. First, Angelopoulos acknowledges that modernism did not provide answers to the post-war impasse that many filmmakers and scholars presumed the cinematic medium had reached. Angelopoulos' films have become more intimate because he believes their ability to affect large-scale political and cultural change is 'negligible'. Nonetheless, his films still retain the modernist ideal of questioning the nature of film art itself. Secondly, Angelopoulos acknowledges the importance of empathy and contemplation in his new filmic language. What the recent films demonstrate, therefore, is an updated form of modernism, or a more malleable form of modernity, one that attempts to remain relevant and reactive to the society in which we live. Bordwell is adamant that the work should not be defined as postmodern, but he also acknowledges that Angelopoulos no longer adheres to a hardened modernist agenda. The filmic language has developed whilst simultaneously 'integrating several lessons from a slightly older modernist tradition'.[9] Likewise, Jameson recognizes a nebulous middleground, claiming that it is an extraordinary development for a filmmaker who had 'already achieved a distinctive oeuvre at the end of the modern period, to have been sufficiently receptive to the deeper swirling currents and trends of history after postmodernity itself'.[10] Angelopoulos' liquid modernity allows him to blur boundaries as well as absorb and inflect a variety of influences.

This shift in style to a nebulous middleground can also be traced in Angelopoulos' use of music. The director explains that when he made his first films he was heavily influenced by the visual style of Westerns, yet he became quickly tired of the manipulative scores that accompanied them, citing a particular dislike for Dmitri Tiomkin's music.[11] As a reaction against the bombastic nature of the classical Hollywood score, Angelopoulos rejected the use of non-diegetic music in his own films and experimented instead with music that issued purely from the diegesis. This stance was, of course, influenced by the approach of other modernist filmmakers and also by the distanciation theories of Brecht.[12] However, on *Taxidi Sta Kithira* Angelopoulos changed his approach and the music forms part of a warmer filmmaking strategy as outlined above. The most significant change is that Angelopoulos began a detailed working relationship with the composer Eleni Karaindrou, and made a commitment to the use of non-diegetic music. Whilst this sudden shift may seem like a complete abrogation of Angelopoulos' earlier beliefs, there is much that links it to his earlier strategy. The music shares some of the dramatic functions of mainstream narrative cinema, but it also originates from a rejection of Hollywood codes and has its own distinctive set of functions and aims. Karaindrou and Angelopoulos eschew many of the standardized approaches of classical film scoring and define their own values for the music, particularly in relation to structure, silence and contemplation. This places Karaindrou's music at an interesting crossroads that is not defined adequately by the existing research in the field. There have been many definitions of the functions of film music, but few that attempt to explain the use of music in European film or, indeed, in art film. This should not be entirely unexpected, as the vast majority of film music research has been based on the narrative Hollywood film score. However, the fact that the existing functional models of film music are largely irrelevant to the understanding of many filmic texts is problematic. Increasingly, scholars (such as Cook, Davison, Everett, Kassabian, and Smith) are concerned by the inadequacies of the various theoretical frameworks and definitions of the objectives of film music and seek to broaden the discussion. By examining the music within *Eternity and a Day* and the collaborative processes that led to its creation, we can begin to move towards a definition of the qualities of music in Angelopoulos' films as well as contributing to a burgeoning debate on the function and nature of music in film.

The journeys

Eternity and a Day tells the story of a poet named Alexander (Bruno Ganz) who makes a final meandering journey, in one day, before he is admitted to hospital where he will eventually die. This journey is physical, philosophical and metaphorical. Much of the film involves Alexander's memories of his dead wife and his regrets at not having been a better husband to her. As he looks back on his life, he comes to recognize his inability to connect with her on a deep emotional level. We are constantly provided with images and motives focusing on the notion of *Exitis*, that is, one who is in exile everywhere. Alexander feels like an outsider who is emotionally divorced from the world in which he lives. The title of the film refers to his wife's response to the question, 'how long does tomorrow last?'

The film also deals with Alexander's friendship with an Albanian street orphan (Achilleas Skevis) who is, in a very real sense, an outsider. Alexander's regrets about not connecting with his wife are channelled into a newfound ability to care for and make a profound change in the life of this child. Alexander's past, present, memory, imagination and reality all blend seamlessly into a contemplative, sensory filmic poem. Accordingly, the complicated personal turmoil and emotional situations that the film displays do not resolve or provide closure, but only create further questions. These open-ended structures and textures inevitably have a profound effect on both the nature and the process of creation of the score. Indeed, what is fascinating about Angelopoulos and Karaindrou's collaborative process is its exploratory nature. Just as the central character Alexander takes an unpredictable trip, so did the director and composer. As Karaindrou explains, the collaborative process 'seemed like a magical journey, whose destination neither of us knew, and surely, what seemed to be the first priority in the "journey" was the instinctive and intuitive course – not some conscious and well planned creative process'.[13] This suggests that the director and composer did not have fully defined functions for the music, but rather that these evolved through their working partnership. Angelopoulos further explains the nature of some of this collaboration.

> We have a very close relationship. First I tell her the story of the next film. She has a tape recorder and records it. She does not want to read the script – she insists she needs to hear the sound of my voice and my inflection when telling the story. Strangely enough, I have the same request from all the actors in my films. It is not the scenario they want to familiarize themselves with, but my interpretation of it. It is probably because when I am telling a story, I do not do it in a logical, linear sequence. I am trying to create an adequate climate for it. The words I choose to express my thoughts, the structure of the phrases, the silences, all these establish a direct contact between me and my listeners, something they cannot get by reading a manuscript.[14]

The difference between this approach and that of mainstream film scoring is particularly striking. First, the composer is involved at a very early stage of the filmmaking process, well before any of the film has been shot. In most mainstream filmmaking the composer is not brought in until the last stage of post-production where they have no choice but to react to a largely completed product, and *decorate*, rather than grow and develop the score *with*, the film. Karaindrou and Angelopoulos' approach obviously provides them with some significant advantages and opportunities. The composer can be involved in the development of both diegetic and non-diegetic music and can exploit the fluid boundary between these two worlds. This is especially important given Angelopoulos' filmmaking style, which frequently aims to blur boundaries in order to challenge the audience's reading of the text. Furthermore, because the music has not been created in direct response to technical concerns, such as scene lengths or editing rhythms, it is able to retain a distinct sense of its own musical structure, which allows it to work with and against the image as an equal partner. This is the kind of association where the music exists in what Brown describes as a 'parallel/aesthetic universe', rather than acting as a 'generator of narrative affect'.[15] The fact that Karaindrou (and Angelopoulos' other collaborators) prefer to listen to an oral recitation of the story rather than reading the script, further accentuates this point. It is not the plot or causal narrative structures that are of relevance to Karaindrou but the film's sensory aspirations; the way the story is told is more important than what the story is. The process of recording Angelopoulos' voice clearly allows Karaindrou to 'penetrate in deeper spheres of *his* psyche',[16] in order to bring inner situations to the surface. It is as if the discovery of the hidden motivating factors inside the director's mind are employed as a means of individualizing the telling of the story. This is as much a mode of scoring the director's personality as the film that the director is making. Of course, this approach raises some challenging questions with regard to our understanding of the structural and narrative concerns of the score.

Structure, silence and narrative agency

One of the fundamental functions of music as defined by virtually all film scholars is its role in assisting, supporting, guiding and shaping narrative. Film music is designed primarily to interpret and illustrate narrative events. 'Narrative cueing', as Gorbman puts it,[17] relates to referential cues, such as indicating point of view, supplying formal demarcations, and establishing settings and characters. Likewise, Kalinak emphasizes music as a feature of narrative agency, claiming that one of the main structural principles at the heart of the classical film score is 'musical illustration of narrative content, especially the direct synchronization between music and narrative action'.[18] That this theoretical construct also influences practitioners' thinking about the functions of film music is supported by Burt and Davis, who write from the perspective of the composer. They define interpretive processes that a composer might employ in the creation of narrative structures. These include music entrances, accent by omission, actor's inner rhythm, supra-rhythmic structure, pacing, suspended and real time, and point of release in the dramatic shaping of a cue.[19]

Whilst there is a great deal of merit in the comments of these scholars, the concept of music as an exclusively narrational force can be problematic when we examine films that do not subscribe to traditional narrative structures. As narrative transitivity is not the major defining feature of Angelopoulos' filmmaking or Karaindrou's compositional strategy, understanding the functions and characteristics of the score requires some further examination. I do not wish to suggest that the music in *Eternity and a Day* does not perform any traditional narrative functions. Indeed, contemporary audiences would inevitably ascribe narrative qualities to any music in any context, but narrativity, in the conventional sense, is not the focus for Karaindrou's score. The music is primarily designed to establish the concepts and the general philosophical outlook of the film rather than moment-by-moment character or setting. The score's connotative function is established at a macro level, a likely consequence of the working methods that the director and composer employ. Consequently, the music's relationship with the image is neither abstract nor representational but *encapsulating*. In this context the appearance of musical gestures that mirror physical action (mickey-mousing), music that smooths over transitions, or music that reflects detailed narrative events become irrelevant, because the connection of the score to the filmic text always functions at a deeper, philosophical level than this.

Example 9.1   *Eternity and a Day*, **Theme A 'Eternity'**
Reproduced by permission of Eleni Karaindrou

There are four main musical ideas in *Eternity and a Day*. The main thematic material, Theme A 'Eternity' (see Example 9.1), is defined by its simple, cyclical quality with repetitive, sequential, ascending–descending patterns that ebb and flow. This rocking motion is also a feature of the harmony which alternates between B♭ minor (tonic) and E♭ minor (subdominant). It is not surprising that this material grows out of the film's opening sound of waves lapping on a shore. Associations with memory and the passing of time are clearly being referenced here, and the material is further developed into a series of variations that emphasize these concepts throughout the film. Derived from the 'Eternity' theme, A¹ 'Parting' is a slower, rhythmically free version of the main melody played (usually by accordion or mandolin) over a static minor drone. Theme B 'Borders'

Example 9.2 *Eternity and a Day*, **Theme B 'Borders'**
Reproduced by permission of Eleni Karaindrou

(see Example 9.2), is a free, pentatonic melody (played on the clarinet, which frequently exploits its *chalumeau* register)[20] that is also heard over a minor drone. Indeed, such is the importance of drones to Karaindrou's score, that they can themselves be defined as a thematic element. Finally, there are numerous composed diegetic elements in the score that are often derived from or grow into the 'Eternity' theme. The interlocking of musical materials across the film's diegetic/non-diegetic spaces creates a thoroughly unified score with an obsessional quality that serves to support the film's larger conceptual framework (see Figure 9.1).

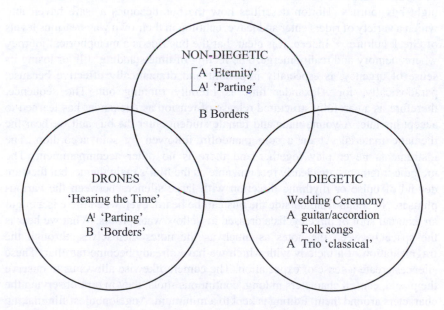

Figure 9.1 *Eternity and a Day*, **structural/thematic unity**

One of the most obvious features of *Eternity and a Day* is how little music there is. The film itself is two hours and eight minutes in length (short for Angelopoulos) with only thirty-six minutes of music (including all diegetic, non-diegetic and meta-diegetic music). It would be common for a mainstream narrative film of similar length to use at least twice as much music. Given the lack of music, it is not surprising that the material is so closely related thematically. In addition, the application of silence and space is so striking that when music is heard the audience is automatically forced to question its significance. But silence is not solely used as a structural device to highlight the score, it also forms part of a broader filmmaking aesthetic, as Angelopoulos explains:

> In today's cinema, the so-called dead time – silence and pauses – has become obsolete. This undefined time that functions between one act and another has disappeared. For me, even silence needs to function in an almost musical way, not to be fabricated through cuts or through dead shots but to exist internally inside the shot.[21]

Angelopoulos contrasts his own filmmaking style with techniques that he believes flatten and deaden the cinematic space. For him, silence and space are devices that can drive contemplation and bring the cinematic experience to life. Cavalcanti's famous comment that 'silence can be the loudest of noises, just as black, in a brilliant design, can be the brightest of colors',[22] seems especially relevant here. A good example of this creation of a living space through both image and sound can be found towards the end of the film as Alexander and the orphan child take a late-night bus journey. Horton describes how the bus becomes a 'safe haven into which a variety of riders enter and leave, echoing in their own ways various levels of Greek culture'.[23] Indeed, it is clear that the bus ride is a metaphorical journey where memory and reality merge. The feeling of time standing still, or losing its sense of urgency, is especially important and dramatically effective because, paradoxically, for Alexander time is literally running out. The sequence, therefore, is a carefully structured release of tension as Alexander has learned to accept his fate. A young male and female student enter the bus and we hear the thematic material A^1 on a solo mandolin followed by solo accordion. The instruments never play together and there is no other accompaniment. The melodic fragments are clearly recognizable as the film's main theme, but they are devoid of pulse or rhythmic direction with large silences between the various phrases. No sound from outside the bus can be heard, even when there is a cut to an external shot of three cyclists dressed in yellow waterproofs. What we hear is the space between the notes as much as the notes themselves, through the fragmentation of a melody with which we have already become familiar. These silences create a sense of expectation. The camera likewise allows us to observe the placid, central characters in long, continuous shots, they in turn observing the characters around them. Editing is kept to a minimum. Angelopoulos' filmmaking is constantly anchored in 'stillness, in an effort to have us experience and contemplate his images in a new way'.[24]

What does a drone mean?

An insight into the score's relationship to narrative agency, in terms of the structure and space that is defined above can be found in the scene in which Alexander has taken the young orphan boy to the Albanian border with the intention of reuniting him with his grandmother. The border zone is a wintry, misty landscape where we see a large wire fence upon which, at different heights, numerous children are hanging motionless. It is as if a photo still had caught them climbing the fence in an attempt to cross the border; the shadowy figures contrasting with the hazy, white background. Typical of Angelopoulos, this frozen, ghostly image is revealed to us in one long, slow shot. There are no close-ups, changes of focus or editing rhythms to disturb the audience's contemplation of the sequence. The meaning of this imagery is, of course, open to interpretation, but Angelopoulos explains that the border is a fantasy that represents a 'frontier in Alexander himself'.[25] Horton, likewise understands the sequence as reinforcing concepts of the border as a physical, metaphorical and cultural, 'transitional and ambiguous territory',[26] and it is the score that he believes helps to magnify this meaning.

> This scene is made even more haunting by the minimalist musical soundtrack, composed by the talented Eleni Karaindrou with an almost instinctive feeling for amplifying Angelopoulos's visuals with equivalent sounds.[27]

Karaindrou's music used throughout this sequence could certainly be described as minimal, although perhaps not minimalist. It consists of a simple D minor string orchestra drone at a consistent *pianissimo* volume and in which the strings do not shift voices or register; the cue consists literally of one primary chord. The only slight fluctuations that can be heard are the inevitable bow re-takes and harmonic overtones, of which the ear becomes more aware as the sequence progresses. The drone itself although minimal in content is conceptually rich. The first track on the *Eternity and a Day* soundtrack CD is particularly instructive in this regard, as it also features a D minor drone and is entitled 'Hearing the Time'.[28] Drones, of course, are free from the temporal constraints of bar structures, harmonic rhythm and pulse, and are, therefore, metaphorically timeless. In a film that poses questions about the passing of time this device, much like the fragmentation of the main melodic material in the bus cue, speaks more powerfully than the simplicity of the material would initially suggest.

Nonetheless, the use of the drone in this sequence is an incredibly sparse mode of scoring. Given this approach, Horton's comments about the scene raise some interesting questions. How can music that does so little 'amplify' the visuals? Why is this drone 'equivalent' to the visual sequence? What does Horton mean when he describes the music as having an 'instinctive' feeling? Part of the strength of the music in this context is precisely that it does not attempt to provide narrative commentary. There are no narrative themes that can be associated with it; the music has no transitional function. It could be argued that the composer amplifies the images by having the courage to let the director's slow revelation of the landscape speak for itself. It is the antithesis of modes of scoring that reinforce, or represent, or overpower. As an audience we are drawn into the image and forced to find meaning within it rather than being told by the composer how to interpret it. Just as the lack of editing requires us to see further than the single shot, so the static nature of the music requires us to hear beyond the meaninglessness of the notes. The drone enjoys its condition as an 'unconsummated symbol',[29] waiting to be imbued with significance. To a certain extent, this is true of all musical gestures, but the drone in this particular context demands the audience's input into its meaning.

I am reminded of Gorbman's argument that the appearance of any music in any filmic context is by definition a signifier of emotion and is 'the obverse of logic'.[30] However, I do not understand the music for this sequence as a signifier of emotion so much as a signifier of structure. There can be no doubt that the appearance of the drone highlights the importance of this sequence over others in the film. The very act of choosing to use music here, no matter how unobtrusive or 'unheard', gives the scene more purpose and meaning than the numerous other slow contemplative sequences that exist throughout the film. Structurally, Karaindrou's music frequently functions in this way by appearing at moments where metaphorical, political or philosophical issues need to be highlighted, but not necessarily where emotional response is to be elicited. Indeed, if there is one defining feature of Karaindrou's music, despite its conventional attractiveness, is that it refuses to make the audience feel comfortable with its emotional reaction to the filmic text. The music does not provide 'formal and rhythmic continuity – between shots, in transitions between scenes'.[31] It is precisely these awkward gaps that interest Angelopoulos and Karaindrou. The music does not apologize for the slow pace of the film by attempting to speed up the audience perception of its temporal structure (a common feature of mainstream scoring). The music does not aim to anaesthetize the audience helping them to suspend disbelief, it requires them instead to engage with the content at the heart of the film.

Where is the diegesis?

We have briefly touched upon the fact that Angelopoulos and Karaindrou's collaborative process allowed them to experiment with music in terms of the film's diegetic spaces. One of the first musical sequences in the film immediately defines some of this playfulness. Alexander looks out of the window of his apartment and presses a button on his hi-fi system. The 'Eternity' theme, which we have previously heard only once as a non-diegetic piece for solo piano, is now heard in a diegetic version for full orchestra. He presses another button and stops the music, preventing it from reaching its climax and resolution. We then see a view of the harbour from Alexander's window. The camera gradually focuses on the terrace of the apartment opposite, with its curtains billowing in the wind. The same orchestral musical material is heard, but on this occasion no diegetic source is disclosed. However, this is not simply a non-diegetic reprise of the music, as Alexander's voiceover reveals:

> **Alexander (v.o.)** Lately … my only contact with the world is this stranger opposite who answers me with the same music. Who is he? What's he like? One morning I set out to find him. But I changed my mind. It's better not to know … and to imagine. A loner like me …. Maybe it's a little girl dabbling with the unknown before leaving for school.

The musical sequence embodies the text. Of course, the device is metaphorical and uses a diegetic/non-diegetic mirror image in order to highlight the notion of Alexander's journey towards self-discovery and self-awareness. The 'stranger opposite' is Alexander himself. As a whole, the scene makes the apparatus of the non-diegetic visible, as if to illustrate to the audience that the music is not designed to be emotionally manipulative. Furthermore, we cannot tell if the musical reprise emanates from a diegetic source or if it exists only in Alexander's mind.[32] The sequence toys with the concept of where the diegesis is located and where the music sits within this. It is these dramatic tensions that Karaindrou and Angelopoulos use as a means of forcing us to question the nature and purpose of the music in *Eternity and a Day*, and it is why music in Angelopoulos' films often sits in a meta-diegetic space.

In addition, Angelopoulos enjoys using the performance of music within his filmic structures. The bus sequence discussed earlier features a curious recital by three conservatoire students who board, set up their music-stands and then begin to play a 'Classical' trio for flute, violin and cello. The child examines the musicians expectantly and the flautist looks back at him accusatorily, as if performances on moving buses are commonplace. Interestingly, when the camera cuts away from the trio to Alexander and the child watching and listening to them, a full orchestral version of the 'Eternity' theme is heard. Once again we have a diegetic/non-diegetic mirror image, perhaps suggesting that Alexander has made progress in his journey of self-discovery.

In the examples I have highlighted in this chapter, the contrast between diegetic and non-diegetic music functions as a metaphor for Alexander's internal struggle and character development. However, one sequence in *Eternity and a Day* is particularly striking because it seems completely unrelated to Alexander. The plot development pauses in order to allow the audience to delight in a remarkable wedding ceremony. We see the bride dancing down the street followed by a procession of her family members and accompanied by raucous, fidgety accordion music. Suddenly, the groom dances into the opposite end of the street accompanied by a violinist playing equally restless figurations. The groom's movement and music are a direct response to that of the bride. Family members observe from windows overlooking the street. Successive iterations of dancing and musical performance act as symbols of both courtship and sexual consummation. Finally, accordion and violin play and bride and groom dance together in an ecstatic representation of their marital union. Horton understands the sequence to be a 'kind of carnival of renewal and happiness', which he contrasts with a scene in *Taxidi Sta Kithira* where an exile 'dances on the tomb of his long-departed good friend from the past'.[33] Certainly, the wedding sequence demonstrates just how far the softened modernity of Angelopoulos' filmic language has developed. But the energy and exhilaration of the wedding is also particularly effective in a film where an imminent and inevitable death hangs over the central protagonist. The sequence is more than just an optimistic contrast, it is part of Angelopoulos' strategy to create an uplifting, sensory experience notwithstanding the solemnity of Alexander's final journey. With relation to the main 'Eternity' theme, for example, Angelopoulos explains:

> I asked her [Karaindrou] not to write a sad piece, despite the fact that it might have seemed to be the obvious choice for a film dealing with a person who faces the distinct eventuality of death. In my eyes, however, the film is almost an invitation to life.[34]

The wedding sequence is indeed an invitation to life and there are other scenes that perform the same function. The final sequence of the film, for example, allows Alexander to open up his emotions to his dead wife as he relives and rewrites his memories of her. By the same seashore that opened the film, where we saw the child Alexander swimming with friends, we now see the adult Alexander intimately dancing with his wife Anna, accompanied by a diegetic version of the 'Eternity' theme played by accordion and guitar. The sequence is symbolic of his journey from childhood to adulthood, as well as his newfound ability to connect emotionally with Anna. He tells his wife that he is not going to go into the hospital and that he would like to make plans for tomorrow. Diegetic music and dance become Alexander's ultimate expression of intimacy and affection, and his invitation to life. In most mainstream filmmaking non-diegetic music always functions as indicator of truth. Whatever the characters say or do, their real motivations, concerns or emotional reality are signalled by the underscore. In *Eternity and a Day*, however, diegetic music, albeit located internally within Alexander's mind, speaks truthfully about his emotional development and represents the personal journey that he has made.

Conclusions

Nicholas Cook has observed that meaning is not exclusively a feature of musical sound 'nor in the media with which it is aligned, but in the encounter between them'.[35] The most striking and important feature about the function of the music in *Eternity and a Day* is that this encounter works on a large-scale, philosophical level, where music encapsulates the central issue(s) that the filmmaker wishes to highlight. This dramatic function partly derives from the collaborative working processes that the filmmaker and composer adopt, but also from the modernist sensibilities that Angelopoulos has honed. The result is a filmic language that aims both to encourage contemplation, and to challenge the audience. Inevitably, this approach means that music does not actively seek to perform the dramatic functions that are generally associated with film scores, such as narrative cueing or emotional re-enforcement; the filmic language does not require it to do so. Furthermore, the desire to allow the audience to contemplate sound and image has led to the powerful use of silence, space and sparse modes of scoring, as well as the deliberate blurring of boundaries between the diegetic and non-diegetic. Although the music of itself may not be challenging, it is through its carefully conceived juxtaposition with the image that it finds new significance, as Cook suggests. The audience must test a variety of ways in which to imbue this composite filmic poem with meaning, because the nature of the collaboration continually questions the function and form of film music.

Notes

1. Bordwell, D. 'Modernism, minimalism, melancholy: Angelopoulos and visual style', in A. Horton (ed.) *The Last Modernist: The Films of Theo Angelopoulos*, Trowbridge: Flicks Books, 1997, 11.
2. Ibid., 11.
3. Horton, A. (ed.) *The Last Modernist: The Films of Theo Angelopoulos*.
4. See Fainaru, D. (ed.) *Theo Angelopoulos Interviews*, Jackson: University Press of Mississippi, 2001.
5. Bordwell, D. 'Modernism, minimalism, melancholy: Angelopoulos and visual style', 11.
6. Wollen, P. *Signs and Meaning in the Cinema*, London: BFI Publishing, 1998, 112.
7. Stratton, D. 'Eternity and a Day', in *Variety*, 25 May 1998, 18.
8. Fainaru, D. *Theo Angelopoulos Interviews*, 49.
9. Bordwell, D. 'Modernism, minimalism, melancholy: Angelopoulos and visual style', 15.
10. Jameson, F. 'Theo Angelopoulos: the past as history, the future as form', in A. Horton (ed.) *The Last Modernist: The Films of Theo Angelopoulos*, 94.
11. Theo Angelopoulos in conversation with Geoff Andrew, National Film Theatre, London, 26 November 2003.
12. The playwright and poet Bertolt Brecht (1898–1956) used a number of techniques, including songs and direct addresses to the audience, in order to prevent the audience from empathizing with the characters or abandoning themselves to the narrative and thereby missing the political content of the drama.
13. Karaindrou, E. e-mail to author, 4 February 2003. Also attrib. *Classic CD*, January 1999, interviewed by Mark Funnell.
14. Angelopoulos, T. 'And About All the Rest', in D. Fainaru (ed.) *Theo Angelopoulos Interviews*, 139.

15. Brown, R.S. *Overtones and Undertones: Reading Film Music*, Berkeley: University of California Press, 1994, 239.
16. Karaindrou, E. e-mail to author 4 February 2003 (my emphasis). Also attrib. *Classic CD*, January 1999, interviewed by Mark Funnell.
17. Gorbman, C. *Unheard Melodies: Narrative Film Music*, Bloomington: Indiana University Press, 1987, 73.
18. Kalinak, K. *Settling the Score: Music and the Classical Hollywood Film*, Madison: University of Wisconsin Press, 1992, 187.
19. Burt, G. *The Art of Film Musc*, Boston: Northeastern University Press, 1994; Davis, R. *Complete Guide to Film Scoring: The Art and Business of Writing Music for Movies and TV*, Boston: Berklee Press, 1999.
20. The clarinet has three registers, the lowest of which is known as the *Chalumeau* range (from the E below middle C to the E above). This corresponds roughly to the range of the former seventeenth-century single-reed instrument known as the *Chalumeau*, which was the precursor to the clarinet.
21. Angelopouolos, T. 'Angelopoulos' Philosophy of Film', in D. Fainaru (ed.) *Theo Angelopoulos Interviews*, 72.
22. Cavalcanti, A. 'Sound in Films' in E. Weis and J. Belton (eds) *Film Sound: Theory and Practice,* New York, Columbia University Press, 1985, 111.
23. Horton, A. *The Films of Theo Angelopoulos*, Princeton: Princeton University Press, 1999, 218.
24. Horton, A. *The Last Modernist: The Films of Theo Angelopoulos*, 4.
25. Angelopoulos, T. 'I Shoot the Way I Breathe: *Eternity and a Day*', in D. Fainaru (ed.) *Theo Angelopoulos Interviews*, 118.
26. Horton, A. *The Films of Theo Angelopoulos*, 217.
27. Ibid., 218.
28. *Eternity and a Day*, Eleni Karaindrou, ECM Records, 1998, ECM New Series 1692 465 125–2.
29. Langer, S.K. *Philosophy in a New Key: A Study in the Symbolism of Reason, Rite, and Art*, Cambridge, MA: Harvard University Press, 1957, 240.
30. Gorbman, C. *Unheard Melodies*, 79.
31. Ibid., 73.
32. This scene could be a homage to Tarkovsky's last film, *The Sacrifice* (1986), where the central character is also called Alexander and non-diegetic/diegetic Shakuhachi music also accompanies his internal struggle towards sacrifice. I am grateful to David Burnand for drawing my attention to this point. The film also represents for Tarkovsky a more softened form of modernism. For more information, see Truppin, A. 'And Then There Was Sound: The Films of Andrei Tarkovsky', in R. Altman (ed.) *Sound Theory, Sound Practice*, New York: Routledge, 1992, 235–48.
33. Horton, A. *The Films of Theo Angelopoulos*, 218.
34. Angelopoulos, T. 'And About All the Rest', in D. Fainaru (ed.), *Theo Angelopoulos Interviews*, 140.
35. Cook, N. *Analysing Musical Multimedia*, Oxford: Oxford University Press, 2000, 270.

Chapter 10

Preisner–Kieslowski: the art of synergetic understatement in *Three Colours: Red*

Jon Paxman

Three Colours: Red (1993) was the last collaboration between the late director Krzysztof Kieslowski and composer Zbigniew Preisner. It was also the final instalment of a filmic trilogy based on the French revolutionary ideals of liberty, equality and fraternity, as symbolized in the French Tricolour. The three films (including *Three Colours: Blue*, 1992, and *Three Colours: White*, 1993) explore these ideals not on a large communal scale, but on a very intimate level – how they relate to the individual.

This chapter is essentially an examination of music–image communication. It will focus exclusively on the first music cue of *Red*, which begins some six minutes into the film (there is no titles music), lasts approximately four and a half minutes and spans six scenes. The analysis will detail the remarkable variety of technical, narrative and sub-narrative roles that the music fulfils, as well as subtle methods of filmic development through music–image synergy and dialectical tension. These scenes serve as a lucid example of the possibilities of music–image discourse, in that they contain virtually no dialogue.

Due to the many layers of meaning and communication within this sequence, the analysis will call to attention the same material repeatedly, but within separate areas of study. The first section will provide segmentation of the sequence into its various scenes and will consider the narrative and characterizational functions of the music. It will identify both the role the music plays within the diegesis, and the way in which it expands our appreciation and understanding of the visual narrative. The second section will focus on various sub-narrative roles of the music, detailing the means by which it encourages sub-textual readings of what we are witnessing. The third section will examine the manner in which narrative momentum is created through synergetic and dialectical signs within the film's sub-narrative, and the extent to which music operates in this function. It will also consider the synergetic connection between the analysed sequence and *Red*'s narrative form.

In order to approach this analysis it would be valuable to review first something of the filmmaking philosophy behind *Red*. In fact, to consider the style and content of *Red* is to appreciate the defining characteristics of Kieslowski's fiction filmmaking, stemming from his fascination with morality, spirituality and metaphysics. He said of his work that he was 'perhaps [trying to capture] the soul. In any case, a truth which I myself haven't found'.[1] It is this agenda that inspired Kieslowski to downplay surface narrative in order to avoid facile and superficial treatment of what is often mysterious, irrational and complex. At the same time, this approach invites the audience to look deeper within the film's subtexts, and it is predominantly here that the most profound themes and ideas are contemplated. As Kieslowski himself commented, 'Things are very rarely said straight out in my films. Very often everything that's most important takes place behind the scenes, you don't see it.'[2]

Red is a beautiful model of understatement, allusion and communicative subtlety. And while narrative direction, on the one hand, seems uncertain, the film progresses with mystical purpose. This quality is achieved both through implied direction and development within the film's sub-narrative layers, and through the repetition of themes, ideas, incidents and signs, which together produce an unfolding filmic discourse. Consequently, the very methods of narrative and sub-narrative communication become aligned with the inherent mystery of the underlying subject matter itself. It all combines in an attempt to steer away from the (inevitably) literal nature of film. As Kieslowski explains:

> The goal is to capture what lies within us, but there's no way of filming it. You can only get nearer to it …. Literature can achieve this, cinema can't. It can't because it doesn't have the means. It's not intelligent enough. Consequently, it's not equivocal enough. Yet, at the same time, while being too explicit, it's also too equivocal.[3]

In part, it is because of this paradox that Preisner's contribution rose above and beyond that of conventional film-scoring practices. The traditional music–image relationship is one that has been called 'mutual implication',[4] which reflects the tendency of music to emphasize what is already apparent in other filmic media. Although this role does not preclude the writing of interesting and arresting music, the resulting overstatement (or, as Hanns Eisler termed it, 'hyperexplicity'[5]) may be thoroughly inappropriate for weighty, complex subject matter. In the case of *Red*, this problem is avoided in part as Preisner only occasionally underscores the already downplayed surface narrative drama. On a sub-narrative level he does a great deal more; however, the other channels of filmic discourse with which the music interacts are often so subtle in their (connotative) communication that the overall combined effect remains understated. Throughout *Red*, Preisner deftly interweaves his music into the surface and sub-narrative layers, both within and outside the diegesis, combining it intricately and synergetically with a variety of filmic media. The result is a filmic language of outstanding sensitivity.

Although the following focus of study will be attributing various filmic ingredients to either Kieslowski or Preisner, it should be acknowledged here that

Kieslowski commonly collaborated with various personnel from very early stages of the filmmaking process. Virtually all his screenplays were co-written with Krzysztof Piesiewicz (*Red* included), and Kieslowski would usually employ his cinematographer and producer in a creative/advisory role to the script from the very outset of a project.[6] Such an inclusive approach is not unusual to Polish filmmaking and this integration applied also to the artistic contribution of Preisner.[7]

Analysis: musical functions in music cue 1 of *Three Colours: Red*

Introductory brief

The first few minutes of *Three Colours: Red* focus primarily on the character of Valentine, a dance student and part-time model living in Geneva. We are also introduced to a young man who lives in an apartment opposite Valentine's, but there is no indication that they know each other, or are even consciously aware of each other's presence. We learn that Valentine has a boyfriend who is abroad in England. As they talk on the telephone it becomes apparent that he is a rather possessive character, although she misses him a great deal. In his absence she seems to lead a busy lifestyle, and one in which she allows a certain amount of control to be exerted on her by others. We see her being instructed in a dance class and told what emotions to express during a photo shoot. Further insight into her character comes indirectly from a moment when she loses on a fruit machine in a bar, but is happy she has lost. The implication is that she feels this represents a good omen, and therefore we are informed of Valentine's superstitious sensibilities; the moment also demonstrates a degree of simplicity and optimism in her world-view. Nevertheless, there is clearly an emotional depth to Valentine, and when asked to think of something sad during a photo session, this seems to come to her very naturally.

1   Narrative and characterization

Scenes 1 and 2   Valentine, thirsty after a dance class, drinks from a bottle of water which sparkles in the sunlight. We soon hear a faint bolero rhythm on orchestral strings and the film cuts to a fashion show where we see her step out onto a catwalk, modelling a light coat. A melodic theme is introduced over the bolero accompaniment, soon after which the music becomes more full-bodied. The catwalk itself takes up a great deal of space in a large room and has enormous, low-hanging chandeliers as centrepieces around which the models walk. Half a dozen models occupy the platform at a time, walking in choreographed sequence while onlookers applaud and camera flashes abound. Valentine smiles enigmatically as she makes her way around the catwalk. On her return she stumbles slightly, but quickly regains her balance. She exits and remarks to a dresser 'I nearly fell'.

Indications are that the music we hear during the fashion show emanates from the diegesis (since we expect music to accompany models on a catwalk). The principal theme embodies striking beauty, resonance and warmth (see Example 10.1).

Example 10.1   *Three Colours: Red*, fashion show
Reproduced by permission of Zbigniew Preisner

On the most superficial level, the music simply supplies suitable fashion show accompaniment. The bolero underpinning provides a fitting rhythmic momentum to the steady and constant movement on the catwalk, and the theme itself embodies a lyrical grace that blends perfectly with Valentine's elegance, the refined clothes and the ornate fashion show decor.

On a purely denotative level, that is about as far as this scene goes. However, on a connotative level there is a great deal being communicated here about the character of Valentine. This is in part emphasized by the *mise-en-shot* camera direction that tracks Valentine throughout the scene, encouraging connections between her, the music and accompanying/peripheral visual elements.

One of the main connotative communications here is that of purity and goodness. We see Valentine drinking from the sun-lit bottle of water, which visually anticipates the sparkling chandeliers and camera flashes. There is an overwhelming aspect of light and beauty in the fashion show itself. Indeed, there is a striking to Valentine, suggesting an index of her angelic nature. Additionally, the elevated, celestial catwalk conveys a somewhat removed, idealistic perspective. Together with the beautiful models, fashionable clothes, admiring and applauding onlookers, we discern a visual metaphor of her optimistic, insular and perhaps naive outlook.

The accompanying music parallels and emphasizes Valentine's purity, idealism and world-view in a number of ways. The simple focus on D major tonic/subdominant harmony fuses with the connoted sense of Valentine's insular perspective, but also her optimism, because of the bright major key tonality. Both optimism and purity are paralleled by the fact that the mellifluous theme emanates grace and beauty through its expansive, consonant melodic architecture. The quality of purity is also accentuated through the high and resonant instrumental registers, due to our tendency to associate 'high' with light and goodness (and conversely 'low' with darkness and impurity). Importantly, therefore, there are no signs of harmonic restlessness or destabilizing rhythms that would otherwise contribute a sense of ambiguity or discomfort. Instead, we simply hear lucid, uninhibited movement: there is a sense of openness here, that Valentine has nothing to hide or be ashamed of.

Scene 3 It is (probably) late evening and Valentine sits in her car after the show, massaging first her wrists and then her head. She looks tired, but also pensive. The theme of the fashion show is heard on guitar, supported by harp and clarinet, but without bolero accompaniment. We first observe Valentine from a perspective looking through the windscreen of the car, and then from behind some revolving doors. She starts the car and drives off.

This scene is noteworthy on a technical level in that it conveys something new simply through a change of instrumentation, rather than the use of thematic variation. With a shift of key to A mixolydian/major, Preisner takes the melodic theme unequivocally out of the diegesis and affirms its leitmotivic relationship to Valentine. By excluding the bolero rhythm he brings into focus a very delicate quality of the theme, enhanced through the gentle interplay of guitar and harp/clarinet accompaniment. The guitar brings out meditative qualities within the theme by virtue of its soft timbres and laconic utterances from short sustaining power. The result is music that breathes, pauses, and encourages us to feel a depth of sensitivity and reflection that does not exist simply within the visual context. Furthermore, it also emphasizes Valentine's solitude. Up to this point in the film we have seen her in company, but not gained any sense of companionship or closeness with others. The closest she seems to anyone is her boyfriend – and he is away in England. In this scene the guitar is therefore effectively singled out and further asserts a sense of this solitude. Preisner has stated that he likes to 'connect a special instrument with the film, something that will guide the listener to the soul of the story. Like something metaphysical.'[8] Although there is not such an obvious instrumental protagonist in *Red*, the occasional use of guitar – often instrumentally exposed and voiced either *piano* or *pianissimo* – manifests aspects of this approach by emphasizing a sense of isolation: a theme relevant to all three main characters of this film.

Scene 4   Valentine drives up to a set of traffic lights on red (we see this from a camera angle behind the red rear light of the car). A motorcyclist also waits, in front of her. From the start of this scene a new musical theme is heard with bolero accompaniment. The lights change and the motorcyclist and Valentine drive off, at which point we see a man crossing the road carrying some books, tied together in a bundle. We soon recognize this man as Valentine's neighbour, to whom we were introduced earlier. The string around the books snaps and they fall onto the road. One book falls open at a certain page, and he begins to read it with apparent interest.

Example 10.2   *Three Colours: Red*, **second theme, part 1**
Reproduced by permission of Zbigniew Preisner

In the early stages of this scene the diegetic/non-diegetic status of the music becomes ambiguous, as we see Valentine tapping her fingers on the steering wheel. We therefore sense that the music may be emanating from her car stereo (see Example 10.2). This is clearly a modal theme wherein Preisner exploits murky, dissonant intervallic relationships. Certainly from Western perceptions and sensibilities of tonal language, minor seconds and diminished fifths – built around chords on the tonic and flattened supertonic degrees – do not manifest sentiments of stability, promise and optimism. Instead they convey a restless quality, and, compounded by the slow melodic rhythm (and prominent reverb in the music's recording), consequently suggest something ominous: the presence of danger. The resumed bolero, now in a higher register, also enhances something of this ambience through the incorporation of the rather eerie microtonal movement. Indeed, other media are at this moment compounding this communication, most notably the ubiquity of the colour red (this will be considered in much greater detail in Section 2). Initially, however, the expectation of danger is interrupted at the book-dropping incident. The music fades out, and silence marks this as a significant moment.

Scene 5 Valentine is driving, listening to music on the car radio. We can instantly recognize that the music is related to the second theme we have just heard. The radio experiences static interference and Valentine fiddles with it to improve the reception; we even see her hit the radio, with obvious frustration. While momentarily preoccupied, the car hits something in the road. Valentine, startled, quickly stops and begins to reverse.

Example 10.3   *Three Colours: Red,* **second theme, part 2**
Reproduced by permission of Zbigniew Preisner

With the shift of focus back on Valentine, the second music theme (now undoubtedly diegetic, on the radio) has progressed into something rather martial and aggressive (Example 10.3). Purely in terms of musical expression, this idea would seem to be signalling, loud and clear, impending danger or disaster. However, it is unlikely that the music actually *heightens* the audience's expectations of this, in comparison with the previous scene. For a start, emanating from the diegesis, the music assumes a denotative function, simply as 'music heard on the radio, experiencing interference'. This, to a significant extent, buries the connotative communication of danger. Added to this, the music now occupies a more middle-ground auditory perspective, having receded from the previous foreground auditory perspectives of scenes 2 to 4. So, although the abstract qualities of the music point towards something both imminent and ominous, together with the fact that we are now conditioned to hear music as something highly relevant to Valentine, we are not tense with expectation. The effect at this point is altogether more subtle. As we hear the car 'thump' and see Valentine's startled reaction, the music pulls out. Silence marks another significant moment.

Scene 6   A German Shepherd dog lies injured on the road. Valentine gets out of the car and approaches it. She shows immediate concern and tenderness, stroking the wounded dog. During this we have heard high string pedals, with thematic allusions to the second theme on clarinet. After a moment's thought she opens up the back door of her car and then tries to pick up the dog. The dog yelps with pain. She manages to get the dog into the car and sees the name Rita on the dog collar, with an address. Now we hear fragments of the first theme on guitar. Valentine studies a map as Rita licks her hand.

Throughout this scene we are wrapped up in the narrative event. We see the cause of the 'thump' and are concerned for the wounded dog. We also witness narrative confirmation of Valentine's goodness, which so far has been largely communicated through the use of filmic metaphors.

Initially, it may seem that the thematic musical references do not carry any narrative or characterizational relevance. After all, such referencing at least retains musical continuity and coherence. Nevertheless, by scoring in this way, Preisner is deliberately making a point. First, the reference to the second theme connects the connotations of impending danger to an outcome, or at least an event. Secondly, as Valentine tries to do the 'right thing' – help the dog – the accompanying musical reference to the first theme enforces the leitmotivic qualities of goodness and purity that were established in the fashion show scene.

Scenes 1 to 6: a question of musical continuity

To conclude this section, it is of interest to note that each scene change from the fashion show onwards is accompanied by a change in musical dimension or subject matter. In other words, Preisner does not seem to stress musical continuity over spatial/temporal discontinuity. This procedure seems to go against the grain of one of the time-honoured roles of film music. As Claudia Gorbman writes:

> The bath or gel of affect in which music immerses film narrative … rounds out the sharp edges, smoothes roughness, masks contradictions, and masks spatial or temporal discontinuity with its own sonic and harmonic continuity. Film music lessens awareness of the frame, of discontinuity … .[9]

However, there are two important considerations here. First, 'sharp edges', 'roughness' and 'contradictions' are not really of issue in this sequence – the narrative is clear and the various scenes play themselves out in an unhurried manner (indeed, this is typical of Kieslowski's filmmaking style). Secondly, whilst Preisner does not compose 'across' various scene changes, he nonetheless asserts continuity within the music's thematic and harmonic structures. Significantly, the modulatory shift at scene 3 takes the key to the closely related dominant key, and also the first theme is repeated, albeit with changed instrumentation. And whilst the second, contrasting theme may further delineate the next scene change (that is, to scene 4), Preisner maintains the new tonic key and utilizes the bolero device to stress compositional connection with the first theme. Musical continuity is therefore very much intact, which in turn provides added coherence to the filmic sequence.

2   Metonymy and musical subtexts

The mixolydian quality of Valentine's theme (scenes 2 and 3) is one that could well be passed over, were it not for the fact that the second theme is so blatantly modal in character. Instead, we have to acknowledge a slight connection between the two themes in so much as they avoid, to different extents, defining characteristics of the Western tonal system. In Valentine's theme, the modality is defined by the use of the flattened seventh within a major key context. Although confined to the first section of the theme (see Example 10.1), this harmonic quality is exposed almost immediately above the bolero, which pulsates on the D tonic. Within the harmony itself the major third is felt rather than heard, and although the melody incorporates the major third degree, this does not enforce the tonal implications of the flattened seventh as a modulatory (and therefore destabilizing) dissonance. Of course, we do perceive tonal qualities within this theme, primarily because the mixolydian mode is so closely connected to the familiar tonality of major keys. However, because the occurrences of the flattened seventh are never immediately followed by chord IV (which would thereby emphasize its tonal implications), the modal quality remains firm.

Whereas the mixolydian references hark back to the early, Greek-influenced church modes, the second theme (see Examples 10.2 and 10.3) reminds us of something further east. Indeed, the these intervallic qualities can also be found in the Arabic *Hedjaz* mode (one used by the Muezzin in a call to prayer), in Syriac-Orthodox church-songs, and in the second tone of the Greek Church tunes.[10] In short, there exists within this theme a veritable religious/mystical metonymy. It could be argued that this not only brings into focus similar undertones within the first theme, but also the mystical quality of the bolero's microtonal movement (as used in accompaniment to the second theme), considering the established use of microtones in Oriental and Oriental-Semitic traditions. However, what is categorical is the fact that the second theme, appreciably infused with religious/mystical qualities, steers our interpretation of events away from a materialistic perspective to one inclined towards mystical and incorporeal realms.

Alongside the second theme and bolero there are important developments of music–image association relating to the incidences of chance, and the proximity of Valentine to her 'unseen' neighbour. When the second theme enters, it initially leads up to the point where the man drops his books. We have indications that the music is diegetic, but this is not certain. As Valentine drives away, the music remains momentarily with the man picking up his books (now certainly non-diegetic). It thereby stresses, through association, a thematic relevance to both characters and consequently (due to the pronounced modal language) a mystical link between them.

At the same time, by virtue of symbiosis, the second theme becomes associated with incidences of chance. The first association coincides with the linking process, as the string holding the neighbour's books together breaks and one of the books coincidentally falls open at a page of interest. In the following scene (scene 5), the altered second theme leads us to another incident of chance – the accident – one that, as opposed to the earlier coincidence, seems on all accounts to be negative. On the one hand, the mystical second theme casts a certain metaphysical relevance on these apparently random, chance events. But, in turn, these associated events imbue the second theme with connotations of design and even purpose – it is as though these things were meant to happen – and it thus takes on an added metonymical suggestion of fate.

It should be noted that there are two other mediums significantly contributing to our reading of events in the third scene of this sequence. First, the very title of the film suggests that the colour scheme of red may bear narrative/dramaturgical significance. Indeed, like the other films of the *Three Colours* trilogy, the eponymous colour carries cultural metonymy: red for love, danger/warning, blood, passion – and also fraternity.[11] And it is no coincidence that the lead female character is called Valentine, a name or word that for many implies the theme of romance. Within the context of this sequence, the metonymical implications of blood and danger are of course particularly significant. However, Kieslowski also develops additional associations with the colour red. In the opening scenes of the film we see that Valentine's flat is situated over a café with a red awning; we learn that she has slept with the red coat of her absent boyfriend; we watch her posing for a photo shoot in front of a red sheet, and so on. We have also seen the young man, her neighbour, driving a red jeep. In the fourth scene of this sequence, such connections are emphasized as we approach the traffic lights from a camera perspective behind the left (red) rear light of Valentine's car, and ultimately come to rest at the end of the scene on a shot that encompasses both a red traffic light and the red frame of a large billboard. The first shot carries with it implications of danger, partly because of the accompanying (ominous) music, but also due to the rather disorientating camera perspective and the aggressive engine revving of a motorbike that enters the shot. By the close of the scene the music has faded, but the red light and billboard operate in part to bracket together Valentine and the young man. Consequently, the colour of red is developed as a metonymical construct to signify destiny, suggesting as it does a mysterious, portentous connection (perhaps involving love, passion, danger ...) between the two characters.[12]

Secondly, Kieslowski's use of *mise-en-shot* camera direction within the fourth scene also compounds the sense of connection between the two characters. As a communicative mechanism, such camera direction becomes established very early on. In one impressive *mise-en-shot* sequence in the opening few minutes of the film, the camera's viewpoint shifts from an outdoor observation of Valentine's neighbour exiting his house and crossing the street, to one which, having climbed and passed through an open window into Valentine's first floor flat, settles close up in front of a ringing telephone. The same shot records a further minute's worth of her telephone conversation before a cut to another camera angle takes place. Although a much simpler example, a *mise-en-shot* of this fourth scene takes us from Valentine's car (pulling away from the traffic lights) to the neighbour dropping his books. This manoeuvre compounds the growing catalogue of such shots that serve to highlight the proximity of Valentine to her neighbour – how they so often occupy the same space and yet remain oblivious to one another. Taken within its own context, this might be as much as we would read into the situation; but because this particular camera direction interacts with the prominent mediums of colour scheme and music, it serves as an additional corroborating channel to deeper, mystical connections.

Another notable and pervading aspect of these six scenes is that of the changing diegetic/non-diegetic status of music. The complete sequence incorporates the following musical shifts in and out of the diegesis:

Valentine drinks water (cat-walk music anticipated)	Non-diegetic (or diegetic overlap)
Cat-walk	Diegetic
Valentine in car – drives off	Non-diegetic
Approaches traffic lights	Diegetic (?) to diegetic overlap = non-diegetic
Valentine fiddles with radio	Diegetic
Attends to wounded dog	Non-diegetic

The fact of this musical omnipresence is interesting because, to some extent, the music becomes part of the metaphysical world of signs to which the characters themselves may be subliminally aware. This role can be observed in the use of diegetic music in scene 5. By this time, we, the viewers, can already recognize that the second theme carries a metonymical connotation of fate. The character of Valentine would not know this, having not been witness to all the relevant events and signs; nevertheless, the music she hears still embodies a mystical quality and is additionally aggressive and foreboding. So by appreciating the diegetic, metaphysical significance of the music, we can infer the action of Valentine struggling with, and even hitting, the radio to improve the reception, as a sign of her unconsciously – and unsuccessfully – struggling with fate.[13] Such use of diegetic music thereby contributes to a central metaphysical theme of the film concerning the intangibility of meaning and purpose, within a seemingly chance-ridden existence.

In the accident aftermath (scene 6) we may infer that there is more to the moment than meets the eye. An accident has occurred and a dog lies wounded in the road: such is the denoted event. But Preisner's referencing of the second theme (with everything that it now implies) calls into question a deeper significance of what we are witnessing – perhaps that this is a catalytic moment. Taken in isolation, the music falls short of communicating this unequivocally, primarily because it is only faintly heard. However, it is compounding a sense of syntagmatic expectation that is arguably not resolved by the accident itself. In other words, surely, from all the previous connotations of warning and danger, we expect something more than a wounded dog? This question will be discussed further in Section 3.

As a point of general interest, the atmospheric reverberation heard throughout the cue (and throughout *Red*) is in some ways of incidental importance to the sub-narrative, in that it is a standard characteristic of Preisner's recording technique. Together with his tendency towards sparse scoring and contrasting layers of instrumentation, it is a stylistic feature that anyone familiar with his work will naturally expect. Preisner has stated that the reverb gives his music a 'breathing' quality.[14] Not to deny this aspect, in the context of *Red* (and indeed within other films of Kieslowski) the pervasive reverb also suggests the resonances associated with religious buildings, such as churches and temples, and it consequently helps assert the mysterious, metaphysical undertones of both the musical themes and the subject matter itself.

3   Methods of filmic development

Synergism

> You can describe something which … doesn't exist in the picture alone or the music alone. Combining the two, a certain meaning, a certain value, something which determines a certain atmosphere, suddenly begins to exist.[15]

This quotation of Kieslowski sums up a great deal of what has so far been discussed in this analysis. Nevertheless, it should be noted that synergism itself is an inevitable consequence of the marriage of music and image. Even if the music simply adds another layer of pathos to an already pathetic situation, the resulting quality of pathos will not lie solely within either channel of discourse. Ideally, Preisner would not want his music to function in such a narrow manner. As he has commented: 'If the music [tells] the audience what is already visible, there is no use listening to it.'[16] Hence the nuanced manner in which Preisner musically compounds visually connoted themes.

But there are further dimensions to the synergetic processes, which raise questions and directional expectations. There are two main signifiers of the sequence to consider. The first example is found in the connoted signs of chance and destiny that seem to link Valentine to her neighbour. There has been nothing explicitly communicated thus far in the narrative, but the sub-narrative bracketing together of these characters through the synergetic activity of music, *mise-en-shot* camera work and colour scheme results in a question that the sequence itself does not answer: What is the connection between these two characters? The second case concerns the connoted elements of impending danger in scenes 4 and 5. To summarize, there is the metonymical implication from the colour red; the rather disorientating visual perspective from the rear light of Valentine's car; the aggressive engine noise of the motorbike at the traffic lights; and the ominous second musical theme. Furthermore, the unsettled ambience is intensified because it is dark, so Valentine seems all the more vulnerable. This combination of signs thereby creates a sense of expectancy for the viewer. In scene 5, Kieslowski diminishes in part the connotations of danger by reducing the presence of red in the visuals and increasing the 'denotative' function of the music (becoming unequivocally diegetic radio music). On one level, Kieslowski is merely avoiding an inexorable crescendo of tension to an inevitably negative outcome. Nonetheless, as mentioned earlier, the ensuing accident does not seem to adequately resolve the weight of the synergetically compounded signs of danger throughout scenes 4 and 5. Perhaps, if the music had not played a part in this, then the weight of the visual metonymical signs would seem just about proportional to the subsequent event. But the interaction of the second theme significantly increases the implication of danger and its consequentiality. By satisfying our expectations only in part, the narrative achieves an added sense of forward momentum: we await further resolution.

Dialectical development

There is an additional interconnectedness of elements within the sequence that gives rise to implied narrative/sub-narrative development. It can be seen that the overall structure of the music, with its contrasting first and second themes, asserts a dialectical relationship. This relationship is both confirmed and emphasized not only through the bolero accompaniment to both themes, but also through the simple juxtaposition of themes, in almost sonata-form fashion (first theme stated in D mixolydian/major tonic; shift with first theme into dominant key of A mixolydian/major; followed by statement of contrasting, modal second subject). In other words, we hear the dark, ominous 'metaphysical' second theme in pronounced dialectical opposition to the light, serene first theme.[17] Simply on a musical level we therefore feel a desire for development, if not resolution, which in itself is a directional component. But when considering the entire cue in context, a great deal of impending opposition and confrontation is implied within the sub-narrative because in addition to the linear, syntactic construction of the sequence, the dialectical musical structure consolidates the relationship of visual signs in scenes 1 to 3 with those of 4 and 5. So elements of light, purity, optimism and beauty are set against elements of darkness, aggression, danger and ugliness (that is, the accident). Such dialectical structuring also encourages the idea that Valentine's stumbling in the fashion show represents a synecdochic dialectic – a sign that Valentine's world-view (as metaphorically indexed by the fashion show itself) is about to be shaken.

While there is extensive variety in what could ensue after the events of these scenes, the synergetic and dialectical structures of this sequence seem to indicate that:

● Valentine, pure and idealistic, is heading towards something that will confront who she is and what she believes;

● there will be development of the mystical connection between Valentine and her neighbour;

● an element of danger will play a part in future events;

● the whole will be immersed in questions of chance and destiny.

It is valuable to remind ourselves that dialogue has played no part in this communication process. Furthermore, because these sub-textual directional qualities cannot be seen to exist within any one part, the communication of such remains poetically understated.

However, it is not important that we *consciously* discern all this. What is important is the fact that the sequence communicates something that will later become corroborated, contextualized and viscerally understood.

Further development of narrative/sub-narrative

We have seen how unresolved dialectical tension, manifested through music and image alone, lends a certain directional quality to the film by the creation of expectation. But whereas the element of danger (which, to an extent, certain signifiers carry throughout *Red*) is not fully realized until a ferry disaster occurs towards the very end of the film, other dialectical and metaphysical implications of the sequence become realized much earlier. This process happens through a developing conflict of personal perspectives between the film's two main characters. In the ensuing scenes, Valentine finds the owner of the dog to be a reclusive and misanthropic retired judge. On their first meeting, the judge shows no interest in his wounded dog and Valentine, repulsed by him, takes the dog to a vet herself. On a second meeting, she finds the judge eavesdropping on a neighbour's telephone conversation, using specialized equipment – an activity that he clearly spends a lot of time doing. In terms of his pessimistic and cynical outlook, the judge seems to be the very opposite of Valentine. But, wishing to understand him, Valentine begins to spend time with him. As a result, the dialectical structures that were introduced in the opening scenes of the film develop further, as the two characters find themselves challenging each other's views and actions. Initially, the confrontation seems to be one way. The judge, though highly intuitive, is incredibly stubborn and Valentine is noticeably shaken by the man's lack of morality and his persuasive cynicism. Later, we come to appreciate that Valentine's purity, openness and optimism are taking effect on the judge. Within this context of moral argument, a further dimension to the narrative emerges as we see the judge take particular interest in the affairs of Valentine's neighbour (a lawyer called Auguste), and his girlfriend, on whose telephone conversations he also eavesdrops. We discern that the judge seems to have some degree of control over various events in the life of Auguste, who himself becomes a judge during the course of the film. Consequently, the mystical undertones of these circumstances are manifest. So as the narrative/sub-narrative develops, the connoted signs and themes of the opening scenes of *Red*, and in particular the dialogue-free scenes of the analysed sequence, become further substantiated and contextualized.

In the same way, Preisner's bolero device also becomes further contextualized in later stages of the film. The similarities and recurrent situations we notice between the retired judge and Auguste – paralleled by the subtle repetition of signs, metaphors and sounds – become an increasingly stronger presence, to the extent that by the end of the film it is as though Auguste is reliving a version of the retired judge's life. The bolero therefore stands as a metaphysical signifier that parallels the recurrent events within the narrative through its own repetitions of rhythmic motif.[18] Its application is therefore leitmotivic; but whereas the leitmotivic qualities of the two themes it accompanies are fairly clear, this particular metaphysical significance of the bolero is never explicit and certainly cannot be understood solely by its use in the opening cue: it exists at this point alongside other nascent metonymical constructs that become progressively meaningful to the viewer (on either a conscious or subconscious level) as the filmic drama unfolds.

What may now be appreciated is that within this music cue there exists a kind of abstract parallel fiction of the film's narrative. During the course of this analysis, qualities such as serene, beautiful, pure, innocent and isolated, have been attached to the first theme, and to the second theme, adjectives such as ominous, mysterious, spiritual and aggressive have been applied. Such terms seem appropriate because they describe fairly accurately the various characteristics of the two themes, given their particular contextualization. Nonetheless, I have attempted at various stages to qualify the more abstract nature of the themes, very much within music's 'Westernized' representational capacity. The dialectical relationship between these two themes, enhanced by a cohesive musical structure, is very clear, and we have also seen how the bolero embodies a contextual significance on the metaphysical theme of recurrent events and experiences. So we hear a repeated event – the bolero – itself containing repeated events in the form of motivic repetitions, contextualized within a mystically and metaphysically infused thematic dialogue. Therein lies a mirror of recurring narrative events and the dialectical struggle we witness between Valentine and the retired judge. Preisner thereby creates a symbolic musical structure that both prefigures and parallels the film's narrative discourse.

In summary

During the course of this analysis of *Three Colours: Red* a number of musical roles have been identified. These can be isolated and summarized on eight distinct levels, as shown below:

1. The technical role within the filmic composition. Music (regardless of its connotative meaning) is used to structure and stress the relationship of visual events and connoted themes.

2. The diegetic functional role. In this respect I have applied the term 'denotative'. In other words, there is a level on which the music does not assume any connotative meaning, because it is fulfilling a functional role within the context of the fashion show, and likewise, later on, for in-car entertainment.

3. The (non-diegetic) surface narrative role. A prime example of this is found in scene 6, where Preisner underscores a sense of tension as the dog lies wounded in the street.

4. The corroborating sub-narrative role. The music compounds other filmic media to connote the personality, disposition and outlook of Valentine, and later, to imply impending danger.

5. The discrete sub-narrative role. It is essentially the music alone that imparts a mystical quality to various signs within the sub-narrative. It therefore

contextualizes them in such a way that we begin to discern a sub-textual metaphysical discourse.

6. The diegetic connotative/metaphysical role. Music operates as a subliminal sign to Valentine (in scene 5) and therefore assumes a connotative role within the diegetic context.

7. The directional role. Whereas filmic direction/development is traditionally conveyed though surface narrative, in *Red* it not only becomes a sub-narrative aspect, but one that is sometimes conveyed exclusively through music–image synergism.

8. A parallel discourse. There exist within the music certain parallels of the film's narrative. Due to the symbiotic mechanisms of this sequence, many of the central ingredients – purity and innocence, isolation, mysticism, antithetical/dialectical struggle, the theme of recurrent events perceived within a spiritual dimension – become identified and consolidated within the music. In turn, the music parallels them all in a structural synecdoche.

While the first five roles listed are common to many films, it is not so often that one finds them all in the same cue. But not only does Preisner's opening cue fulfil these more regular demands in a beautifully artistic and individual manner, it also reaches far beyond into highly innovative forms of filmic development. It is because of this integration and interaction that the analysis has been able to demonstrate something of the nature of *Red*'s narrative form. In most films, direction is achieved by raising questions and creating expectation within the surface narrative alone. Often, if there are underlying themes, they carry no structural weight or significance. In *Red*, there are very few questions and even fewer expectations raised in the surface narrative; instead, these are developed in a subtle, understated manner within the film's sub-narrative, which in turn provides momentum and meaning to the narrative events. Throughout *Red*, therefore, we experience an inventive approach to narrative form, synergetically created by the interplay of surface and sub-narrative, not itself contained within either part. Kieslowski himself said in 1994: 'physicists are starting to look for the relationship between microscopic elements to try and explain life's mysteries. Perhaps in my films I'm trying to do the same.'[19]

Notes

1. Mensonge, M. 'Three Colours Blue, White and Red: Krzysztof Kieslowski and friends', *Cinema Papers*, June 1994, 27.
2. Stok, S. *Kieslowski on Kieslowski*, London, Boston: Faber & Faber, 1993, 216.
3. Ibid., 194.
4. Gorbman, C. *Unheard Melodies: Narrative Film Music*, Bloomington: Indiana University Press, 1987, 15.

5. Eisler, H. and Adorno, T. *Composing for the Film*, New York: Oxford University Press, 1947, 14.
6. *Red* cinematographer: Piotr Sobocinski; *Three Colours* trilogy producer: Marin Karmitz.
7. Mensonge, M. 'Three Colours Blue, White and Red: Krzysztof Kieslowski and friends', 32.
8. Carisson, M. and Holm, P. 'Interview with Zbigniew Preisner', *Music from the Movies*, May 1997, 39.
9. Gorbman, *Unheard Melodies*, 59.
10. Idelsohn, A. *Jewish Music in its Historical Development*, London: Henry Holt & Co., 1929, Ch. 2.
11. As symbolized in the French Tricolour.
12. As the film develops, the colour of red also symbolizes the conditional mood – a metaphor for the question 'What if ...?'
13. As for Valentine herself, a further chance to recognize this incident as a 'sign' comes later, as she enters the house of the dog's owner, a retired judge. Looking for the occupant, she hears static interference coming from what seems to be a radio. The sound is remarkably similar to that heard on the radio before the accident. This is one of the first indications that either the judge is somehow drawing Valentine to himself, or the hand of destiny is upon them both.
14. Carisson, M. and Holm, P. 'Interview with Zbigniew Preisner', 39.
15. In Stok, S. *Kieslowski on Kieslowski*, 179.
16. Carisson, M. and Holm, P. 'Interview with Zbigniew Preisner', 42.
17. This is not to suggest that the tonal conflict, inherent within the exposition section of sonata form, has any bearing on the thematic dialectic here, as it is the first theme that introduces the new key of A mixolydian/major.
18. Carisson, M. and Holm, P. 'Interview with Zbigniew Preisner', 41. Preisner confirms this role of the bolero: 'I chose a bolero to describe the circular movement ... it's about things coming again and again.'
19. Mensonge, M. 'Three Colours Blue, White and Red: Krzysztof Kieslowski and friends', 28.

Chapter 11

'The Rhythm of the Night': reframing silence, music and masculinity in *Beau Travail*

Heather Laing

'Here I am, Commandant. Like a watchdog. Looking after your flock.'[1]

In the final scene of Claire Denis' 1999 film *Beau Travail*, remorseful protagonist Sergeant Galoup (Denis Lavant) bursts into action on an empty dance floor. Watching himself in the mirrored walls he dances in an increasingly frenetic style before disappearing from the screen into the blackness that will herald the closing titles. This is the dance floor that has been seen throughout his memories in the film – populated by his fellow legionnaires, the women of Djibouti and his girlfriend Rahel (Marta Tafesse Kassa) – where he has remained always on the sidelines, unable to relinquish his self-control to join the dancing. The scene is notable in both stylistic and narrative terms as an emotional representation of Galoup's suicide. As Denis herself says: 'It's as if his soul is freed from his body. It flows out with the blood from his veins.'[2] The cathartic value of this scene is often attributed to the violent athleticism of his dance, but this does not seem fully to explain why it comes as such a shock, a relief and why, despite his tragic circumstances and the anger of his movements, we feel so uplifted as he dances to his death.

The fact that such a moment is played out through music and dance immediately calls into question the role of the soundtrack in Galoup's emotional and behavioural trajectory throughout the film. This film adheres to neither the thematic conventions of the classical score nor the self-expressive diegetic numbers of the musical to encourage our identification with or sympathy for its characters. Its methodology is more obscure. It integrates the functions of sound, diegetic music and silence to both represent and undermine Galoup's view of himself, his past and his masculine identity. The non-diegetic score and *mise-en-scène* also both represent and critique Galoup's behaviour, through an intertextual examination of masculine emotion and containment. This chapter examines this methodology – both as a unique means of placing Galoup at the centre of an entire 'soundworld' from which there is only one means of escape, and as a development on conventional codes of film scoring relating to gender, excessive emotionality and silence.

The structural thematic of silence

Although Galoup's narration structures the entire film – so that we hear his voice almost constantly – he rarely remembers himself as a speaking subject. His self-representation is of a man of few words, economically delivered. In his contemporary Marseilles setting he also speaks only once, and then in the briefest of terms. He does not even, within the space of the film, *speak* his own voiceover. His story is drawn from the diary that he writes in both past and present, but we never see him read from this or recount its contents to anyone within the diegesis. His voiceover, which often accompanies scenes in Marseilles as well as in the past of Djibouti, remains an interior monologue. Such self-definition and representation through silence reflects the masculine mould in which he casts himself. As a sergeant of the French Foreign Legion, he exists in a context of institutional silence where recruits are famously 'asked no questions'. It is, as Kent Jones puts it, 'the universe of men silently faced towards one another and away from life'.[3] And Galoup is 'a perfect legionnaire'[4] – disciplined, focused, controlled in mind and body, emotionally self-contained and intensely private. He writes down rather than discusses his thoughts and is often alone. But the silence that signifies strong, controlled masculinity to Galoup is reframed by the film, perhaps under the influence of its literary source, as a sign of weakness and vulnerability – an emotional repression that leads to an *inability* to speak rather than a *choice* not to – a '[r]ecoil from the world of self-revelation'.[5]

Herman Melville's 1891 novella *Billy Budd, Sailor (An Inside Narrative)*, on which the film is based, turns on a central narrative device – the eponymous Billy's ultimately fatal stammer. Billy, although perfectly able to express himself under normal circumstances, stammers terribly when faced with highly emotional situations. As a result, when faced with Master-at-Arms John Claggart's attempt to frame him with an accusation of mutiny, he is rendered mute and can do nothing to express himself but strike out, delivering the fatal blow to his persecutor that eventually costs him his own life. In *Beau Travail*, this emotional stammer becomes a structuring principle of Galoup's character and, by extension, of the film's overall exploration of masculinity. No one actually stammers, but the idea of emotional silence – forcibly induced from either within or outside the self – and the violence resulting from such suppression, pervades the narrative. Its primary issue therefore lies in the act of repression itself, rather than the specificity of the emotions being repressed.[6]

The constant redistribution of silence intensifies its destructive power. Galoup is silenced in his attempt to communicate on the subject of Gilles Sentain (Grégoire Colin) – the innocent recipient of his instinctive jealousy and hatred – with his Commandant Bruno Forestier (Michel Subor), who uses the Legion's code of honour as a means of admonishment for this very modest, if corrupt, 'outburst' of feeling. Galoup in turn enforces his repressive silence on his men, most pointedly in both actual and metaphorical terms through his repeated response to any kind of indiscipline or dissent with silent or near silent exercise sessions.[7] Most importantly, however, Galoup imposes silence upon Sentain. Particularly during moments of social interaction between the men or when Sentain himself speaks, Galoup glares at him in silence, thus ensuring his subordinate's compliance. Finally, when Sentain attempts to speak on two occasions in defence of fellow legionnaire Comb (*sic*),[8] Galoup silences him first by overriding him verbally and secondly with a slap in the face. The displacement of the silencing emotional stammer from Billy Budd to Galoup results in the latter's inability to break out of his emotional repression and corrupted code of self-control, so that he too resorts to violent self-defence. In turn, his slap places Sentain in a similar defensive position and, suffering the same inability to speak, he performs a parallel act of violence towards his superior.

Holding on: the gendered soundscape and musical interludes

Galoup's masculinity informs his subjective representation of the past. His memories are almost entirely determined by the contrast of silence and sound – or perhaps more accurately 'noise'. Sound becomes associated with those things that threaten the idea of containment: personal conversation between both women and men; the diegetic pop and folk music that accompanies night-time Djibouti and Forestier's indulgence in drugs; the disco and its female sirens. It has a physical corollary in what might be termed 'visual noise' – the intense colours of the local women's clothing, the inky darkness and multi-coloured lights of the town at night[9] – and a behavioural equivalent in disorderly conduct or loss of 'edge'.[10] But the film does not allow his subjectivity to have sole authority and places his representation under constant strain. He represents the army camp as largely monochrome and often verbally silent. It is juxtaposed, however, not only with the vividness and diegetic music of the town but also with the impossibly bright turquoise sea. Even within its confines, the rank-and-file legionnaires chat, laugh, joke, sing and whistle – if only occasionally – and there are surreptitious instances of bright colour.[11] Finally, one of the most striking areas of pressure on Galoup's masculine containment comes from the film's use of non-diegetic music.

The balance of Galoup's subjectivity and the wider view of the film is introduced in the opening sequence of scenes – before his narration begins – and reiterated through a related series of musical 'interludes'. The film opens with titles on a black background, to the sound of blowing wind and faint orchestral music taken from Benjamin Britten's 1951 opera *Billy Budd*, his own adaptation of Melville's novella.[12] The first image is then revealed as a frieze painted on a wall, showing legionnaires deployed across a desert landscape. The accompanying music is a non-diegetic male chorus singing the legionnaires' song '*Sous le soleil brûlant d'Afrique*'.[13] It is unaccompanied, its volume is even and moderate, it has the rhythm and tempo of a march and its timbre suggests the outdoor location of its obviously untrained singers. These factors suggest musical functionality. It bonds the men mentally and physically into a robust and proud group. It expresses their principles and historicizes their image; they are part of a long tradition and an established code of honour that is the stuff of popular legend – a point that is later emphasized when their exercises are accompanied by a solo male voice singing another verse of the song. They are also, on the other hand, something of a thing of the past. The paintwork of the frieze is peeling and the Djibouti regiment no longer goes to war but engages in an apparently endless and redundant routine of 'training intensively for nothing in particular'.[14] As we reach the end of both the frieze and the song, the screen returns to black and we are presented in silence with a column of names – those of the four men who will head the cast. This offers a very particular idea of how the film will be. Military men – specifically of the French Foreign Legion – are its subject matter. At stake are issues of their community, their particular brand and code of masculinity and their image. The aura of the film is stark, even bleak, and its tone is austere.

Everything changes, however, when the black screen gives way to a close-up of a young African woman in a disco. She mimes a kiss at nobody in particular in time with the overblown kissing sound of Tarkan's disco track 'Simarik'[15] then laughs mockingly as she begins to dance. This is the first image of an actual person and the cut to close-up is unexpected, as is the sudden and dramatic increase in the volume of the soundtrack for both the kiss and the following music. The implied time is evening, the disco is dark and women in colourful, seductive clothing dance alone or with legionnaires. Its introduction through the face of a woman and the dominant presence of women on this and later occasions suggest the disco as a female space. Their music, rather than connoting a collective identity in honour and duty, evokes a mood of sensual enjoyment, interaction, frivolity and recreation.[16] When not dancing in front of the mirrored walls in narcissistic self-contemplation, they adopt highly sexualized modes of dance in response to the soldiers. Despite the sexual spectacle that they present, however, they are by no means passive. On the contrary, the female space is represented as just as suggestive of battle – in its own particular way – as the male space.

The disco scene rudely interrupts the film's reverent, historicized imagery of masculinity with a real, present-day woman. As the camera passes through the disco, two women dancing with legionnaires direct kisses in a humorous style directly to the camera. They therefore remove their attention from the men, who seem unaware of these apparent moments of surreptitious and humorous complicity with the (female?) film viewer.[17] The song meanwhile speaks of sexual game-playing and incorporates an unusual shift of gender in its address. Although it is sung primarily to and about a female subject, it shifts once into the use of the masculine version, in Turkish, of the pronoun 'you'. The singer therefore appears to direct his comments towards, by turns, a female and male lover, suggesting both heterosexual and homosexual love interests.[18] As well as the disco threatening Galoup with the idea of emotional and sexual interaction with women, the song therefore poses the additional 'threat' to his masculinity of homosexuality. As we return to the disco on later occasions, the sense of sexual power implicit in this initial air of gentle mockery seems to gather strength in the dramatic re-presentation of the women. The music always bursts onto the soundtrack at significantly greater volume than the surrounding scenes and cuts out all other diegetic sound. The women's unified style of dancing evokes the image of a highly sexualized battalion and their constant gaze at their reflections in the mirrored walls renders them their own, obviously appreciative audience. As they await the arrival of the men, they therefore present a kind of army of sirens advancing into war. The disco both adopts and subverts signifiers of the army and military activity. In Galoup's view, the women are on parade, are marching into battle, are psyching out the enemy – but in an offensive that threatens emotional and sexual '*interaction*'[19] rather than war.

Galoup's discomfort in this environment – the reality that threatens his imagery – is reflected in his constant self-marginalization. As he appears in the opening scene, he approaches Rahel from behind and touches her hand to attract her attention. She turns in response before casually disengaging from his touch. She then dances with no further attention to him and fades into the background while he stands rooted to the spot, seemingly agonized and barely managing to repress his own apparent desire to move in time with both her and the music. This offers a physical corollary of his verbal and emotional repression – he cannot express himself in words, neither can he 'let go' of his own body. As his tendency towards silence becomes more apparent, this contributes to the idea of a gendered division of both space and soundtrack that, unlike the other legionnaires, Galoup is unable to cross with any success. He is, by his own admission, 'narrow minded':[20] he fails to 'see' colour and the kind of detail that defines a landscape[21] and, despite having a girlfriend, his memories present disco music, and indeed diegetic music, as part of a 'feminine' world that threatens his self-containment and control. Such a threat is emphasized by his reaction to the music of the funeral procession, which causes him to contemplate his own and Forestier's deaths. The masculine space is the daytime, outdoor, spartan place of work, exercise and self-discipline. The feminine space of the night-time sees all discipline lost – the men drink, dance with women and fight. His view of the world in fact evokes a rather extreme version of Jacques Attali's conception of the relationship of music and 'noise'. Whereas Attali contends that music attests to the possibility of masculine civilization by its organization of feminine 'noise' into an ordered system of sounds,[22] Galoup eschews even music to see order only in silence. To retain the correct masculine order of both himself and the other men, he must subdue 'noise' with actual and/or metaphorical 'silence'.[23]

This often involves the channelling of his and his men's energy into the overtly muscular activity of combat exercise. These all-male episodes take place in bright daylight and, if not in silence, with only minimal or necessary sound. In the first such episode, the men are introduced by their own gaunt shadows on the desert sand. They stand, arms aloft, eyes closed, in an exercise of stamina and balance. In one sense, and no doubt to Galoup, this is a display of strength, self-discipline and endurance carried out in harsh conditions and stark silence. What we seem to be shown by the film, however, is a group of isolated bodies, made vulnerable by closed eyes and exposed torsos. They sway precariously in the wind and in some cases look fit to drop, but they must not move. Unlike the women of the disco, they are separated, isolated, denied an active relationship either to each other or the film audience. This offers an interesting variant on Richard Dyer's suggestion that being in action may preserve the masculinity of male bodies presented for spectatorial consideration.[24] The 'action' undertaken by these men presents them as more than normally passive. Their excessive vulnerability in fact evokes the imagery of crucifixion which, as Leon Hunt has pointed out, is essentially contradictory in its offsetting of passivity with control.[25] In this initial positioning, therefore, the men are represented as both actively muscular and yet passively vulnerable to our gaze and examination. While Galoup encourages only their strength, forbearance and silence, he unwittingly presents them as, in Yvonne Tasker's terms, 'both feminine and masculine',[26] thereby signalling the film's concern with the examination of the true nature of 'strong' masculinity.

This contradictory *mise-en-scène* is underpinned by a subversive use of non-diegetic music. Existing as it does at a physical 'distance' from the diegetic world, the non-diegetic score is not bound to support the emotions or intentions of characters but is able instead, if required, to comment upon or even criticize their behaviour. In this case, intertextual references to Britten's opera belie Galoup's outward control and suggest the truth of the contained chaos and latent violence that characterize his masculinity. Most of the exercise sessions are accompanied by choruses that crystallize the dynamics of disorder/fear of disorder and control that underpin the narrative of *Billy Budd*, so that the fear of mutiny that allows Claggart to frame Billy in both Melville's novella and Britten's opera translates in *Beau Travail* into Galoup's terror of his own emotional eruption.[27] As with the volcanoes that stand 'like sentinels'[28] over Galoup's attempt to separate Sentain from Forestier, there is a great deal of molten lava beneath the crust of control that he forces upon himself and his troops, and his attempts to quiet disorder or indiscipline in his men reflect his strenuous efforts to maintain control of himself.

The first hint of this problematic dynamic actually precedes even the first exercise session, coming as it does at the very outset of the film. The opening music comes from Act Two Scene Two of Britten's opera and its low volume, minor tonality and motivic repetition cast an ominous tone over the beginning of the film. This is qualified by reference to its place in the opera. It forms part of an interlude between two scenes that builds up into the conclusion of a shanty, 'Blow Her to Hilo, Riley', sung by the sailors. The shanty has been heard in the previous scene while the officers discuss their terror of mutiny. The intermittent sound of singing from below deck convinces them that all is well; that, and the fact that the men are so effectively policed by Claggart, the 'veritable Argus' with 'a hundred eyes'.[29] The portentous association of this introductory music with a false impression of equilibrium and control foretells the issues of masculinity with which the film will deal and casts an immediate shadow over the subsequent disembodied singing of the legionnaires.

Galoup's first group exercise is then accompanied by the chorus 'Oh Heave, Oh Heave Away Heave' from Act One Scene One of the opera. This belies the disciplined silence of its already paradoxical display and inflects it with a sense of arduous, possibly enforced labour, suffering and repetitious ritual. It also opens out its investigation to a more universal level. The shadows that first introduce us to the men recall the 'clear-cut shadows horizontally thrown of fixtures and moving men' on Melville's man-of-war.[30] The men of *Billy Budd* and *Beau Travail* are united in the anonymity of their shadows just as they are in their historicized images: the legionnaires of the desert; the sailors and impressed men of the man-of-war. Musically also, the shanty offers the seafaring equivalent of the legionnaires' song, and its use as a form connects *Beau Travail* not only to Britten's opera but also to Peter Ustinov's 1962 film adaptation of the same story, *Billy Budd*. The legionnaires and sailors symbolize displaced and disenfranchised men throughout history – fleeing or being forced out of society to serve in isolated, all-male enclaves. The cut to the following scene, made seamless by the continuation of the same operatic chorus, continues the recollection of their forebears as Galoup brings the men to the camp by sea. It is perhaps appropriate that the specific site of the film's test of masculinity is crystallized here, as the music reaches its climactic chords over a shot–reverse shot exchange of glares between Galoup and Sentain.

The final chorus is perhaps the most telling and is saved until later in the film. This makes explicit both the danger of the outbreak of masculine emotion and the force of control necessary for its containment. In the context of the opera, it follows immediately after Billy Budd's execution, witnessed by his fellow sailors, who now really do threaten to rise up in mutiny. The commands of the officers cut forcibly through the rising rabble of angry voices and, eventually, a return to their work routine distracts the men from their own emotions.[31] In the film, it appears for the first time accompanying an exercise session following Galoup's removal of his men from the army camp in his attempt to separate Sentain from Forestier. The power of the men is emphasized by the matching of the increasingly loud and angry chorus with unusually close shots of their faces, arms and hands, the slightly low angle of some of the shots and the expansive, muscular movement of their exercises. The commands of the officers then coincide with the appearance of Galoup and lead to the calmer image of the coastline at night. All the energy of this visual/musical combination is later invested in the specific relationship between Galoup and Sentain as it returns to accompany the intensity of their encircling, 'battle of wills' exercise. Although a temporary calm follows this episode, it is soon disturbed by Galoup's victimization of Comb as a means of entrapping Sentain. The final loss of his self-control that begins with this action is underlined by the following exercise session. Beginning with a painfully dissonant chord of the 'Hilo' sea shanty over a high-angle shot of Comb, this suggests his 'silencing' punishment for his alleged abandonment of his post. As the shot opens out, however, we see all the men engaged in a series of graceful stretching exercises. The joyful voices of Britten's chorus are calmed as Galoup's men lie slowly back on the ground – their painfully stretched torsos and bent legs resembling a scattering of dead bodies. Galoup's corrupt code of conduct threatens to destroy the legion and the positions of the men prefigure the position in which Galoup will later contemplate and perhaps commit suicide. The lie is finally given to the assurance of calm promised to the opera's officers by the sound of the shanty, and the true progenitor of mutiny has sealed his own fate.

Letting go: Galoup's journey from discipline to freedom

The one threat to order that Galoup cannot still is himself. His repressed hatred of Sentain is so great that it eventually erupts in an action of violently irrational and self-destructive fury. His desperate, ill-conceived attempt to send his innocent victim to his death in the desert, however, ultimately leads to Galoup's own pitiful downfall. His progress towards this eruption is suggested through a series of transgressive moments in which hints of his contained violence break through his veneer of self-discipline. His most important flaw is his possessiveness of Forestier and the jealousy that arises from his belief that Sentain has caught his superior's eye. After Forestier has congratulated Sentain for bravery we see Galoup, back in his room, viciously slam down his jacket onto a chair before forcibly regaining his composure. He resorts to breaking his usual silence in an attempt to sway Forestier against Sentain, although this is only reported in his voiceover – the only thing we see and hear 'live' is Forestier's admonishing response. Silenced once again, he confesses his next plan in his diary. Finally, it is an adoption of music and relatively free movement that signals his ultimate moment of triumph in his vengeful trajectory. With Sentain banished to the desert, Galoup strolls alone at night and, in an unprecedented moment of 'frivolity', *sings* – albeit almost inaudibly – and skips a step.

This loss of control in the past is mirrored by a similar trajectory of transgressive moments in the present. In the context of his regretful voiceover, however, these suggest a redemptive liberation from the codes that have previously bound him. As we see him for the second time in Marseilles, he listens in an almost tentative manner to diegetic pop music on the radio. Later, although the clothes that he washes are still military khaki, the washing bowl is a vivid pink, the pegs are blue and yellow, the clothes that he puts on are black – the colour of night – and as he gazes appreciatively at himself in his bathroom mirror, he is framed against a bright, multicoloured wall hanging. Added to this, Eran

Tzur's hypnotic, non-diegetic score suggests his surrender of control – be it over the course or content of his memories, his actions in the past or his hold on life in the present. This music first appears, for example, after we see him drunk and out of control in night-time Djibouti, drawing the disapproving gaze of Forestier in what Galoup terms 'a harbinger of things to come'.[32] With the entrance of the music, his memories become impressionistic: Rahel dances; Galoup roams the streets of Djibouti in the black outfit that he is currently ironing in Marseilles. His memories then meander through scenes that seem influenced by his present-day washing and ironing and how they relate to what he has lost: the men exercising on lines; the washing lines, domestic duties and multi-lingual conversations of the camp; Rahel's more colourful laundry and his tenderness towards her.[33]

The most striking mirroring of his moments of transgression in Djibouti, however, comes with the final bizarre recollection of his tiny 'song and dance' on Sentain's grave. As he contemplates suicide, the camera focuses on a vein pulsing in his arm. This – perhaps the ultimate sign of the inside on the outside – seems to become the source of the imaginary final song, which fades in with the words: 'This is the rhythm of the night .... This is the rhythm of my life.'[34] In Galoup's final emotional and corporeal release, he embraces those things that his repressive masculinity proscribed: the darkness and lurid, coloured lights of the night; music; self-expression; free movement. This is indeed the 'freedom' that he has heard perhaps 'begins with remorse'.[35] But it is not a complete disavowal of his past. As if to make up for lost time, his dance is the wildest possible display of the physical power that the Legion has given him. Like crucifixion, his suicide is a paradoxical death – it signifies both loss of control and ultimate control over his body.

Galoup, masculinity and music

Galoup's spiritual and, we may assume, corporeal release permit him a very particular kind of redemption that marks him out from the character in *Billy Budd* to whom he is most often compared – John Claggart. This is in part due to the fact that Galoup is by no means a straightforward successor to Claggart. Just as Forestier seems to be as much modelled on the wise, elderly Dansker (particularly as he appears in Melville's novella and Ustinov's film) as Captain Edward Fairfax Vere, in Galoup the most painful qualities of three characters intersect: Billy's emotional stammer, Claggart's jealousy and Vere's regret. It is perhaps Galoup's combination of regret and the 'inability' to speak that overrides the destructive power of his jealousy and makes him a sympathetic character – albeit reservedly. *Beau Travail* adopts the confessional flashback structure of Britten's opera, with Galoup taking Vere's place as the narrator who carries the burden of conscience for the death of an innocent man in the past.[36] Both in his narration and largely in his flashbacks, however, Galoup remains 'silent' – with his interior monologue in the present giving some substance to his lack of words in the past. The combination of voice and silence places him in an unusual narrative position. Most notably, he is spared the indignity of diegetic examination to which such narrators are often subjected. No one actually hears his confession, so there is no ultimate diegetic 'diagnosis' or judgement of his flaws, sins, remorse or eventual decision – although we may assume that this will follow when his diary and body are found. The 'privacy' of the narration allows him to maintain his own masculine code of silence even as he 'speaks', as well as to control its flow and continue uninterrupted and unquestioned.

Galoup's positioning as both vocal and silent is also reflected in his relationship to the film's non-diegetic music. Although the legionnaires' songs and excerpts from Britten's opera give voice to his self-image and self-repression respectively, the separation of the music from actual images of him – particularly in isolation from the other men – means that they do not emphasize identification with his specific emotional trajectory. His emotions are therefore 'represented to' rather than 'identified with by' the film audience. Similarly, as he marches his men through the arid landscape to the sound of Neil Young's 'Safeway Cart',[37] we may understand the sad futility and smallness of his frenetic, vengeful activity. The lack of connection between the music and Galoup, however, suggests that, rather than identifying with a painful moment of self-awareness, this music is offering perhaps the most objective commentary on his actions and emotions. Rather than representing what he feels, it pities his futility. While these interludes are often likened to musical numbers, they seem more reminiscent of the non-diegetic male choruses of Westerns. These tend not to be identified with single characters but seem to 'fill in' for the typical diegetic taciturnity and emotional awkwardness of the male characters.[38] The effect, like that of the confluence of Britten's shanty and the shadows of the men at sea and in the desert, is one of universalizing the trials of masculinity. The nearest that the film comes to a conventional matching of non-diegetic music to character interiority is Eran Tzur's non-diegetic scoring. The potential for close emotional identification is prevented, however, by the lack of a close shot of Galoup's face as he imagines his past. We see what we assume he remembers and follow the random associations of his thoughts, but we do not see him in any close facial detail, accompanied by non-diegetic music, while he reconsiders his past. Neither is the music lyrical, sentimental or recognizably melodic – Galoup has no theme to represent the development of his emotional trajectory.

This is not particularly unusual for a male character but does raise some problems considering the degree of Galoup's emotionality. His verbal silence relates him to a wide variety of mainstream Hollywood representations of masculinity. In their introduction to *You Tarzan*, for example, Pat Kirkham and Janet Thumim talk of the 'variants of tortured and silent suffering, which for many contributors [to the edited collection] seem to be telling signifiers of the masculine'.[39] Such verbal silence can be compensated for by the presence of music, but this often operates at the diegetic level; making a man a musician – amateur or professional – is an extremely popular and emotionally versatile method of characterization. Allowing a male character to express his interiority through the performance of music rather than words, however, still enables him to maintain his self-control and regulate the degree to which he reveals himself. It is only at the non-diegetic level that the character loses such musical-narrational control and moves, in film music terms, into a state of emotional excess that implies 'the feminine'.[40] Whereas the association of femininity through non-diegetic music with female characters is common, if problematic, the potential threat that it represents to masculinity means that it is used only sparingly and in very particular circumstances with male characters. This is not to say that a lack of representation through non-diegetic music implies that male characters are emotionless. Rather, it implies that they are emotional to a 'normal' rather than 'excessive' degree. [41]

Although Galoup's emotional responses to both Forestier and Sentain are clearly at a level that would normally warrant the term 'excessive', they are not signalled as such by a conventional use of non-diegetic scoring. This puts Galoup in a rather strange position not only with regard to the soundtrack of *Beau Travail* but also in terms of comparison with characters that may be considered partial references for his characterization and very particular situation. In William Wellman's 1939 version of *Beau Geste* – arguably the most famous of Hollywood's French Foreign Legion films – heroic, principled legionnaire masculinity is also shown to encompass personal devotion between men. The fraternal love of the Geste brothers is emphasized, however, rather than understated, through the use of a lyrical orchestral theme. Overt feminization is avoided by the sourcing of this theme in the diegetic performance of their beloved adopted sister, but this does not detract from the highly sentimental tone that it sets for certain interactions between the men. Although the eponymous character in Ustinov's *Billy Budd* is far from overtly masculine, his simple and straightforward emotions are fully expressed in his own words. These are not usually deepened by the use of non-diegetic music and so he remains his own emotional spokesman. The only exception to this comes when he stammers and 'can't find the words, for what [he] feel[s]'.[42] On the second and last occasion that this happens, as he faces Claggart's accusation, the non-diegetic score builds to its most dramatic point in the whole film, ending only when Billy strikes out with all the force of suppressed fury that the music suggests. In *Beau Travail*, only the campfire percussion music seems to offer an unfettered representation of Galoup's specific interiority.[43] He is so lost in his own brooding that he seems unaware of the increasingly frenetic music around him. However, as he throws a stick onto the fire, its crash into the flames coincides with the beat of the music and seems to effect a change in its rhythm. Although in one sense this opens him to our gaze, his potential feminization is avoided on three counts: the music is diegetic; it is not actually performed by Galoup; it is incredibly 'muscular' and the emotions implied are violent and aggressive rather than desperate and vulnerable.

Galoup's non-diegetic musical silence forms part of the narrative strategy by which Denis maintains him as an example of a *too* self-contained masculinity. The conventional codes of scoring male characters are given to him as a means of representing and characterizing himself before being turned on him as an indicator of his own lack as a man who is, as he himself says: 'Unfit for life. Unfit for civilian life.'[44] In Denis' terms, he is just as unfit for military life. He does not realize that their greater emotional freedom does not make the other men inadequate soldiers. On the contrary, he is evidently pleased by their ability to match his own silent stealth during a combat exercise in a ruined building. Their flexibility of behaviour between what Galoup would undoubtedly envision as masculine and feminine modes, rather, marks them out as representative of a kind of inclusive masculinity more capable of survival. With his diegetic incapacity for 'normal' self-expression elevated to extreme repression by his lack of musical 'release' at the non-diegetic level, Galoup's excessive emotions must become the source of his downfall. His non-diegetic silence suggests a failed masculinity – a level of emotional containment so over-forced that it cannot work. Rather than minimizing the turbulence of his emotions, therefore, this places the burden of their expression onto an increasingly loaded silence both diegetic and non-diegetic. The containment of the silence is so powerful that it becomes a more active element of the soundtrack as the film progresses: it is not that there is 'no music', it is that there is 'silence'.

Galoup therefore retains something of his privacy. Although his motivations have been in one sense clear they are also incomprehensible, and we have not been allowed 'into' his experience, but only to watch as he represented it. This is true even of the apparent emotional explosion that marks his death. He abandons himself to the 'rhythm of the night',[45] the music and dance of 'feminine' chaos, but now it is not even diegetic – he has retreated instead into the realm of the meta-diegetic.[46] This imaginary release allows him to retain control over the terms of his abandonment of his own masculine code. It is, therefore, in many ways a more meaningful catharsis, since he relinquishes his former self in the only way that is relevant for him rather than being dictated to by the wider voice of the film. The tension of its score, narration and representation of masculinity lies in concepts of control and lack of control. In this respect, Galoup does not just battle with Sentain and himself, but with the film itself for control of his own destiny. We respect him, even at the end, because he willingly embraces chaos rather than be overwhelmed by it. As he dies, he finally learns how to be a better man – in giving in to femininity he is not weakened but strengthened. The violence that his physical and verbal silence suppressed is now vented in self-expression and release.

By denying Galoup the 'pressure valve' of occasional non-diegetic musical release, Denis reconfigures the Hollywood convention of 'normal' masculine emotion. Rather than a lack of 'feminine' non-diegetic scoring signifying an everyday level of emotion, it trades places with the 'symptom' of excessive emotion that finds Hollywood women constantly accompanied by music. *Excessive silence*, in *Beau Travail*, is the symptom that attests to the repression of excessive emotion in the man. This is why to break through that silence, and to let go of all that it entails, allows Galoup an end that is at the same time tragic, uplifting, sympathetic and redemptive.

Notes

I would like to thank David Burnand and Miguel Mera, as well as Tim Ayling, Valerie Orpen and Robynn Stilwell for their comments on an earlier draft of this chapter.

1. All quotations from *Beau Travail* are taken from Galoup's voiceover narration, using the English translation by Andrew Litvak that appears on the UK Artificial Eye DVD release of the film.
2. Denis, C. in Taubin, A. 'Under the Skin', *Film Comment*, **36** (3), May/June 2000, 22.
3. Jones, K. 'The Dance of the Unknown Soldier', *Film Comment*, **36** (3), May/June 2000, 27.
4. Galoup in *Beau Travail*.
5. Jones, K. 'The Dance of the Unknown Soldier', 27.
6. Many accounts of the film attribute Galoup's jealous behaviour to his homoerotic feelings for Forestier and his sense that Sentain poses a threat as a rival in this respect. My own sense is that Galoup's emotions are more akin to a son's jealous desire for paternal attention, affection and approval. Nevertheless, for the reason stated in the chapter, I have purposefully chosen not to debate Galoup's motivations in this analysis.
7. These are frequently carried out in silence but at best allow for no more than grunts from the men or terse instructions from Galoup.
8. In the film itself, this character's name is spelled/pronounced Kombé. Andrew Litvak's subtitles, however, translate this as Comb. I will use Litvak's version throughout this chapter.
9. The entrance to the Bar des Alpes, where we assume the disco is located, represents the division of monochrome and colour in all its implications. The street outside and the stairs to the bar are dull grey, but the string of lights leading to the top of the stairs is brightly coloured. The stairs, in Galoup's scheme of silence and noise, lead from masculinity to femininity, from order into chaos.
10. Galoup does not chew the local *qat* leaves as Forestier does because, he says, he does not like to 'lose [his] edge'. He certainly stamps on any loss of behavioural self-control or disorder amongst the men, such as the fighting that seems to break out directly from the wild percussion music that they play around the campfire. The episode to which he refers as a 'harbinger of things to come', accordingly, is the one occasion when he is seen in town at night, drunk and out of control.
11. It seems particularly contrary to Galoup's style of masculinity that the men should learn to speak each other's languages, thus facilitating full and open communication across all sorts of boundaries. Their general banter undermines the military discipline of their domestic routines and links them to the activities and conversation of the local women. Such a traversing of gender boundaries is also signified by factors such

as: the brightly coloured clothes pegs, party tablecloth and serviettes for the birthday celebrations for one of the legionnaires; the cigarette glowing in the increasing darkness that suggests Forestier's existence between the restrictions of the military and the freedoms of the local nightlife; the blood that signifies the breaking of the body as the helicopter crashes into the sea.

12.   I will be referring to the original 1951 four-act version of the opera throughout this chapter.

13.   '*Sous le soleil brûlant d'Afrique*' is sung on the soundtrack by members of the film's cast.

14.   Jones, K. 'The Dance of the Unknown Soldier', 27.

15.   '*Simarik*' by Turkish artist Tarkan, published by Universal Music France, incorporates kissing sounds into its lyrics.

16.   It should be noted that the women do not create their own music, but dance to songs by various male pop singers. Although they are conceptualized as sirens, therefore, they are not given an actual musical voice. Within the terms of the film, this could indicate Galoup's mistaken impression of their threat; they are, after all, dancing to men's music.

17.   As a possible acknowledgement of a female viewer this would also, of course, offer an extension of the possibility of the women's complicity with their female director.

18.   I am indebted to Yalçin Ozdemir for his translation of this song and for drawing my attention to this point.

19.   Jones, K. 'The Dance of the Unknown Soldier', 27. As Jones quite rightly states, it is '*interaction*' – rather than women as such – from which the men of the Legion 'recoil'.

20.   Galoup in *Beau Travail*.

21.   He says: 'What did I see of wild camels, of shepherds appearing from nowhere? Women in bright colors [*sic*] in fields of stone, all those images.'

22.   See Attali, J. *Noise: The Political Economy of Music*, trans. B. Massumi, Minneapolis: University of Minnesota Press, 1985.

23.   Examples of 'disorder' followed by exercise include: the men's presence in the disco; Galoup's outburst following Forestier's commendation of Sentain; the men fighting on the beach at night; Galoup's nightmare and Forestier's call to him to 'wake up, my boy'; Comb's alleged abandonment of his post.

24.   Dyer, R. 'Don't Look Now', *Screen*, **23** (3–4), September/October 1982, 66–7.

25.   Hunt, L. 'What are Big Boys Made Of?', in P. Kirkham and J. Thumim (eds) *You Tarzan: Masculinity, Movies and Men*, London: Lawrence & Wishart Ltd, 1993, 73.

26.   Tasker, Y. *Spectacular Bodies: Gender, Genre and the Action Cinema*, London and New York: Routledge, 1993, 80. Tasker finds this contradictory imagery in the representation of the body of the male action hero in 1980s Hollywood cinema.

27.   The concept of 'mutiny' must be understood in metaphorical terms. Catherine Grant, for example, perhaps takes the concept too literally when considering whether or not the film's use of music from the opera adds anything to its meaning. On both occasions when the chorus following Billy Budd's execution is used in the film, Grant states that: 'mutiny is not at issue' and therefore deduces that an understanding of the music cannot add to an understanding of the film. Also, unfortunately, by wrongly identifying the opening music of the film as the same as the opening music of the opera, she does not consider it in the dichotomous terms of its correct context in Act 2. Grant, C. 'Recognizing *Billy Budd* in *Beau Travail*: Epistemology and Hermeneutics of an Auterist "Free" Adaptation', *Screen*, **43** (1), Spring 2002, 60–61; 63.

28.   Galoup in *Beau Travail*.

29. Captain Edward Fairfax Vere in Forster, E.M. and Crozier, E. *Billy Budd* (libretto), London: Hawkes & Son Ltd, 1951, reproduced in booklet accompanying 1997 live recording, © Paris: Erato Disques SA, 1998, 111.

30. Melville, H. *Billy Budd, Sailor (An Inside Narrative)*, edited with Introduction and Notes by H. Hayford and M.M. Sealts Jr., Chicago and London: Phoenix Books, The University of Chicago Press; Toronto: The University of Toronto Press, 1962, 116.

31. In Ustinov's film, the issue of whether the men can be dispelled by the commands of their officers alone is avoided by the timely appearance of a French fighting ship. The men take up arms against it in revenge for the fact that its arrival was too late to interrupt and prevent Billy's execution.

32. Galoup in *Beau Travail*.

33. Many critics have commented upon the comparison of domestic chores that links the legionnaires in Djibouti and Galoup in Marseilles. In particular, Amy Taubin points out how this emphasizes his isolation now that he is removed from the 'corps that moved as one body' in Djibouti. 'Under the Skin', 22.

34. 'The Rhythm of the Night' by Corona. Published by Warner Chappell Music Ltd/Extravaganza Pub/Intersong Music Ltd.

35. Galoup in *Beau Travail*.

36. In *Beau Travail*, Sentain is actually shown to have survived his ordeal. It is not clear, however, whether Galoup is aware of this or indeed whether Sentain's rescue is actually concurrent with Galoup's suicide.

37. 'Safeway Cart' by Neil Young and Crazy Horse. © Silver Fiddle Music c/o BMG Publishing France.

38. Laing, H. 'Wandering Minds and Anchored Bodies: Music, Gender and Emotion in Melodrama and the Woman's Film', unpublished PhD thesis, University of Warwick, 2000, Chapter 5.

39. Kirkham, P. and Thumim, J. 'You Tarzan', in P. Kirkham and J. Thumim (eds), *You Tarzan: Masculinity, Movies and Men*, 24.

40. Laing, H. 'Wandering Minds and Anchored Bodies'.

41. Ibid.

42. Billy Budd (Terence Stamp) in *Billy Budd* (Peter Ustinov, 1962).

43. Obviously the non-diegetic music that accompanies the 'battle of wills' exercise also does this, but the sentiment is shared between Galoup and Sentain. Furthermore, this music rehearses the re-containment of emotion rather than its free expression.

44. Galoup in *Beau Travail*.

45. The lyrics of Corona's song seem to offer a particularly apt description of the world that Galoup must face.

46. Claudia Gorbman explains music as being meta-diegetic when it '"takes over" part of the film's narration' by representing the musical thoughts of a character. Gorbman, C. *Unheard Melodies: Narrative Film Music*, Bloomington: Indiana University Press; London: BFI, 1987, 23.

Chapter 12

Scoring *This Filthy Earth*

David Burnand

This chapter charts the decision-making processes involved in the music scoring of *This Filthy Earth* (2001), from the initial treatment stage through to post-production. The author, as one of the sound designers and as composer for the film, had unique access to the practical and creative interactions of the director, producers, sound team and – of course – the composer, with respect to sound and music. It is hoped that these insights will lead to a fuller understanding of music's dramatic, narrative and discursive functions in cinema; the exploitation of digital technologies in contemporary film scoring; the fusion of sound design and music; and the working relationship of composer and director, after several years of collaboration on independent films.

As a rare example of practice-led research in contemporary film scoring, it is intended that this chapter will provide insights into the dynamics between intention, process and outcome. This immediately raises the problem of how a composer can discuss their own work, in hindsight, without descending into anecdote and self-regard, or post-rationalization. There is inadequate space in the current chapter to provide a critique of the methodology itself. Others will do so, perhaps. Suffice it to say that, just as an archaeologist cannot fully comprehend the significance of a flint tool without knowing – quite possibly through developing the skills and insights of a flint-knapper – what is discarded during the process, or reused in a different context, so the study of film music cannot rely solely on readings of the text.

This Filthy Earth was commissioned by The Lab, Robin Gutch's department of FilmFour, which had been attempting to resurrect British art-house cinema. To quote *Times* critic James Christopher, The Lab's purpose '[is] to fry the wits of most multiplex audiences'.[1] Gutch asks: 'Where will the Ken Loaches, Mike Leighs, Nic Roegs and Steven Frears come from in 20 years time? ... These people don't just happen accidentally.'[2] Regrettably, just a year after the release of *This Filthy Earth*, the FilmFour distribution arm was closed due to lack of funds. Whilst it is hoped that the work of The Lab will continue, many felt at the time that this was a black day for UK cinema. John McVay, chief executive of the Producers Alliance for Cinema and Television, stated: 'the budget cuts will seriously reduce opportunities for independent film producers ...'.[3] At the time of writing, tax breaks and exchange rates have encouraged Hollywood to come to the UK to make films. This is excellent news for British studios and production staff, but appears to be doing nothing to foster local independent filmmaking, and may even serve to eclipse it further.[4]

This Filthy Earth was directed by Andrew Kötting, an idiosyncratic filmmaker who has attempted to maintain his independent status during a period of variable support for cinematic experimentation in the UK. The film was written by Kötting and comedian-actor Sean Lock, and is broadly based on Emile Zola's novel *La Terre*, which first appeared in serial form in France in 1886. Zola's story was set in the plain of the Beauce near Chartres, on the eve of war in 1870, and deals with peasant farmers' relationships with the land and each other, especially that obsessive greed which challenges their humanity. An elderly farmer divides his land between three children, who he then lives with in turn, and with increasing suffering, until murdered by his youngest son, Buteau. The tragic heroes of the original story are a young girl, Françoise, and the outsider Jean Macquart. Zola manages to combine lyricism with violence and the grotesque. There is humour but, above all, an honesty and directness about the conditions and motivations of these characters that shocked many readers at the time. The English translation of 1888 was vilified by those who sought to protect public morality,[5] leading to a fine for the publisher Vizetelly and withdrawal of the book. A widely available and unabridged English version did not reappear until 1954.

Whilst the prescient social realism of Zola's original does not fully translate to the indefinite, yet more modern era of its reworking, the following extract from a review of *This Filthy Earth* gives an indication of the approach that Kötting and Lock took in the adaptation, which maintains many features of the original, and which deliberately attempts to disturb a contemporary audience, just as Zola did in his day:

> anyone deluded enough to expect a plush heritage film … will probably go into toxic shock. *This Filthy Earth* is a true phantasmagoria inhabited by rural monsters and grotesques so backward they seem prehistoric. It's virtually impossible to find one's bearings in this floating nightmare. Kötting chips away at our ordinary filmgoing security with a screechingly abrasive technique that combines slow and speeded-up motion, time-lapse photography, changes in film stock, non-synchronous sound and archival inserts.[6]

In a handwritten note on the cover of draft eight of the screenplay,[7] the director provided the following general indications for the film's style:

> moon and the sledgehammer meets unforgiven in a spud western landscape – inter apocalypse inspired serbian berserk melodramatic epic …

> (p.s. with a cum shot in the first four minutes)

My first collaboration with Andrew Kötting was *Hoi Polloi* (1990), an experimental short film for BBC2. This was an opportunity to explore our mutual interests in the later films of Tarkovsky, especially their sound design, and to see whether digital sound sampling might enable a meaningful fusion of music and sound design through the use of *musique concrète* techniques. Some years later, while working on the soundtrack CD for Kötting's *Gallivant* (1996), it was mooted that we might work on a sixth film together, based on *La Terre*. Having recently reread the book, and seen an early silent version of the story,[8] I suggested that music and sound design might be minimal, representing the beautiful but brutal indifference of the earth to the machinations of these dysfunctional characters. There would be no place for music representing the characters themselves, their relationships or actions. In representing the landscape musically, there would be an emphasis on drones acting as fixed sonic horizontals. This was agreed at the time, and continued to be the working brief when the script was first in development. However, what directors say and what they actually want can be very different things, once the exigencies of production and post-production present themselves.

As the script developed, it became clear that the director wanted a much wider range of musical types and functions than originally agreed, and that the soundtrack was to feature a great deal of existing music. My role was rapidly developing into providing mere interstices for these second-hand materials. This held little interest as a composition project, but there was always a chance that the situation might change. I had noted on previous projects that Kötting sometimes tires of music that is agreed early in production, and often changes his mind as a result of hearing the same thing over and over during editing. It became a matter of devising cues that might commend themselves as alternatives to the found music on the temp track, some of which I had suggested myself. In all but one case, this is what happened.

This Filthy Earth is 106 minutes in duration, and comprises six reels ranging in length from 13 to 20 minutes.[9] Thirty-one original music cues survived the post-production filtering process, amounting to over 40 minutes of music, out of some 90 minutes of demos and masters submitted. This excludes the single cue that uses non-original music, that is, Burkhardt Kiegeland's *Kanon* (1995), which is the only part of the temp track that failed to be replaced, despite several expensive attempts to do so. The stylistic range of the film's soundtrack, which is typical of Kötting's work, allowed for this intrusion on the original music score without attention being drawn to its separate provenance, no matter how galling it was to concede the fact.

Table 12.1 provides an outline of the film's original music cues. Borders indicate either the continuity of a cue across scenes or the grouping of successive cues into continuous music. A single discrepancy between a scene description and its associated music title indicates that the cue was shifted from its originally intended position and purpose: that is, cue 15, *Pull the Church Down*, an intense organ piece reminiscent of a distorted Bach chorale prelude, was moved by the director from a later part of the story and used, instead, to accompany the wedding photograph scene. The dramatic justification for this was that both scenes feature intercuts of the priest ranting in disgust at the villagers. However, the full sound of a large organ is at odds with the diegetic implication of the cue's relocation, as this is a small village church that would be hard-pushed to offer a harmonium; but such considerations worry musicians more than they do filmmakers, or film audiences for that matter. Notwithstanding the many changes that were likely to occur between completion of the screenplay and completion of the film, the opportunity to plan ahead, building musical–narrative coherence in advance of fitting music to the eventual picture edit, was a rare opportunity. This forward planning reveals itself in the relationships that exist between many cues, as will now be detailed, but the inclusion of unrelated and orphaned material[10] demonstrates the extent to which audio normally accompanies, rather than drives, narrative and visual decisions.[11]

Table 12.1   Music cues for *This Filthy Earth*

No.	Scene description	Music cue title	Key (indicative)
1	Front Credits; mud, a child and a woman	The Earth Sounds	E♭m
2	Fran sees Lek for the first time Fran's voiceover	Lovers Meet (*Iwan Gamus* v1) Lovers Meet (*Iwan Gamus* v1) contd	Fm Fm
3	Buto at work in the fields	Buto Builds a Wall v1	E♭m
4	Buto at work in the fields	Buto Builds a Wall v2	E♭m
5	Megan and blind Joey (outsiders)	The Smoke of Time v1	E♭m
6	Armandine shows her dislike of Lek (outsider)	The Smoke of Time v2	A♭m
7	Fran ponders her future by a pond	The Announcement	Am/Fm/A♭m/Em
8	Circus	Circus	F
9	Etta (Kath's bastard daughter) feeds the geese	Etta Feeds the Geese	B♭
10	Armandine pisses in the graveyard	Wedding Morning v1	Dm/E♭(Lydian)
11	Buto leaves for church	Wedding Morning v2	E♭(Lydian)/Dm
12	Fran, Kath and Molly walk to church	*Burkhardt Kiegeland 'Kanon'*	Dm
13	Wedding service commences	Are You Welcome in the House of God?	B♭m/Fm
14	Wedding service continues	Are You Welcome in the House of God?	B♭m/Fm/B♭m
15	Buto and Kath kiss; photos; priest berates all	Pull the Church Down	atonal/C
16	Wedding reception	Wedding Dub	Ebm
17	Lek watches Buto and Papa trade insults	Wedding Morning v3	Dm/E♭(Lydian)

Table 12.1   *concluded*

No.	Scene description	Music cue title	Key (indicative)
18	Fran sits & thinks while Etta feeds the Geese	Etta Feeds the Geese	B♭
	Cut to Papa feeding hens	Etta Feeds the Geese contd	B♭
	Cut to Fran & Buto ploughing	Etta Feeds the Geese contd	B♭
	Fran moves earth by hand	Etta Feeds the Geese contd	B♭
19	Megan and Joey by a pond looking for food	Ripples in the Pond	E♭m
20	Fran alone in bed; dreams of meeting Lek	The Lovers Dream (*Iwan Gamus* v2)	Fm
21	Fran wakes; watches Buto and Kath having sex	Midnight	F
22	Harvest time	Harvest Morning (Roll Me Over)	D♭/Fm/Dm
23	Buto shouts at Megan to work harder	Heat and Death intro	D♭
24	Megan collapses and dies	Heat and Death contd	Fm
	Fran drags Megan's body away as the storm returns	Heat and Death contd	Fm
25	Joey mourns Megan	Lament	Am
26	Fran works alone in the rain	Regrets and Rain	Dm
27	Armandine drags a bath tub through the woods	Armandine's Cottage	Am
	Lek approaches Armandine's cottage and enters	Armandine's Cottage contd	Am
	Lek discovers radios, cats in buckets etc.	Armandine's Cottage contd	Dm/Am
28	Lek is beaten by the mob	The Beating	atonal/Em
29	Lek shouts for help, whilst tied to a revolving wheel	Joey Frees Lek (*Ar Verjelen* v1)	A♭m
	Lek is released by Joey and confronts Armandine	Joey Frees Lek (*Ar Verjelen* v1) contd	A♭m
30	Kath tries to talk to Buto, but he is silent	Buto Builds Another Wall	E♭m/A♭m/D♭m
31	Lek asks Fran to leave with him, but she declines	The Lovers Part (*Ar Verjelen* v2)	A♭m
	Lek leaves the village with Joey; Fran is left alone	The Lovers Part (*Ar Verjelen* v2) contd	D♭m/A♭m
32	End credits; Buto's brother chases sheep	Jesus! You're the Pig Up in My Tree	E♭m

Cue 1: the front credits cue was conceived as a musically autonomous piece, in other words independent of any specific picture obligations, though the director had provided a clear indication of purpose and style. Rough timings were available in advance of post-production, and the hope was fulfilled that changes would be made to picture edits in order to accommodate the music as submitted. *The Earth Sounds* is a contemporary overture, setting the mood and introducing materials and processes that will be heard later, but in this case the sounds are both conventionally musical and *concrète*. Samples of gramophone scratches and a faulty television set, typical of recent electronica by bands such as Pansonic, connect with the distressed 8mm visual style of the opening, but without any attempt at synchronizing audio and visual glitches. This choice of sounds sets up a complicated link with the film's title, theme, setting and style, as was intended by the director. The audio and visual glitches are 'dirty', but not at all pastoral. The background to the credits changes from black to impressionistic images of a young girl and a young woman working in the mud. A low, throbbing, synthesized drone adds to the tension between sound and picture. The rather dated, pastoral setting[12] is at odds with these modern, technologically-derived sounds, suggesting that this is a story about the recent past and the countryside, but from a modern urban perspective, and tuned to the sensibilities of a modern urban audience. Nevertheless, this audio-visual combination has the effect of introducing the theme of filth and corruption at a tactile level, forcing the audience to feel the sticky, black mud that has invaded the cinema screen, and wonder what this might mean. To have used the sound of mud itself, would have risked comedy and tautology.

A variety of pseudo-environmental sounds emerge, acting as accompaniment to a muezzin-like call to prayer, derived from multiple time-stretching and compression treatments of a 'lowing cow' sound effect.[13] This digital processing depletes the sound of its original bovine formants, leaving the melodic outline intact. Indeed, the process reveals the melodic line by removing the source's identity.[14] This is the first of several veiled symbols within the soundtrack. As the drone and other incidental sounds continue, a slowed-down treble recorder takes up the portamento style of the first melody. This gives way to a Second World War air-raid siren that is played in two versions simultaneously, each with a slightly varied, random time-stretch applied to it, which emphasizes the effect of distant warning by suggesting long and multiple paths from source to listener. The siren is both recognizable sound effect and musical line, its final pitch carefully judged to dissolve back into the musical texture on the tonic $E\flat$. These three sound sources (animal, instrumental and mechanical) share a plaintive quality that sets the scene for the dark and tragic story that will follow. In addition to its foreboding, this opening music also points to the deliberate vagueness of time and place in *This Filthy Earth*, with a hint of impending war, as suggested by Zola's original setting.

Very late in post-production the executive producer persuaded the director that the mood of this cue was too dark, and suggested the addition of a toy piano, as we see glimpses of the little girl Etta during the opening credits. Had this been a conventional overture from the Golden Age of Hollywood, a fuller range of emotions would undoubtedly have been quilted together, but this would be part of the musical plan rather than a last-minute overdub. In the absence of the director and the executive producer, it was agreed with the supervising sound editor[15] to make no change, and see if anyone noticed as the end of post-production loomed. Climaxing, as the music and film title do, on a close-up of a bull's erect penis dripping semen, it seemed entirely appropriate that musical expression should be as uncompromising as possible, thus leaving the audience unsure of how to react to the following comic scene of the cow's insemination, and the light-hearted first meeting of Francine and Lek, the tragic lovers of *This Filthy Earth*. Whilst there was every intention of engaging the audience from the outset, this was not to be achieved by rendering them 'untroublesome (less critical, less wary) viewing subject[s]'.[16] Additionally, any musical focus on the child Etta, in this context, might have suggested that the ensuing story was about her jeopardy, which is not the case. At the final review of sound and music no one raised any objection to the absence of toy piano. A cynic might conclude that film scores are the product of non-musicians' whims or musicians' subterfuge.

Cue 2: as Francine wipes the bull's wasted semen off her hands, the foreigner Lek arrives on his employer's tractor, applauding the young woman whilst shouting 'bravo' and then several words in Russian. As Francine smiles, the second cue begins. A drone, a tone higher than cue 1, lighter in texture and less menacing, accompanies a single phrase of *Iwan Gamus*, a Breton folk song, the eponymous hero of which learns of his lover's death and wishes to join her in eternity.

A moment needs to be taken here, in order to explain the background to this and the other Breton folksong setting in the film. Originally, the director had wanted to use several traditional Breton songs recorded by Denez Prigent. Their stories tell of knights, shepherdesses and unrequited love. The unfamiliar language was intended to express Lek's role as foreigner and outsider, without identifying a specific nationality. Kötting had tried unsuccessfully to use Prigent's recordings in our previous collaborations, but here he felt there was the perfect opportunity to do so. However, whilst the songs and their simple drone-based accompaniments seemed ideally suited to the soundworld imagined for this film, my initial reading of Lek's character suggested that a lower, rougher, more world-weary and less spiritually aspirational voice was needed. By chance, whilst on a field trip collecting recordings of Corsican polyphony, I came across an amateur singer named Andre Ebrel, who had the vocal qualities I was searching for. Remarkably, Ebrel had grown up in Brittany and knew some of the songs that were already temp-tracked to the film. A quickly arranged recording session in a chapel in Bastia provided the source material needed, and on returning to the UK it was not difficult to persuade the director to agree to my replacing Prigent's voice and reworking the arrangements. Clearly there was an advantage to being involved in the project over a sufficiently long period to allow for this degree of input. However, with hindsight it could be argued that Prigent's pure tenor voice might have worked equally well, if differently, had it been primarily a vehicle for expressing the character of Lek. On screen, Lek turned out to be innocent and childlike, rather than experienced and resourceful as initially suggested by the screenplay. No doubt, a degree of professional and financial self-interest lay at the root of my determination to create original arrangements of these songs. Nevertheless, it will be shown that these cues ended up doing more than merely representing Lek's character and his 'other-ness'.

Returning to cue 2, the concealed subject of loss in the Breton lyrics is reflected in the mood of the music, and used to contradict any expectation that this will be a simple love story. The character of the melody, especially in Ebrel's version, is stoical rather than sad, and in this cue it is reduced to just the first phrase, which introduces Iwan Gamus but not his fate. The drone continues through to the next scene showing Francine alone on a hill above the village, talking to herself (and the audience) in voiceover, about her family and the smiling foreigner that she met at the farm. This conventional use of music to suture shifts of time and place may seem at odds with Kötting's vaunted abrasive style. However, the issue here is not so much about supporting discourse as about supporting narrative. The audience is being introduced to the characters in a conventional way, through acting and voiceover. Herein lies a problem for Kötting and his collaborators, as this was his first adaptation of a conventional story. The style of his previous work suited an unconventional approach to plot and character, and often involved deliberate confusions of fiction and documentary.[17] In *This Filthy Earth* the tension between Zola and Kötting is ever present, and lies at the heart of difficulties with the design and reception of this film. As one critic put it: 'Kötting is no storyteller, but the film exhibits so bold and singular a talent that it hardly matters.'[18]

Jumping ahead some fifty minutes to cue 20, the *Iwan Gamus* melody returns in extended form for the dream sequence in which Francine and Lek meet in a field. This is the closest thing to a love scene in the film. Considerable reworking of the track was necessary at the last minute when a small re-edit of picture was required to make it absolutely clear that this was Francine's dream, rather than reality. The need to insert a shot of Francine, restless in bed, was unproblematic in itself, as the introductory drone could be readily extended, but other minor changes were introduced to the dream sequence without regard to previously agreed music synchronization. In order to avoid clashes with dialogue, Ebrel's recorded voice had to be minutely rephrased using digital editing. In addition, accompaniment detail such as harp and prepared piano flourishes had to be repositioned or erased altogether. Consequently, some of the harmonic detail that had been added in order to avoid closure to the vocal line in this cue was lost.

Two settings of another Breton folk song, *Ar Verjelen*, form a readily recognizable association with cues 2 and 20, owing to shared intervallic features, the drone accompaniment and Ebrel's easily recognized voice. This provides a stylistic and sonic link throughout the film, which is always associated with Lek or with attitudes towards him, though not in the manner of simplistic cinematic leitmotif. *Iwan Gamus* is about the loss of a lover, and accompanies earlier scenes where Fran and Lek may be forming a relationship, real or virtual. In other words, it is predictive of their inevitable failure to fall in love, whilst also expressive of the attraction that exists between them. *Ar Verjelen*, on the other hand, concerns a humble shepherdess who becomes a queen. These settings occur later in the film, first where the blind and hitherto helpless Joey frees Lek from captivity (cue 29). A little later (cue 31) an extended version of *Ar Verjelen* sutures the visual shifts from: (a) Francine declining Lek's offer to leave with him; (b) a shot of Joey smiling for the first time, having avenged Buto's brutal treatment of his partner Megan, and having saved Lek's life; and (c) Lek and Joey leaving the village together, at which point the song is taken up by a female voice for the first time. This voice[19] continues through the shot of Francine crying and alone on a hilltop, forming an audio-visual symmetry with the second part of cue 2.

If the stylistic similarities between the two songs reinforce a narrative connection across the film as a whole, then their subtle differences are just as important. The contrasts in melodic trajectory and range are expressive of their contrasted sentiments, which are paralleled in more complex form in *This Filthy Earth*. *Iwan Gamus* is in F minor and has a range of a minor 7th (see Example 12.1). The highest point is reached four times in the first half of the melody, but always with a sense of resignation in falling back to the tonic. The remainder of the song oscillates around the tonic, expressing an overriding sense of lost purpose. *Ar Verjelen*, on the other hand, is more excursive, passionate and fulfilled in character (see Example 12.2). It is in A♭ minor, has a range of a minor 9th and works its way steadily towards the top of the singer's range, finally falling to the tonic as its musical and narrative quests are realized. The upward range is widened further when the female voice takes over, with a modulation to the subdominant.

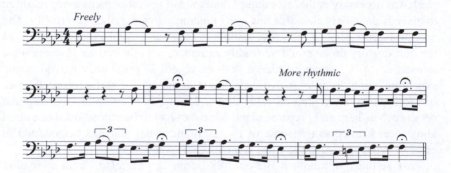

Example 12.1   *Iwan Gamus*

Example 12.2 *Ar Verjelen*

The temp track littered the film with Prigent's songs, without specific placement of them for dramatic effect or narrative purpose, as is often the case where a director's liking of certain music overrides more appropriate cinematic considerations. In replacing the temp track, the concentration on just two carefully chosen songs from the same repertoire enabled an integrated and functional approach to their use. It was suggested above that the *Iwan Gamus* settings are expressive of the would-be lovers' feelings whilst predictive of their inevitable failure to fall in love. The reasons for Francine's final rejection of Lek remain deliberately vague on the face of it. Therefore, the extent to which the setting of *Ar Verjelen* supports a reading that has the heroine triumphing by getting her land, but not her man, and thereby facing up to the vicissitudes of life in inevitable misery and loneliness, helps to place the film outside mainstream narrative cinema. In addition, music adds to the complex of interpretations that can be drawn from this deliberately confusing ending: for example, a reading that has a minor character, blind Joey, prevailing over the bully Buto, where the main protagonists could not. Perhaps the music represents Joey's triumph, rather than Francine's. There is even the suggestion that shared antipathy may form a stronger bond than mutual attraction, considering that it is Lek and Joey who leave together, walking off into the sunrise of a new day.[20] More generally, the traditional folk-music origins of these two songs speak of a bygone age, and so add to the effect of a timeless myth of land and mankind.

A number of other relationships between music cues provide narrative cohesion over the course of the film, drawing attention to certain behaviours, beliefs and emotions. Cues 3, 4 and 30 are variations of a soundscape composition titled *Buto Builds a Wall*. Breath-like gestures are derived from the treatment of slowed-down machine noises, some of which were heard in their original form in cue 1, representing Buto's efforts, but also his alienation. In the first two variations, the anti-hero Buto is indeed building a drystone wall, while we are introduced to the more distasteful characteristics of his father, brother and the evil Armandine. When a further variation of this cue returns towards the end of the film, Buto's life is falling apart and he sits silently indoors, trying to ignore his wife and his predicament, thus building an emotional wall. Highly processed voices, reminiscent of the unworldly shepherd cries in Tarkovsky's *The Sacrifice*

(1986),[21] provide these three scenes with intimations of the spirits of nature, over which we have no control. These distant cries are heard elsewhere, as well: for example, cue 18, as Buto and Francine plough a field and crops magically appear (through the use of time-lapse photography); cue 19, as Megan and Joey scavenge for food in a pond; cue 25, the voices are pitch-shifted down to a male register, as Joey mourns Megan, just before a series of stomach-churning transformations of animal flesh; cue 29, as the bloodied and abused Lek revolves on a wooden wheel, just before Joey frees him; and cue 31, acting as a bridge to the uncharacteristically tongue-in-cheek music for the end credits. As with the digitally treated cow sound in cue 1, the stretching process cloaks the voice's human origins, enabling it to represent a mediating presence between the extremes of landscape and the human condition.

Another distinctive sound forms part of the several drones that are heard throughout the film. It is derived entirely from sine waves, using frequencies based on the proportions of the floor plan of Chartres Cathedral, in Just Intonation.[22] The sound was originally created with a Yamaha synthesizer, several years earlier, as part of an electroacoustic piece.[23] Given the setting of Zola's original story near Chartres, the desire to work with drones, and the director's interest in hidden symbols, the opportunity to re-use this material was eagerly taken. On its own, the sound is similar to that of prayer bowls. The slow, independent fade-ins and fade-outs of each sine wave create an ambiguous sense of continuity and change. The frequency relationships of Just Intonation introduce strong amplitude modulation between certain tones, rhythmicizing the texture from time to time. The harmony of the spheres is suggested, and with it an expression of indifference to mankind. In addition, sine waves connote a purity that no other sound can achieve. This contrasts with the gravel voice of Ebrel, who sings of lost love and unlikely triumph while hinting at the corrupting tendency of hard lives. Equally, the distortions of prepared piano,[24] the scratches and glitches heard throughout the film, and other elements of the drones stand in stark contrast to these pure sine waves.

Finally, mention must be made of the key plan, which is indicated in Table 12.1. Past experience had shown that Kötting, and many other directors, seem unaware of any need to consider continuity and contrast of keys between cues, even where these run directly into one another. However, in this case, sufficient forward planning enabled some musical-dramatic sense to be made, despite a few changes in the order of scenes, and the shift of one cue to a scene for which it was not originally intended. To take just one example, the director's initial desire to use an existing pop song by Baby Bird[25] for the closing credits, would have required an upward semitone shift of key that was at odds with the gentle visual transition from the lovers' parting to the drunken lurching of Jesus Christ (Buto's brother) in a field of sheep, as the end credits roll.[26] Of course, the Baby Bird song could have been pitch-shifted down to A♭m, in order to segue with the end of cue 31. However, by replacing found music with an original dub reggae track fulfilling the same 'throwaway' function as Baby Bird's song, a more apt transition was achieved from A♭m to E♭m. This signals both change and relatedness between the later scenes, as the wastrel Jesus Christ now has to look after his dead brother's farm. It also returns to the film's opening key, a fact that may appear musically gratuitous at face value, especially as the styles of the opening and closing cues are highly contrasted. However, some of the sounds from cue 1 reappear in this new context, for example the warning siren that dissolves back into the musical texture on the tonic E♭. This suggests a connection to the very start of the film, perhaps reminding the audience that they have been moved from foreboding to farce, via tragedy, and that this journey will repeat itself cyclically in the lives of women and men, just as the seasons of this Earth change, yet come full circle.

Notes

1.   Christopher, J. 'Brits out for the Lab', *The Times*, 8 November 2001, 15.
2.   Ibid.
3.   McVay, J. cited in Plunkett, J. 'FilmFour distribution arm closed', *Guardian Unlimited*, 9 July 2002, http://film.guardian.co.uk/News_Story/Exclusive/0,4029, 752164,00.html (accessed 30 May 2003).
4.   During the editing of this chapter, it became apparent that UK tax loopholes were to be addressed, thus reversing the trend that encouraged Hollywood to come to the UK.
5.   For example, The National Vigilance Association and the *Pall Mall Gazette*.
6.   Matthews, P. 'This Filthy Earth', *Sight and Sound*, www.bfi.org.uk/sightandsound/ 2001_12/filthy.html (accessed 4 December 2002).
7.   Received by the author in June 2000, as the film went into production.
8.   *La Terre* (André Antoine, 1921).
9.   Despite technological advances in post-production and distribution, it is still the case that music cannot be scored across reel changes. A reel lasts just 10 minutes, though double and triple reels are in common use nowadays.
10. For example, cues 25 and 26.
11. The education of student filmmakers needs to address this issue, if better use of music and sound is to be made in the cinema, for the sake of making better films.
12. Somewhere rural and isolated in the north of England, sometime in the last twenty to sixty years.
13. With digital processing it is now possible to stretch and compress the duration of sound files independently of pitch-shifting.
14. Before Tarkovsky, Robert Bresson argued that the 'noises must become music'. See Bresson, R. *Notes on the Cinematographer*, trans. J. Griffin, London: Quartet Encounters, 1986, 20.
15. Jeremy Price (Videosonics), who was an invaluable collaborator in the process of determining relationships between music and sound, including his own superb, naturalistic sound design.
16. Gorbman, C. *Unheard Melodies*: *Narrative Film Music*, Bloomington: Indiana University Press; and London: BFI, 1987, 58.
17. For example, *Gallivant* (1996).
18. Matthews, P. 'This Filthy Earth'.

19.   Opera singer Heather Johnson, imitating Ebrel's diction and style.
20.   A 'queer' interpretation may also be considered.
21.   A favourite film of both the director and the composer, not least for the magnificent sound design. See Burnand, D. 'Tarkovsky's Gift', in L. Sider, D. Freeman and J. Sider (eds) *Soundscape*, London: Wallflower Press, 2003, 118–20. In this case, Heather Johnson imitated Gabon yodel calls, which were then time-stretched and filtered.
22.   Just Intonation constructs diatonic scales with a combination of 3:2 and 5:4 pitch ratios. Therefore, it is more attuned to the harmonic series than Equal Temperament.
23.   *One Equal Light: in memoriam John Lambert*, 1996.
24.   A technique, introduced by John Cage, in which screws and other objects are placed between the strings of a piano, in order to create percussive, inharmonic and muted effects.
25.   The stage name of New Zealander Stephen Jones.
26.   In fact, exactly that shift of key had occurred between cues 6 and 7, in order to match the jolt experienced by Francine at the announcement of her sister's wedding to Buto.

Bibliography

Albrecht, G. *Nationalsozialistische Filmpolitik*, Stuttgart: Enke, 1969.

Alvares, R. *La harmonía que rompe el silencio: Conversaciones con José Nieto*, Valladolid: Semana Internacional de Cine, 1996.

Anderson, P.A. *Deep River: Music and Memory in Harlem Renaissance Thought*, Durham, NC: Duke University Press, 2001.

Andrew, G. *The Three Colours Trilogy*, London: British Film Institute, 1998.

Ashcroft, B., Griffiths, G. and Tiffin, H. *The Empire Writes Back: Theory and Practice in Post-Colonial Literatures*, London: Routledge, 1989.

Attali, J. *Noise: The Political Economy of Music*, trans. B. Massumi, Minneapolis: University of Minnesota Press, 1985.

Austin, G. *Contemporary French Cinema: An Introduction*, Manchester: Manchester University Press, 1996.

Bacon, H. *Visconti: Explorations of Beauty and Decay*, Cambridge: Cambridge University Press, 1998.

Barr, C. *Ealing Studios*, New York: Overlook Press, 1977.

Barthes, R. 'The Realist Effect', trans, G. Mead, *Film Reader* 3, Evanston, IL: Northwestern University Press, 1978, 131–5.

Belach, H. (ed.) *Wir tanzen um die Welt. Deutsche Revuefilme 1933–1945*, Munich: Hanser, 1979.

Berresford Ellis, P. (ed.) *James Connolly: Selected Writings*, Harmondsworth: Penguin Books, 1973.

Bhabha, H.K. *The Location of Culture*, London: Routledge, 1994.

Biamonte, S.G. (ed.) *Musica e film*, Rome: Edizioni dell'Ateneo, 1959.

Biskind, P. *Down and Dirty Pictures: Miramax, Sundance, and the Rise of the Independent Film*, New York and London: Simon & Schuster, 2004.

Bock. M. (ed.) *CineGraph Lexikon zum deutschen Film*, Munich: edition text und kritik, 1984.

Bordwell, D. *Making Meaning: Inference and Rhetoric in the Interpretation of Cinema*, Cambridge, MA: Harvard University Press, 1991.

Borgna, G. *Storia della canzone italiana*, Milan: Arnoldo Mondadori, 1992.

Bourdieu, P. *Distinction: A Social Critique of the Judgement of Taste*, trans. R. Nice, Cambridge, MA: Harvard University Press, 1984.

Brenner, H. *Die Kunstpolitik des Nationalsozialismus*, Reinbek: Rowohlt, 1963.

Bresson, R. *Notes on the Cinematographers*, trans. J. Griffin, London: Quartet Encounters, 1986.

Brophy, P. (ed.) *Cinesonic: The World of Sound on Film*, Sydney: Southwood Press, 1999.

Brown, F., Compitello, M.A., Howard, V.M. and Martin, R.A. (eds) *Critical Essays on the Literature of the Spanish Civil War*, East Lansing: Michigan State University Press, 1989.

Brown, R.S. *Overtones and Undertones: Reading Film Music*, Berkeley: University of California Press, 1994.

Brunette, P. *Roberto Rossellini*, New York: Oxford University Press, 1987.

Burgoyne, C.B. and Routh, D.A. 'National Identity, European Identity and the Euro', in K. Cameron (ed.) *National Identity*, Exeter: Intellect, 1999, 107–24.

Burnand, D. and Sarnaker, B. 'The Articulation of National Identity Through Film Music', *National Identities*, **1** (1), 1999, 7–13.

Burt, G. *The Art of Film Music*, Boston: Northeastern University Press, 1994.

Calabretto, R. *Pasolini e la musica*, Pordenone: Cinemazero, 1999.

Carisson, M. and Holm, P. 'Interview with Zbigniew Preisner', *Music from the Movies*, May 1997, 38–42.

Casares Rodicio, E. (Director and Coordinator) *Diccionario de la música española e hispanoamericana*, Madrid: SGAE, 2001.

Caughie, J., Kuhn, A. and Merck, M. (eds) *The Sexual Subject: A* Screen *Reader in Sexuality*, London: Routledge, 1992.

Chiarelli, C.G. *Musica e memoria nell'arte di Luchino Visconti*, Milan: Archinto, 1997.

Chion, M. *La musique au cinéma*, Paris: Fayard, 1995.

Coats, P. *Lucid Dreams: The Films of Krzysztof Kieslowski*, Trowbridge: Flicks Books, 1999.

Colón Perales, C., Infante del Rosal, F. and Lombardo Ortega, M. (eds) *Historia y teoría de la música en el cine: Presencias afectivas*, Seville: Alfar, 1997.

Cook, N. *Analysing Musical Multimedia*, Oxford: Oxford University Press, 2000.

Cooke, D. *The Language of Music*, Oxford: Oxford University Press, 1959.

Cooper, D. *Bernard Herrmann's Vertigo: A Film Score Handbook*, Westport, CT: Greenwood Press, 2001.

Corrigan, T. (ed.) *The Films of Werner Herzog: Between Mirage and History*, New York: Methuen, 1986.

Coyle, R. (ed.) *Screen Scores: Studies in Contemporary Australian Film Music*, Sydney: AFTRS, 1998.

Cronin, P. (ed.) *Herzog on Herzog*, London: Faber & Faber, 2002.

Crouch, D., Thompson, F. and Jackson, R. (eds) *The Media and the Tourist Imagination*, London: Routledge, 2005.

Cueto, R. *El lenguaje invisible: Entrevistas con compositores del cine español*, Alcalá de Henares: Festival de Cine de Alacalá de Henares, 2003.

Curran, J., Gurevitch, M. and Woolacott, J. (eds) *Mass Communication and Society*, London: Open University/Edward Arnold Ltd, 1977.

Daubney, K. *Max Steiner's Now, Voyager: A Film Score Guide*, Westport, CT: Greenwood Press, 2000.

Davis, R. *Complete Guide to Film Scoring: The Art and Business of Writing Music for Movies and TV*, Boston: Berklee Press, 1999.

Davison, A. *Hollywood Theory, Non-Hollywood Practice: Cinema Soundtracks in the 1980s and 1990s*, Aldershot: Ashgate, 2004.

De Santis, G. *Verso il neorealismo. Un critico cinematografico degli anni quaranta*, Rome: Bulzoni, 1982.

Deleuze, G. *Cinema 2: The Time Image*, trans. H. Tomlinson and R. Galeta, London: Athlone, 1989.

Deleuze, G. and Guattari, F. *A Thousand Plateaus: Capitalism and Schizophrenia*, trans. B. Massumi, London: Athlone, 1987.

Dibble, J. 'Musical Nationalism in Ireland in the Twentieth Century: Complexities and Contradictions', in T. Mäkelä (ed.) *Music and Nationalism in 20th Century Great Britain and Finland*, Hamburg: von Bockel Verlag, 1997, 133–44.

Dyer, R. 'Don't Look Now', *Screen*, **23** (3–4), September/October, 1982, 61–73.

———— *Seven* (BFI Modern Classics), London: British Film Institute, 1999.

———— *Heavenly Bodies: Film Stars and Society*, 2nd edition, London: Routledge, 2003.

Dyer, R. and Vincendeau, G. (eds) *Popular European Cinema*, London and New York: Routledge, 1992.

Eagleton, T. *The Ideology of the Aesthetic*, London: Blackwell, 1990.

Egorova, T. *Soviet Film Music: An Historical Survey*, London: Harwood Academic Publishers, 1997.

Eisler, H. and Adorno, T. *Composing for the Film*, New York: Oxford University Press, 1947.

Ellwood, D.W. and Kroes, R. (eds) *Hollywood in Europe: Experiences of a Cultural Hegemony*, Amsterdam: VU University Press, 1994.

Elsaesser, T. *New German Cinema*, Brunswick, NJ: Rutgers University Press, 1989.

Everett, W. 'Songlines: Alternative Journeys in Contemporary European Cinema', in J. Buhler, C. Flinn and D. Neumeyer (eds) *Music and Cinema*, Hanover, NH: Wesleyan University Press, 2000, 99–117.

Ezra, E. (ed.) *European Cinema*, Oxford: Oxford University Press, 2004.

Fainaru, D. (ed.) *Theo Angelopoulos Interviews*, Jackson: University Press of Mississippi, 2001.

Farassino, A. (ed.) *Neorealismo. Cinema italiano 1945–1949*, Turin: EDT, 1989.

Forgacs, D. *Rome Open City*, London: British Film Institute, 2000.

Foucault, M. 'Des espaces autres', *Architecture/Mouvement/Continuité*, **5**, October 1984, 46–9.

Fowler, C. (ed.) *The European Cinema Reader*, London and New York: Routledge, 2002.

García del Busto, J. (ed.) *Escritos sobre Luis de Pablo*, Madrid: Taurus, 1987.

Gargano, P. and Cesarini, G. *La canzone napoletana*, Milan: Rizzoli, 1984.

Gorbman, C. *Unheard Melodies: Narrative Film Music*, Bloomington: Indiana University Press; and London: British Film Institute, 1987.

Governi, G., Lefevre, F. and Terenzi, C. (eds) *Tu musica divina. Canzoni e storia in cento anni d'Italia*, Turin: Umberto Allemandi, 1996.

Grant, C. 'Recognizing *Billy Budd* in *Beau Travail*: Epistemology and Hermeneutics of an Auterist "Free" Adaptation', *Screen*, **43** (1), Spring, 2002, 57–73.

Hagener, M. and Hans, J. (eds) *Als die Filme singen lernten. Innovation und Tradition im Musikfilm 1928–1938*, Munich: edition text und kritik, 1999.

Harris, B. and Freyer, G. (eds) *Integrating Tradition: The Achievement of Seán Ó Riada*, Terrybaun, Bofeenaun and Ballina: Irish Humanities Centre and Keohanes, 1981.

Hawkins, P. *Chanson: The French Singer-songwriter from Aristide Bruant to the Present Day*, Aldershot: Ashgate, 2000.

Heredero, C. and Monterde, J.E. (eds) *Los 'nuevos cines' en España*, Valencia: Institut Valencià de Cinematografia, 2003.

Hewitt, N. (ed.) *The Culture of Reconstruction: European Literature, Thought and Film, 1945–50*, London: Macmillan, 1989.

Higson, A. *English Heritage, English Cinema: Costume Drama Since 1980*, Oxford: Oxford University Press, 2003.

Hill, J., McLoone, M. and Hainsworth, P. (eds) *Border Crossing: Film in Ireland, Britain and Europe*, London: British Film Institute, 1994.

Hinkel, H. (ed.) *Deutsche Kultur-Wacht*. Blätter des Kampfbundes für Deutsche Kultur e.V., Berlin, 1932.

Horton, A. *The Films of Theo Angelopoulos*, Princeton: Princeton University Press, 1999.

——— (ed.) *The Last Modernist: The Films of Theo Angelopoulos*, Trowbridge: Flicks Books, 1997.

Idelsohn, A. *Jewish Music in its Historical Development*, London: Henry Holt & Co., 1929.

Inglis, I. (ed.) *Popular Music and Film*, London: Wallflower Press, 2003.

Insdorf, A. *Double Lives, Second Chances: The Cinema of Krzysztof Kieslowski*, New York: Hyperion, 1999.

——— '*Soñar con tus ojos:* Carlos Saura's Melodic Cinema', *Quarterly Review of Film Studies*, **8** (2), Spring, 1983, 49–53.

Iordanova, D. *Cinema of the Other Europe: The Industry and Artistry of East Central European Film*, London and New York: Wallflower Press, 2003.

Iseminger, G. (ed.) *Intention and Interpretation*, Philadelphia: Temple University Press, 1992.

Jäckel, A. *European Film Industries*, London: BFI Publishing, 2003.

Jameson, F. *Brecht and Method*, New York: Verso, 1998.

——— *Postmodernism or the Cultural Logic of Late Capitalism*, Durham, NC: Duke University Press, 1991.

Jones, K. 'The Dance of the Unknown Soldier', *Film Comment*, **36** (3), May/June, 2000, 26–7.

Jossé, H. *Die Entstehung des Tonfilms. Beiträge zu einer Faktenorientierten Mediengeschichtsschreibung*, Munich: Alber, 1984.

Kalinak, K. *Settling the Score: Music and the Classical Hollywood Film*, Madison: University of Wisconsin Press, 1992.

Kaplan, E.A. *Women and Film: Both Sides of the Camera*, New York: Methuen, 1983.

Karlin, F. and Wright, R. *On the Track: A Guide to Contemporary Film Scoring*, New York and London: Schirmer Books, 1990.

Kassabian, A. *Hearing Film: Tracking Identifications in Contemporary Hollywood Film Music*, New York and London: Routledge, 2001.

Kater, M.H. *Different Drummers: Jazz in the Culture of Nazi Germany*, New York: Oxford University Press, 1992.

Kater, M. and Riethmüller, A. *Music and Nazism. Art under Tyranny, 1933–1945*, Laaber: Laaber Verlag, 2003.

Kehr, D. 'To Save the World: Kieslowski's *Three Colours* Trilogy', *Film Comment*, November/December, 1994, 10–20.

Kelson, J.F. *Catalogue of Forbidden German Feature and Short Film Productions*, Trowbridge: Flick Books, 1996.

Kirkham, P. and Thumim, J. (eds) *You Tarzan: Masculinity, Movies and Men*, London: Lawrence & Wishart Ltd, 1993.

Kolocotroni, V. 'Monuments of Time: The Works of Theo Angelopoulos', in J. Orr and O. Taxidou (eds) *Post-War Cinema and Modernity: A Film Reader*, Edinburgh: Edinburgh University Press, 2000, 399–409.

Kracauer, S. *From Caligari to Hitler. A Psychological History of the German Film*, Princeton: Princeton University Press, 1947.

Kreimeier, K. *Die Ufa Story*, Frankurt am Main: Fischer Taschenbuch Verlag, 2002.

Laing, H. 'Wandering Minds and Anchored Bodies: Music, Gender and Emotion in Melodrama and the Woman's Film', unpublished PhD thesis, University of Warwick, 2000.

Langer, S.K. *Philosophy in a New Key: A Study in the Symbolism of Reason, Rite, and Art*, Cambridge, MA: Harvard University Press, 1957.

Leppert, R. *Music and Image: Domesticity, Ideology and Socio-Cultural Formation in Eighteenth-Century England*, Cambridge: Cambridge University Press, 1988.

——— *The Sight of Sound: Music, Representation and the History of the Body*, London and Berkeley: University of California Press, 1993.

Lev, P. *The Euro-American Cinema*, Austin: University of Texas Press, 1993.

Longley, E. *The Living Stream*, Newcastle upon Tyne: Bloodaxe Books, 1994.

Lunghi, F.L. 'La musica e il neo-realismo', in E. Masetti (ed.) *La musica nel film*, Rome: Bianco e Nero, 1950, 56–60.

Macnab, G. 'Working with Kieslowski', *Sight and Sound*, **6** (5), May, 1996, 16–22.

Malik, I.H. 'Ireland Orientalism and South Asia', *Asian Affairs*, **32** (2), 2001, 189–94.

Melville, H. *Billy Budd, Sailor (An Inside Narrative)*, ed. H. Hayford and M.M. Sealts Jr., Chicago and London: The University of Chicago Press; Toronto: The University of Toronto Press, 1891.

Memmi, A. *The Colonizer and the Colonized*, trans. H. Greenfeld, London: Earthscan Publications Ltd, 1990.

Mensonge, S. 'Three Colours Blue, White and Red: Krzysztof Kieslowski and friends', *Cinema Papers*, Australia, June, 1994, 27–32.

Mera, M. 'Is Funny Music Funny? Contexts and Case Studies of Film Music Humor', *Journal of Popular Music Studies*, **14** (2), 2002, 91–113.

——— 'Representing the Baroque: The Portrayal of Historical Period in Film Music', *The Consort: The Journal of the Dolmetsch Foundation*, **57**, Summer, 2001, 3–21.

Meyer, K. *Ancient Irish Poetry*, London: Constable & Co. Ltd, 1913.

Morcom, A.F. 'Hindi film songs and the cinema', unpublished PhD thesis, London: University of London, 2002.

Morley, D. and Robbins, K. 'Space of Identity: communication technologies and the reconfiguration of Europe', *Screen*, **30** (4), Autumn, 1989, 10–34.

Morricone, E. and Miceli, S. *Comporre per il cinema: Teoria e prassi della musica nel film*, Venice: Marsilio, 2001.

Mulvey, L. 'Visual Pleasure and Narrative Cinema', *Screen*, **16** (3), Autumn, 1975, 6–18.

Newton, M. *Kind Hearts and Coronets*, London: BFI Publishing, 2003.

Nichols, B. (ed.) *Movies and Methods Volume II*, Berkeley, Los Angeles and London: University of California Press, 1985.

Nieto, J. *Música para la imagen: La influencia secreta*, Madrid: SGAE, 1996.

Nowell-Smith, G. and Ricci, S. (eds) *Hollywood and Europe: Economics, Culture, National Identity 1945–95*, London: British Film Institute, 1998.

Ó Buachalla, S. *The Literary Writings of Patrick Pearse*, Dublin and Cork: The Mercier Press Ltd, 1979.

Ó Canainn, T. *Seán Ó Riada: His Life and Work*, Wilton: The Collins Press, 2003.

O'Brien, H. 'Projecting the Past: historical documentary in Ireland', *Historical Journal of Film, Radio and Television*, **20** (3), 2000, 335–50.

O'Sullivan, D. *Songs of the Irish*, New York: Bonanza Books, 1960.

O'Toole, F. *The Ex-Isle of Erin*, Dublin: New Island Books, 1997.

Pachón Ramírez, A. *La música contemporánea en el cine*, Badajoz: Diputación Provincial de Badajoz, 1992.

Padrol, J. (ed.) *Evolución de la banda sonora en España: Carmelo Bernaola*, Alcalá de Henares: 16 Festival de Cine de Alcalá de Henares, 1986.

Pearse, P. *Plays, Stories, Poems*, Dublin: Talbot Press, 1966.

Philips, K. (ed.) *New German Filmmakers: From Oberhausen Through the 1970s*, New York: Frederick Ungar, 1984.

Polster, B. (ed.) *Swing Heil. Jazz im Nationalsozialismus*, Berlin: Transit Buchverlag, 1989.

Premuda, E. *Il coro sulla scala. Il rapporto suono-immagine nella stagione neorealistica di Giuseppe De Santis*, Palermo: Edizioni della Battaglia, 2000.

Randol, E. 'Schoenberg: the Most Famous Thing He Never Said', *International Forum for Suppressed Music (IFSM) Newsletter*, November, 2002, 13–17.

Rizzardi, V. (ed.) *L'undicesima musa: Nino Rota e i suoi media*, Rome: RAI, 2001.

Rockett, K., Gibbons, L. and Hill, J. (eds) *Cinema and Ireland*, London: Routledge, 1987.

Rogers, H. 'Fitzcarraldo's Search for Aguirre: Music and Text in the Amazonian Films of Werner Herzog', *Journal of the Royal Musicological Association*, **129** (1), 2004, 77–99.

Rügner, U. *Filmmusik in Deutschland zwischen 1924 und 1934*, Hildesheim: Georg Olms, 1988.

Sakmyster, T. 'Nazi Documentaries of Intimidation: "Feldzug in Polen" (1940), "Feuertaufe" (1940) and "Sieg im Westen" (1941)', *Historical Journal of Film, Radio and Television*, **16** (4), 1996, 485–514.

Sider, L., Freeman, D. and Sider, J. (eds) *Soundscape*, London: Wallflower Press, 2003.

Silverman, K. 'Masochism and Subjectivity', *Framework*, **12**, 1980, 2–9.

Skinner, F. *Underscore*, New York: Criterion Music Corp, 1950.

Slocom, J.D. (ed.) *Violence and American Cinema*, New York: Routledge, 2001.

Smith, J. *The Sounds of Commerce: Marketing Popular Film Music*, New York: Routledge, 1998.

Spinazzola, V. *Cinema e pubblico. Lo spettacolo filmico in Italia 1945–1965*, Rome: Bulzoni, 1985.

Steinweis, A. *Art, Ideology and Economics in Nazi Germany. The Reich Chamber of Music, Theatre and the Visual Arts*, London: University of North Carolina Press, 1993.

Stilwell, R.J. '*Sense and Sensibility*: Form, Genre and Function in the Film Score', *Acta Musicologica*, **LXXII**, 2000, 219–40.

——— 'Symbol, Narrative and the Musics of *Truly Madly Deeply*', *Screen*, **38** (1), Spring, 1997, 60–75.

Stok, D. (ed.) *Kieslowski on Kieslowski*, London, Boston: Faber & Faber, 1993.

Straniero, M.L. *Manuale di musica popolare*, Milan: Rizzoli, 1991.

Strauss, F. *Conversaciones con Pedro Almodóvar*, trans. P. Jimeno Barrera, Madrid: Ediciones Akal, 2001.

Suchoff, B. (ed.) *Béla Bartók Essays*, Lincoln and London: University of Nebraska Press, 1976.

Tackmann, H. 'Beschluß betreffs Mitgliedschaft der Filmautoren und Filmkomponisten vom 7.11.1933', *Filmhandbuch der Reichsfilmkammer*, Berlin, Allgemeines VI A, 3 a–f, 1938.

Tasker, Y. *Spectacular Bodies: Gender, Genre and the Action Cinema*, London and New York: Routledge, 1993.

Taubin, A. 'Under the Skin', *Film Comment*, **36** (3), May/June, 2000, 22–8.

Tiffin, H. 'Post-Colonial Literatures and Counter-Discourse', *Kunapipi*, **9** (3), 1987, 17–34.

Truppin, A. 'And Then There Was Sound: The films of Andrei Tarkovsky', in R. Altman (ed.) *Sound Theory, Sound Practice*. New York: Routledge, 1992, 235–48.

Uhlenbrok, K. (ed.) *MusikSpektakelFilm. Musiktheater und Tanzkultur im deutschen Film 1922–1937*, Munich: edition text und kritik, 1998.

Venturelli, R. (ed.) *Nessuno ci può giudicare. Il lungo viaggio del cinema musicale italiano 1930–1980*, Rome: Fahrenheit 451, 1998.

Vidal, N. *El cine de Pedro Almodóvar*, Barcelona: Destino, 1988.

Vincendeau, G. (ed.) *Film/Literature/Heritage: A Sight and Sound Reader*, London: British Film Institute, 2001.

Vitti, A. *Giuseppe De Santis and Post-war Italian Cinema*, Toronto: University of Toronto Press, 1996.

Vogelsang, K. *Filmmusik im Dritten Reich. Die Dokumentation*, Hamburg: Facta, 1990.

Volker, R. *'Von oben sehr erwünscht'. Die Filmmusik Herbert Windts im NS-Propagandafilm*, Trier: Wissenschaftlicher Verlag Trier, 2003.

Wayne, M. *The Politics of Contemporary European Cinema*, Bristol: Intellect, 2002.

Weis, E. and Belton, J. (eds) *Film Sound: Theory and Practice,* New York, Columbia University Press, 1985.

White, H. *The Keeper's Recital*, Cork: Cork University Press, 1998.

Willem, L. (ed.) *Carlos Saura: Interviews*, Jackson: University of Mississippi Press, 2003.

Wilson, E. *Memory and Survival: The French Cinema of Krzysztof Kieslowski*, Oxford: European Humanities Research Centre, University of Oxford, 2000.

Wollen, P. *Signs and Meaning in the Cinema*, London: BFI Publishing, 1998.

Index

The definite and indefinite articles are ignored in the alphabetical sequence but are not inverted. For example, *Un americano in vacanza* will be found under 'a'.

References to films are made under the director and, where required, the composer of music for the film.